City Schools and City Politics

STUDIES IN GOVERNMENT AND PUBLIC POLICY

City Schools
and City Politics
Institutions and Leadership in Pittsburgh, Boston, and St. Louis

John Portz, Lana Stein,
and Robin R. Jones

University Press of Kansas

Published by the University Press of Kansas (Lawrence, Kansas 66049), which was
organized by the Kansas Board of Regents and is operated and funded by Emporia
State University, Fort Hays State University, Kansas State University, Pittsburg State
University, the University of Kansas, and Wichita State University.

Library of Congress Cataloging-in-Publication Data

Portz, John, 1953–
    City schools and city politics : institutions and leadership in
  Pittsburgh, Boston, and St. Louis / John Portz, Lana Stein, and
  Robin R. Jones.
        p.   cm. — (Studies in government and public policy)
    Includes bibliographical references (p.   ) and index.
      ISBN 0-7006-0979-2 (cloth : alk. paper). — ISBN 0-7006-0980-6
  (pbk. : alk. paper)
      1. Education, Urban—Political aspects—United States Case
  studies.   2. Urban policy—United States Case studies.
  3. Educational change—United States Case studies.   4. Educational
  leadership—United States Case studies.   I. Stein, Lana, 1946–   .
  II. Jones, Robin R., 1946–   .   III. Title.   IV. Series.
  LC5131.P67   1999
  370'.9173'2—dc21   99-31311

British Library Cataloguing in Publication Data is available.

Printed in the United States of America
10 9 8 7 6 5 4 3 2 1

Contents

v

Preface

In the spring of 1993, we were selected to participate in a study of civic capacity and urban education, funded by the National Science Foundation and directed by Clarence Stone of the University of Maryland. Each of us conducted research in our home city. Since Pittsburgh, Boston, and St. Louis share certain historical, political, and economic features, we began writing together about our city governments and school systems and the approach of civic leaders to the decline of public education and possible reform strategies.

The issue of civic capacity remained central to our research. Why do certain cities show greater initiative than others? What are the roles of institutions and leadership in creating and activating that capacity? We begin with the premise that central cities have experienced profound demographic and economic change, leaving them with a significant proportion of the very poor, including many outside the legal economy. The public schools in central cities have exhibited the effects of these changes earlier than the cities themselves and are plagued by high drop-out rates, poor attendance, and low test scores. Although facing common problems, Pittsburgh, Boston, and St. Louis did not respond similarly to the challenge. Pittsburgh was able to make the most strides, followed by Boston. St. Louis consistently lagged behind. In this volume we explore the reasons behind these divergent responses.

Chapter 1 sets the stage by identifying significant features of urban public schools and their host cities. The importance of civic capacity to the development of effective urban regimes is also discussed in this chapter. Urban regime theory, developed by Stone and others, highlights the central role of partnerships among business, government, and community leaders in addressing urban problems. Civic capacity focuses specifically on the regime-building process in which cross-sector alliances are created and institutional resources developed to implement key policies and programs. Civic capacity and urban regimes have been constructed primarily in the area of economic development. The question we pose is whether they also can be created to address challenges of urban public education.

In Chapter 2 we introduce the importance of institutions and leadership in the formation of civic capacity. Institutions, such as school departments, school-business partnerships, and cross-sector networks, provide the foundation for civic capacity. They are enduring parts of the urban setting that empower as well as constrain human actors. Leaders work within this institutional environment to create civic alliances and institutional capacity. Leaders from both inside and outside the school system can create a common vision for a community and build institutions to help realize that vision. The interaction of institutions and leadership takes place within a city's political culture, which can itself vary among cities and over time.

School politics and the development of civic capacity in Pittsburgh, Boston, and St. Louis are examined in Chapters 3 through 6. A brief overview of the three cities, highlighting similarities and differences in governmental structures, economic experiences, demographic trends, and educational practices, is presented in Chapter 3. Chapters 4, 5, and 6 contain case studies of each city. We begin each chapter by exploring the city's urban regime and its experiences with economic development policies. We then turn to the central concern of whether and how civic capacity is extended to address problems of urban education. The roles of institutions and leaders are discussed at length. Pittsburgh emerges with the strongest record of extending civic capacity to include public education, followed by Boston and then St. Louis.

In the final chapter we present a summary of our findings and illustrate how civic capacity can differ among cities and why. Importantly, the path to building civic capacity for public education can vary among cities. In Pittsburgh, the business community played a central role in building civic support for public education, while in Boston the mayor was the key actor. We emphasize the critical role played by leaders but recognize that leaders operate within an institutional and cultural environment that limits and constrains their opportunities.

The authors acknowledge the very important contributions of Clarence Stone to this work. We were very pleased to have been included in his study and to have benefited from his direction and comments. We also thank Jeff Henig, Bryan Jones, and the other members of the Civic Capacity and Urban Education research team for their insights and helpful comments during this research project.

1

Cities, Schools, and Civic Capacity

In the years following the Second World War, central cities in the northeastern and midwestern United States began to experience a significant out-migration to suburbia. The loss of population and businesses led to many efforts to revitalize the city, particularly the downtown area. Business leaders joined elected officials in these efforts. Concomitantly, the public school systems in these cities experienced major changes. The physical infrastructure of school buildings deteriorated, and many school systems witnessed a decline in student enrollment. In addition, student populations became increasingly nonwhite. A new challenge for central cities arose: how to increase overall school effectiveness, particularly in preparing often low-income students for a job market demanding higher levels of skills. Meeting this challenge, like the development challenge posed earlier, would require collective efforts. School officials, mayors, city councillors, business elite, and the wider community would have to view public education as a significant problem and work together to address it.

Yet, cities are not equally endowed with the governmental structures, institutional arrangements, leadership, and political culture to permit this shift from a physical to a social problem. In short, the civic capacity of cities varies. Our task is to explain this variation in the development and adaptation of civic capacity. Using three similar yet disparate cities—Pittsburgh, Boston, and St. Louis—we explore the factors associated with building and applying civic capacity to address problems of urban education.

In this chapter we outline the plight of cities and their schools as a prelude to our focus on the experiences of Pittsburgh, Boston, and St. Louis. We begin with an overview of the problems faced by America's cities and their school systems, particularly those located in the rustbelt, then turn to a closer look at the responses. Our interest in economic development leads to a review of regime analysis as central to understanding urban development responses, and our focus on urban

1

education prompts a brief overview of educational reform efforts that have recently captured the attention of national and city policy makers. This overview highlights the critical role played by community support structures and coalitions—indicative of a city's civic capacity—which in turn is a topic of central concern in the next chapter.

MUNICIPAL CHANGE AND DECLINE

In 1950 many cities, particularly those in the Midwest and Northeast, reached their apogee in terms of population. The density created by returning soldiers and their soon burgeoning families was short-lived, however. Suburbanization, a process that actually began in the early 1900s, "became the quintessential physical achievement in the United States."[1] By 1980, 40 percent of the country's population resided in suburban communities. Available land, market forces, and government policies—particularly guaranteed mortgages and highway construction—joined together to produce metropolitan areas characterized by racial and class segregation.[2] Along with the suburbanization process came significant demographic and economic changes in central cities.

Demographic and Economic Changes

The population movement outward from central cities has strong implications for municipal governance and for public school systems. Suburbanization made more marked the existing patterns of racial segregation in urban areas. Each census subsequent to 1950 documented population losses in industrial cities, a growing percentage of minority residents, and an increasing proportion of people living below the poverty level. By 1980, eight of the ten most distressed cities in the United States were located in the Northeast and Midwest.[3] The trend continued through the 1980s. St. Louis, for example, lost over half of its population between 1950 and 1990, while the percentage of nonwhites in the city increased from 18 percent to 49 percent. Furthermore, by 1990, 21 percent of St. Louis families lived below the poverty line. Employment opportunities in northern manufacturing and the mechanization of southern agriculture prompted many former sharecroppers off the land and to northern cities. Between 1940 and 1970, up to five million African-Americans were part of this migration.[4] At the same time, white middle-class and working-class families turned to the suburbs in large numbers.

The demographic transformation of central cities soon was followed by an economic one of even greater magnitude. Deindustrialization—systematic disinvestment in the nation's productive capacity—became increasingly apparent in the 1970s.[5] Plant closings and consolidations affected basic industries such as automobiles, steel, and tires.[6] These industries were the backbone of a number of midwestern and northeastern cities. As manufacturing capacity declined, investment in the infrastructure of production also decreased. Many urban workers lost their livelihood; between 1958 and 1977, for example, twelve large cities of the Northeast and Midwest lost 2.3 million manufacturing jobs.[7] The blue-collar path to upward mobility that had worked for generations of urban immigrants became a far less certain one. In an increasingly competitive world economy, American corporations sought to enhance their profit margin through mergers, acquisitions, leveraged buyouts, and outsourcing to less developed countries overseas.[8]

The postindustrial era had begun. The production of goods in central cities plummeted, and the service sector increased its share of urban jobs. Service sector employment, however, varied quite dramatically, resulting in two distinct tiers of service employment.[9] The first tier, housed in the growing number of high-rise corporate headquarters in certain cities, involved business and financial services and employed well-educated professionals, such as lawyers and accountants. The second tier contained low-wage jobs in personal services, such as hotel employees and fast food workers. In many locales, suburban commuters often filled the first-tier jobs, while many city residents were left with low-paying, second-tier positions. Jobs in the second tier frequently offered little hope of career advancement.

An Urban Underclass

These economic and demographic changes of the last half century produced an increasingly concentrated and debilitating poverty in urban neighborhoods, referred to by some scholars as an urban "underclass."[10] In its most common usage, underclass refers to that portion of the population that is separated from the legal economy, either because of reliance on public assistance, participation in the informal (or undocumented) economy, or engagement in illegal activities. Christopher Jencks describes the demography and geography of this urban underclass: "Nonwhites are far more likely than whites to have underclass characteristics, and they almost always live in racially segregated neighborhoods. Because the underclass constitutes a relatively large fraction of the nonwhite population, it is a majority or near majority in some nonwhite neighborhoods."[11] According to William Julius Wilson, the situation is aggravated further by the movement of members of the black middle class to the suburbs subsequent to the enactment of the Civil Rights Act of 1968.[12] Among those left in the cities, "rates of crime, drug addiction, out-of-wedlock births, female-headed families, and welfare dependency" increased notably since 1970,[13] paralleling the plummet in blue-collar employment. Jencks notes this connection as well: "Job opportunities declined after 1970 for men without high school diplomas. . . . Unskilled and semiskilled workers had trouble finding steady jobs, and those who found jobs had to accept lower real wages."[14]

In a more recent analysis, *When Work Disappears*, Wilson continues his documentation of the characteristics of high poverty neighborhoods inhabited by minority group members. In these neighborhoods he finds "broken families, antisocial behavior, social networks that do not extend beyond the confines of the ghetto environment, and a lack of social control over the behavior and activities of children and adults."[15] Cities always have had poor neighborhoods, but joblessness today is more acute. In certain urban neighborhoods, "a substantial majority of individual adults are either unemployed or have dropped out of the labor force altogether."[16] In neighborhoods where few adults work, more drug trafficking and higher incidences of drug-related crime occur.[17] The segregation of the poor, and especially African-American poor, has an additional consequence. According to Wilson, "Segregation in ghettos exacerbates employment problems because it leads to weak informal employment networks and contributes to the social isolation of individuals and families, thereby reducing their chances of acquiring the human capital skills, including adequate educational training, that facilitate mobility in society."[18]

Demographic and economic changes present new challenges to mayors and other urban leaders. Population loss and an increase in urban poverty link directly to a decline in city resources and revenues. New York City, Cleveland, Philadelphia, and other cities have faced fiscal crises rooted, in part, in changing economic and demographic conditions. Among the responses, discussed later in this chapter, is a reliance upon cross-sector alliances—urban regimes—that bring together leaders in government, business, and other sectors of the community to address problems facing the city.

Central City School Systems

Demographic and economic changes have had profound effects on city youth and their school systems. Students in urban schools are more likely to be poor and members of minority groups, and available resources have declined along with the fiscal base of the city. Once seen as the great assimilators in American society, urban schools today are often found wanting.

In large cities, public school systems mirror changed municipal demographics and economics. In fact, in most, the school population is more heavily minority and poorer. In 1990, for example, 54 percent of elementary and secondary students in central city schools were African-American or Hispanic, yet only 36 percent of all central city residents fell into these racial and ethnic groups.[19] In the eleven-city study that spawned the current volume, the average percentage of African-American and Hispanic students is 73 percent. In contrast, the cities themselves have an average minority population of 50 percent. In general, minority residents tend to be younger than white city dwellers and have more school-age children. In addition, a number of white parents have abandoned the public schools even while retaining their residence in the city.

Urban youth live in an economic environment that poses formidable challenges. In the fifty largest U.S. cities, 27 percent of children live in poverty, compared with 18 percent nationwide, and 35 percent of city children live in single-parent families, compared with 22 percent nationally.[20] Furthermore, 17 percent of city children live in "distressed neighborhoods," compared with only 5 percent of children nationally.[21] The consequences for city youth are substantial. As a recent foundation report concludes, "Although many factors put children at-risk, nothing predicts bad outcomes for a kid more powerfully than growing up poor."[22]

These conditions have grown steadily worse in recent decades.[23] In 1970, the child poverty rate in the fifty largest cities was 18 percent, compared with 27 percent in 1990. In 1970 only 3 percent of city children lived in distressed neighborhoods, whereas in 1990 this figure had risen to 17 percent. In cities of the Northeast and Midwest the situation is even more critical. Of the fifty largest cities, sixteen are in the Northeast and Midwest. Among this group, 30 percent of children live in distressed neighborhoods. In contrast, only 10 percent of children in cities in other regions of the country live in distressed areas. In some rustbelt cities the problem is particularly acute. In Detroit, for example, 62 percent of children live in distressed areas; in Cleveland, 46 percent; in Buffalo, 41 percent.

These economic and demographic challenges facing urban schools systems are evident in table 1-1. Using data from the Council of the Great City Schools, which represents fifty of the nation's largest school systems, table 1-1 compares all school systems in the nation with the Great City Schools as well as a subset of the Great City Schools—major rustbelt cities, including Pittsburgh, Boston, and St. Louis.[24] Among the Great City Schools, 58 percent of students receive free or reduced-priced lunches, compared with 39 percent of students in all schools nationwide. Similarly, students in urban schools are more likely to be recipients of welfare payments than are students in all schools. Also, as noted earlier, city school

Table 1-1. Characteristics of Sample School Systems (1992–1993)

System	Enrollment	% Free Lunch*	% Limited English	% Welfare	% Black	% Hispanic
Nation	42,734,746	38.6	4.9	21.8	15.2	12.2
Great City Schools	5,763,126	58.4	15.8	31.9	42.1	27.0
Rustbelt Cities:						
Baltimore	110,662	62.0	N/A	23.7	82.3	0.3
Boston	62,407	58.3	22.0	N/A	47.6	22.7
Chicago	411,582	68.1	11.3	N/A	56.2	29.0
Cleveland	70,532	78.0	7.4	N/A	69.6	6.7
Detroit	175,036	57.5	4.5	39.8	88.4	2.6
Milwaukee	100,163	64.0	N/A	N/A	57.8	10.4
Philadelphia	206,898	N/A	3.0	76.3	63.2	10.0
Pittsburgh	41,160	61.3	0.7	36.7	53.0	0.3
St. Louis	42,278	85.0	2.0	51.0	78.3	0.4

*Includes those receiving free or reduced-price lunches.

Source: Council of the Great City Schools, *National Urban Education Goals: 1992-93 Indicators Report* (Washington, D.C.: Council of the Great City Schools, 1994).

students are more likely to be African-American or Hispanic than are students nationwide.

These trends are even more evident in rustbelt cities. Comparing schools in rustbelt cities with all Great City Schools, all but two have a higher percentage of students in the free lunch program. Rustbelt cities also report a higher percentage of students in federal welfare programs. In Philadelphia and St. Louis, over one-half of students live in poverty environments that make them eligible for federal welfare support. And finally, schools in rustbelt cities tend to have larger minority populations. All rustbelt cities, for example, have a higher percentage of African-American students than is true for the average of the fifty Great City Schools.

In general, demographic and economic changes pose a formidable challenge for central city schools. Urban students come from families that often must cope with multiple social problems. As one principal in Boston commented, "Kids come to school with huge burdens on their shoulders." A recent report by *Education Week* and Pew Charitable Trusts highlights this issue: "The biggest challenge facing U.S. cities and their school systems is concentrated poverty. In poor neighborhoods, the deck is stacked against children from the moment they are born."[25] Low birth weights, medical needs, single parents, crime, and a host of other problems confront urban youth. For many students, addressing these social and economic problems becomes a prerequisite to creating a conducive environment for learning and achievement.

Not surprisingly, then, measures of student achievement in central city schools are typically below national norms. Harvey Kantor and Barbara Brengel highlight the inability of urban public school systems to educate a diverse student body with multiple needs: "Achievement in inner-city schools continues to lag behind national norms, and drop-out rates in inner-city high schools (especially among African-Americans and Hispanic youth) remain distressingly high, while many of those who do graduate are often so poorly prepared they cannot compete successfully in the labor market."[26]

Data on student achievement, presented in table 1-2, provide several measures of this situation. Caution is advised in using this information: the data are self-reported; there is no common formula for measuring drop-out rates; and different test instruments are used to measure reading and math ability. However, despite these caveats, the data indicate that school systems are experiencing considerable difficulty in educating urban youth. Students in city schools experience higher drop-out rates than all students in the country, and their reading and math scores are below those of all students. In several rustbelt cities, like St. Louis and Chicago, achievement indicators are even lower. Although there are recent signs of progress, most central city schools continue to trail national averages on key measures of academic achievement.[27]

School system data, as well as the general economic and demographic trends evident in most northern cities, highlight the plight of urban America. Many central cities and their school systems, particularly those in the North, have become

Table 1-2. Achievement Measures of Sample School Systems

System	Average Annual Dropout Rate	Median High School Attendance	Reading, % in Bottom Quartile*	Math, % in Bottom Quartile*
Nation	4.4%	93.2%	25.0	25.0
Great City Schools	8.7%	87.7%	32.9	29.6
Rustbelt Cities:				
Baltimore	N/A	79.3%	38.0	38.7
Boston	8.7%	83.0%	23.0	18.8
Chicago	14.8%	79.7%	42.3	45.6
Cleveland	11.2%	N/A	27.3	26.5
Detroit	N/A	87.0%	28.4	29.4
Milwaukee	17.4%	80.0%	30.1	30.9
Philadelphia	N/A	N/A	46.0	45.2
Pittsburgh	7.0%	79.4%	19.7	17.4
St. Louis	14.1%	79.5%	42.2	36.7

*Based on an average of norm-referenced tests in different grades. See *National Urban Education Goals: 1992–93 Indicators Report,* p. 125, notes for figures 45 and 50, for an explanation.
Source: Council of the Great City Schools, *National Urban Education Goals: 1992–93 Indicators Report* (Washington, D.C.: Council of the Great City Schools, 1994).

smaller and poorer with increased representation of children of color. Urban labor markets now absorb fewer high-skilled workers than in decades past and an even smaller proportion of those with limited skills. The education and economic challenges that face central cities are intertwined. As Charles Kerchner concludes, "Cities are utterly dependent upon an education system to rebuild their neighborhoods and economies."[28] To strengthen the economic base of central cities, steps are needed to enhance a city's educational infrastructure; to strengthen the educational infrastructure, a vibrant economic base is needed to provide jobs and fiscal support. As we argue in the next section, both of these efforts—educational reform and economic development—require the formation of cross-sector coalitions around a common agenda of urban change.

URBAN ECONOMIC DEVELOPMENT

Since the early 1950s, major cities in the United States have used federal programs and local business support to redevelop central business districts, uproot slums, attract corporate headquarters, and enhance tourist-based enterprises. A common theme in many of these efforts is a business-government partnership. Business leaders and elected officials agreed on the means and ends to enhance property values and municipal revenues. Although the projects put forth over the last five decades benefited certain segments of the population over others, business leaders and government officials were able to work together to achieve capital-oriented ends.

The need for such coalitions is well documented. As Clarence Stone points out, the "formal public authority" of local governments in the United States is quite weak.[29] State constitutions and laws circumscribe the jurisdiction of cities and frequently restrict their autonomy and taxing authority. Further, the fragmentation of American metropolitan areas limits the power of central governments. Shrinking resources also limit the ability of cities to act. As population falls and the middle class departs, municipal governments struggle to provide services to residents and maintain the physical infrastructure. Mayors, to govern under these circumstances, must reach out for allies in the community. An extensive literature now exists documenting alliances between urban government officials and their coalition partners, particularly corporate leaders.

Community Power

The study of urban alliances and coalitions has its roots in the community power debate that began in the 1950s. Floyd Hunter's reputational analysis of Atlanta initiated the debate.[30] After a series of interviews, Hunter concluded that Atlanta's business elite dominated policy making in the city. Robert Dahl quickly countered Hunter's elitist interpretation with a pluralist explanation of municipal power.[31] In his classic study of New Haven, Dahl postulated that actors prominent in one sector of city life were not necessarily prominent in another. For example, businessmen were quite active in New Haven's urban renewal but were far less significant in educational policy. He also described how New Haven's mayor, Richard Lee, took the lead in the creation of an urban renewal program and coaxed business leaders on board.

In the 1970s and 1980s, the focus shifted to alliances and coalitions devoted to urban economic development. Harvey Molotch viewed the city as a "growth machine" in which "politically mobilized local elites" pursued a common interest in urban growth.[32] Politicians, local media, and utilities joined property investors, developers, and real estate financiers in this growth machine. Occasionally, universities, the arts, sports teams, and labor unions also became involved in municipal land-use decisions involving their interests.[33] As Molotch and others emphasized, the distributional effects of the growth machine disadvantaged non–capital owning classes.

Paul Peterson's 1981 study, *City Limits,* also contributed to a flowering of work in urban political economy.[34] Peterson postulated that cities must concentrate their energies on development, or they will fail. So dependent on their own resources and in competition with suburbs and other communities, cities cannot afford to sponsor redistributive programs themselves but instead must concentrate on luring new enterprises to town. In response to Peterson's work, the distributional concern was raised again, as many urbanists noted that low-income residents typically did not benefit from a focus on economic activity.[35] John Mollenkopf's work on Boston and San Francisco highlighted the governmental side of development policy, showing how entrepreneurial mayors helped to establish business organizations that supported urban renewal. Working-class neighborhoods in both cities fell sway to plans for office towers and high-priced condominiums and apartments.[36]

Urban Regimes

In recent years, the study of urban political economy has turned its focus to coalition building among public and private actors. Whether led by the mayor or business community, cooperation between the city's chief elected official and prominent corporate heads has become a prerequisite for development efforts to remold the skyline, reshape the riverfront, and move the poor away from the central business district. An examination of the nature of this cooperation lies at the heart of regime theory. Stephen Elkin notes that "city politics is a profoundly economically oriented enterprise" and "that the choices open to political leaders are constrained by the economic arrangements in which the city is situated."[37] Therefore, there is "a strong tendency for political leaders and businessmen, particularly those concerned with land-use matters, to find themselves in tacit or open alliance."[38]

Stone further defines this idea of a regime as "the *informal arrangements* that surround and complement the formal workings of governmental authority."[39] Stone notes that "informal arrangements are held together by a core group—typically a body of insiders—who come together repeatedly in making important decisions."[40] He studied Atlanta and found that its cross-sector coalition, or regime, contained the city's prominent business leaders, who worked with several mayors both to reshape the city physically and to desegregate quietly, thereby enhancing business prospects.

Central to a regime is the ability to achieve shared goals. For the members of the regime, this is a model of production rather than control. Producing results, not simply controlling resources, is key. As Stone notes, the critical task is "gaining and fusing a capacity to act—*power to,* not *power over.*"[41] Since the formal authority of government is limited, regime building stresses that other institutions in the city, particularly in the business community, play a part in making and carrying out civic initiatives.

Most scholars concur that cities have a regime, but the type of regime may vary from city to city or within a single city at different points in time. Stone, for example, identifies several regime types—corporate, progressive, caretaker—that differ in the nature of the coalition and the allocation of costs and benefits.[42] Corporate regimes, as in Dallas, are dominated by business interests; progressive regimes, as in Burlington, Vermont, attempt to expand public services and residential opportunities; caretaker regimes, as in Kalamazoo, Michigan, focus on small-business interests and home ownership.

Regimes differ for a number of reasons. The institutional environment, particularly related to the structure of city government, is key. Reformed government structures are most conducive to a regime with a strong business presence. A city manager or strong mayor, for example, could work more closely with business leaders than could a fragmented government composed of a weak mayor and a large, district-based city council. For example, Atlanta's adoption of at-large elections and other reform institutions was instrumental in the development of that city's regime.[43]

Urban regimes also differ by their membership. The business sector plays a central role, but in some communities neighborhood organizations, labor groups, or others also might play a significant part. The composition of a regime influences its goals and strategies. Robyne Turner, for example, found that the different needs and styles of regime participants in four Florida cities helped explain the variation in which these cities incorporated residential concerns into their agendas.[44] Bringing together the membership of a regime and sustaining that governing coalition are critical and often difficult tasks.

Barbara Ferman's introduction of "arenas" extends regime analysis by focusing on the different settings in which coalition building and governing take place. Ferman describes arenas as "spheres of activity that are distinguished by particular institutional frameworks and underlying political cultures."[45] "Civic" arenas, for example, are typically dominated by private, nonprofit institutions, while "electoral" arenas are dominated by partisan institutions that operate according to various quid pro quo relationships. In the same city, different policies, such as development and education, may be handled in different arenas. Further, because cities differ in their governmental structures and cultures, a particular policy may belong to the civic arena in one city, but in a different community that policy may be part of the electoral arena.

Limitations to Regime Participation

Urban regimes are tenuous undertakings. Alliances that bring together government and corporate leaders are difficult to build and sustain. Civic cooperation among actors with different interests is a "process inbred with uncertainty. Cooperation is always somewhat tenuous."[46] This fragile nature of an urban regime is particularly evident on the business side. Bryan Jones and Lynn Bachelor, for example, group firms by their likelihood of entering into cooperative arrangements with local government.[47] Businesses tied to their location in a particular city—banks, utilities, real estate developers—are more likely to be active coalition partners with local government. In contrast, corporations that export their product to other locations are less likely to enter into coalitions and will tend to be "indifferent to development schemes that are not directly related to their own businesses."[48]

Corporate willingness to join a cross-sector alliance and support regime goals also may be tempered by the advent of new ownership or of chief executive officers who are not hometown products. Mergers, divestitures, and leveraged buyouts, so common in the last two decades, have contributed to the changed nature of certain regimes. Perhaps most important, the ability of many large firms to relocate their headquarters or production facilities makes them less likely long-term coalition partners, at least in the sense of the intensive and intimate collaboration that evolved in Atlanta.

The nature of business associations also can limit regime participation. In most major cities, the largest business enterprises have formed associations that played a pivotal role in urban renewal and subsequent physical development. Yet, there is considerable variation among such bodies, which can affect coalition building. Some are formally organized with a permanent staff, while others have few resources. The case studies that follow capture this range. In Pittsburgh, the Allegheny Conference on Community Development, that city's primary business association, possesses considerable staff and resources, while in St. Louis the counterpart business association, Civic Progress, has limited resources. As we will see later in this book, the resulting regimes demonstrate quite different histories and experiences.

Government also can be a source of instability for the creation and longevity of regimes. Electoral turnover of officials, particularly the mayor, can undermine a development coalition. Mayors often establish a close working relationship with business leaders. Instability in the mayor's office can lead business leaders to question the ability of city government to make and sustain long-term commitments. The structure of local government also can limit regime development. A fragmented form of government typically diminishes the ability of city officials to act on behalf of the city. A weak-mayor form of government, for example, often is characterized by multiple power centers and a limited ability to exercise clear leadership. These qualities handicap city officials in their efforts to establish urban regimes.

Partnerships between local government and business leaders are most prominent in the area of physical development. Almost every major city can point to a cross-sector alliance that produced a significant economic development project. However, a joint attack on problems in the social sphere—such as education— occurs less frequently. In the social realm, problems seem more intractable, funding is less certain, payoffs are not readily apparent, and benefits are less direct to the private partners. Yet, as in the area of development, a considerable body of literature points to the need for outside community involvement in attempts to improve public school systems.

EDUCATIONAL REFORM

The theme of the previous section—the importance of cross-sector coalitions to achieve civic goals—is also applicable to the realm of education. Increasingly, broad community action is seen as critical to successful school reform. As one observer of school reform notes, "To ignore the intimate connections between school and community in the reform and restructuring of urban schooling is to condemn such attempts to almost certain failure."[49] Paul Hill and his associates make the need for cross-sector alliances in education even more explicit through their use of a double helix model. "Like the double helix that combines and re-combines genetic material to renew life, a citywide school improvement strategy must combine two complementary strands. The *outside* strand attracts and mobi-lizes political support and other resources from outside the traditional school bu-reaucracy, from taxpayers, businesses, and the larger community. The *inside* strand focuses on the content of schooling—curricula, academic standards, incentives and work rules for teachers, and a philosophy of school management."[50]

The double helix approach of considering both inside and outside factors relevant to school reform has gained widespread support in recent years. It co-exists, however, with other reform efforts that emphasize different aspects of the educational environment.

TRENDS IN EDUCATIONAL REFORM

The United States has a long history of educational reform, in part because of its faith in education as a remedy for society's problems.[51] The Progressive move-ment at the turn of the century, the equity movement of the 1960s, and the current thrust for excellence have all sought to improve society by changing the educa-tional system.[52] During the early 1980s, educators such as Ernest Boyer, James Comer, John Goodlad, Arthur Powell, Eleanor Farrar, David Cohen, and Theodore Sizer articulated their disappointments with American public education and rec-ommended ways in which individual schools could improve.[53] They founded experimental schools and formed networks of like-minded educators. Some crit-ics, such as Diane Ravitch and Chester Finn, attacked the entire American educa-tional system.[54] Finn later described the system as "flabby," providing children "a diet of educational junk food."[55] Ravitch, Finn, and others advocated a back-to-basics approach and formed the Educational Excellence Network in 1981.

A national call for educational reform occurred in 1983 with the publication of *A Nation at Risk,* prepared by the National Commission on Excellence in Edu-cation. Business leaders, economists, and political leaders issued a strong warn-ing: "Our nation is at risk. Our once unchallenged preeminence in commerce, science, and technological innovation is being overtaken by competitors through-out the world."[56] Rhetorically tied to national economic performance, the drive for excellence spread quickly. The Carnegie Forum on Education and the Economy, the National Governor's Association, and the Education Commission of the States established networks, held conferences, and published reports that called for major changes in the educational system. They were joined by various private sector or-ganizations such as the U.S. Chamber of Commerce and the Business Roundtable.

The plethora of educational reform proposals surfacing since the early 1980s has been described as a series of waves. Larry Cuban spoke of these waves depositing "programs, like skeletons of long-dead sea animals . . . on the coral reef of schooling" and then breaking on the "shores of public attention."[57] The first wave took place at the state level, was driven by governors, and focused on raising standards and other academic requirements. Educational reforms included higher teachers' salaries, tighter teacher certification requirements, increased testing of students, tougher graduation requirements, smaller class sizes, and a longer school year. Some states even mandated homework. These reforms, however, did not alter what was learned, how it was taught, or how schools were governed.[58]

The second wave, in the mid- to late 1980s, resulted primarily from local initiatives and focused on the instructional process.[59] These new reforms concerned changes within the classroom. Although school structure would remain essentially the same, what students were expected to learn and what role teachers would play in this process would change. There was a movement away from basic skills and toward higher order thinking skills. Teachers were to be professionals with more decision-making authority, while principals became their instructional leaders.

The third wave of reforms continued to focus on the local delivery system, but it went well beyond the instructional process. In the 1990s, these reforms sought the "overhaul of most, if not all, of the major aspects of the educational enterprise somewhat simultaneously."[60] Borrowing a phrase from business, the reforms were called "restructuring," most of which changed the decision-making structure of school, empowering those at the "retail level." Centralized school districts established in the Progressive era would be decentralized so that parents could become partners in their children's learning. Teachers would be leaders, principals facilitators, and superintendents enablers.[61] If fully implemented, the restructuring would be systemic, altering the school districts' whole mission.

A variation on third wave themes, constituting a possible fourth wave, is the movement to privatize education. John Chubb and Terry Moe recommend breaking up the public school monopoly through the use of vouchers.[62] In 1991, Chris Whittle began the Edison Project to create two hundred private schools in five years. Privatization experiments in Hartford, Miami, and Baltimore have captured public attention, and voucher programs in Milwaukee and Cleveland also have become closely watched reforms. Some have questioned this new direction. Jeffrey Henig argues that the real danger is not public support for private schools, but that "market-based proposals . . . will erode the public forums in which decisions with societal consequences can be democratically resolved."[63]

Reform in Urban School Systems

At the city level the waves of reform have captured considerable attention. Although some cities are more active participants, reform initiatives have become quite commonplace. In the eleven-city project, reform efforts were evident in virtually all the cities. Henig notes that "in spite of frequent charges that the educational community is reflexively resistant to innovation and reform . . . large-city school districts are virtually overrun with reform initiatives."[64] These initiatives cover a wide range of activities.

Changes in the instructional process, assessment, and evaluation. One group of reforms, like the second wave, directly addresses the instructional process. Some reforms—combining age groups, putting teachers together in interdisciplinary teams, changing course requirements—make incremental changes to the instructional process. Other reforms attempt more dramatic change, such as advocating a substantial reorientation of the curriculum to emphasize higher-order thinking skills and individualized learning.[65] To support these changes, school systems are investing in staff development that goes beyond traditional continuing education classes to include summer institutes, sabbaticals, teachers centers, and other programs that link professional development to a larger reform strategy.

New forms of assessment and evaluation also are important reform components. In place of means-based, basic skills tests, some school districts are developing "authentic assessment" tools that include portfolios, student exhibits, and exit interviews.[66] For these school districts an important question is how to combine such highly individualized assessment tools with state and national subject standards that are currently under development. In addition to individual student assessment, district-wide research and evaluation are important reform initiatives. William Cooley and William Bickel, for example, argue that school districts should develop a system of "decision-oriented educational research" that incorporates and combines data collected at the student, classroom, school, and district levels.[67]

Decentralization. The reform agenda also includes measures that decentralize decision-making authority. There are two major variants in this category: "system-level decentralization" and "market decentralization."[68] System-level decentralization moves authority from the central office to the schools. Site-based management is an exemplar of system-level decentralization. Under site-based management, the principal, teachers, and parents, and occasionally students and community representatives, create a formal decision-making structure for the school. A school improvement plan is developed, and the site council is given authority over certain school-wide policy areas, such as curriculum, budgeting, and staffing. This form of decentralization is widespread, although implementation in many school districts is limited and fragmented. Still, almost all Great City Schools have attempted site-based management, and 40 percent of those school systems have initiated site-based management in at least three-fourths of the schools in the district.[69] The effectiveness of site-based management is the subject of debate.[70] Some educators argue that site-based management is only successful in improving school effectiveness if it is coupled with other reforms that directly address the instructional process. In contrast, other educators argue that site-based management's focus on school-level change reduces the chances for meaningful systemic innovation because it "deprives the system as a whole of the full innovative thrust of proposals for reform and change."[71]

In contrast, market decentralization uses incentives common in a market, such as competition, to restructure the school system. School choice is a prominent example. This form of decentralization can be achieved within one school district through the use of magnet schools or through controlled choice systems, such as in Boston, where parents can choose a school from a large zone within the school district. Alternatively, choice can be extended outside the school district. Minnesota, for example, was the first state to adopt a statewide choice program. Other states have followed, although the flexibility and openness of choice programs vary by state. Voucher programs also are used to enhance parental choice. Milwaukee and Cleveland, for example, provide vouchers to students that can be used for tuition at private schools. Other states and cities are debating the merits of adopting such an approach to decentralization.

Privatization and charter schools are two additional examples of decentralization through market reforms. Baltimore and Hartford pursued privatization options when they contracted with a private firm to operate schools within each district. Both efforts, however, ended after several years of controversy and mixed assessments. A number of states have passed legislation allowing charter schools. Parents, teachers, and others in the community may design a school that best suits the needs of a certain group of students and apply for a charter or contract to establish such a school with public funds. These schools are free from many state and local regulations, although the degree of independence varies from state to state.

Partnerships and linked services. Conditions of poverty in many cities have prompted another set of reforms that link schools with social services. Beyond academic subjects, these reforms provide comprehensive programs that include health, nutrition, employment, and other critical services. As Lisabeth Schorr concludes, "The programs that work best for children and families in high-risk environments typically offer comprehensive and intensive services."[72] Such programs prepare children for the school experience, support them while they are there, and help them adapt to the world of work. Since these programs go beyond the instructional mission of the public school system, they often necessitate partnerships or linkages with other institutions. Head Start is such a program; it joins schools with social service providers to offer health, nutrition, and other social services as well as cognitive training.

In some cities, schools are becoming "one-stop" centers for the delivery of a broad range of health and social services. Houston's School of the Future project, for example, offers integrated health and human services through selected middle and elementary schools, targeting schools with concentrations of at-risk students. In Los Angeles, the Family Service Center at the Murchison Street Elementary School assigns case managers to bring city, county, and community services to the school's children and their families.[73] A 1997 survey identified 913 school-based health centers in the United States, a 50 percent increase in only two years.[74] School districts vary in the extent to which outside services are integrated into the operation of the school itself. In some schools, outside services are "add-ons" to the instructional mission and are kept separate from the classroom. Alternatively, other schools adopt a more collaborative arrangement in which the school and nonschool agencies jointly develop and implement programs.[75]

Another set of partnerships prepares the student for the world of work. Potential partners include postsecondary educational institutions and business employers. Examples include tech prep programs, career academies, cooperative education, and youth apprenticeships.[76] Minneapolis, for example, started Youth Trust in 1989 as a partnership of schools, employers, and youth-serving agencies. Youth Trust fosters school-business partnerships that offer summer jobs for city youth. In Boston, Project ProTech is another prominent example. ProTech links high schools with employers in particular industries, such as medical care and finance. Students complete a four-year program that combines traditional high school classes with apprenticeships in the chosen industry.

Obstacles to Urban School Reform

Despite many reform efforts, the initiatives outlined above have had limited impact on many youth in urban schools. One study refers to urban school systems as "islands of achievement" amidst "oceans of failure."[77] Former Secretary of Education Terrel H. Bell, who commissioned *A Nation at Risk,* admits that the reforms spawned by the report "had no significant impact on the thirty percent of our students who are the low-income minority students. We are still not effectively educating them."[78] As Kantor and Brengel conclude, urban schools are "plagued by insufficient funding and outdated facilities, low academic achievement, and exceedingly high drop-out rates."[79]

Such limited impact, however, is not due to a lack of ideas or reform initiatives. Urban school districts across the country have experimented with all of the reforms cited above. Some school districts even have extended reforms system-wide, as is the case with site-based management. Yet *extending* and *sustaining* reform initiatives remain major challenges for most urban school systems. A recent study of fifty-seven urban school districts highlighted the large number of reforms as well as the limited ability to actually implement and sustain these reforms. As the study notes, the "emphasis on the politically attractive aspects of reform has produced inattention to the details of implementing reform."[80] As Henig concludes, "The problem involves an inability to build small school-based efforts into citywide programs and an incapacity to sustain existing initiatives in the face of competing priorities or hot new ideas."[81] Stone makes a similar point, noting that "efforts at change rarely seem to be more than partial and fragmentary."[82]

There are many potential obstacles to urban school reform. As in our discussion of urban regimes, a formidable challenge is building and sustaining a civic alliance to support public education. A frequent obstacle to building this alliance is creating a common language and agenda among supporters of educational reform. Different reform advocates offer varying perspectives on education. Business leaders, for example, often focus on vocational skill development as well as program and budgetary efficiencies in the system, while government officials typically view the schools through a prism of community stability, election concerns, or constituent services. Educators, on the other hand, often focus on curriculum, measures of student achievement, or institutional survival. It is difficult to create a common frame of reference and language among these actors.

Indeed, it may even be the case that school leaders and other involved parties are more interested in reaping their own benefits than improving teaching and learning in the schools. Wilbur Rich identifies "cartel-like governing entities" that control many urban school districts.[83] Composed of school administrators, union leaders, and school activists, these "cartels" maintain control of school policy to confer "income, status, and perks" on their members.[84] For school reform to take place, this focus on employment and other distributive benefits must be replaced by a concern for academic achievement. Stone describes this as adopting a "performance regime" in which educational leaders turn their attention to excellence in teaching and learning.[85] This focus on educational performance must become a community-wide concern. As David Tyack and Larry Cuban conclude, successful educational reform initiatives must "enlist the support of parents, school boards, and the community more generally [in a] lengthy and searching public dialogue about the ends and means of schooling."[86]

Another frequently cited obstacle is the general decline in external support for city schools. The Council of the Great City Schools, for example, launched a "Marshall Plan" to revive urban schools. Central to this plan are calls for greater state funding, new federal aid, federal support for infrastructure repairs, and a general mobilization of the nation and communities in support of urban schools.[87] As the executive director of the council concludes, America has abandoned its city schools, "leaving them underfunded, isolated and politically disabled."[88] In its statistical study of school systems, the council concludes that "it is patently unfair that inner-city public school children, whose average needs are much greater, receive fewer resources per child than their better-off suburban counterparts. A level playing field should not be too much to expect."[89]

The poverty that surrounds many urban schools and their students is a third major obstacle. Urban youth often lack the family support structure and financial resources available to other schoolchildren. James Comer, for example, highlights the many environmental influences that make urban education so difficult. Many urban youth live in family and community networks that provide only limited support for learning and achievement.[90] Some civic partners see the problems of poverty as pervasive and insurmountable, entailing costs and remedies beyond the resources of a civic alliance. Others, like Comer, argue that addressing these problems is critical to successful school learning and achievement. In either case, urban poverty remains a central obstacle to school reform. As David Berliner and Bruce Biddle conclude, underlying the crisis in education are critical problems of urban America, including income inequality, growth stagnation, racial discrimination, and violence.[91]

Creating the institutional ability to initiate and implement reforms is another key challenge. Opinions differ, however, on the nature of this challenge. The independent structure of many school districts is occasionally cited as an obstacle to reform. The creation of independent school districts was a result of Progressive reform efforts earlier in this century that sought to separate schools from politics.[92] This transformation left "most school systems politically independent, if not fiscally independent, of municipal governments."[93] Some students of school reform claim that this independence isolates school officials from broader community pressures and limits the ability of municipal officials to play a role in reform. In recent years, a number of local government officials have attempted to reduce the independence of school districts. The mayors of Chicago, Baltimore, and Boston, for example, are now directly involved in the appointment of school board members and superintendents, and each exercises considerable control over the school budget. Independence between schools and local governments, however, is praised by others, who argue that it allows school officials to focus their efforts on educational issues. From this perspective, a separation between schools and local governments protects schools from political biases and the manipulation of the educational agenda to serve political ends.[94]

The organizational structure of urban school systems is a related challenge that impacts the institutional ability to achieve school reform. This argument follows two quite different paths depending upon the nature of the school organization. Some reformers focus on the centralized and bureaucratic nature of many school districts. Beginning in the early twentieth century, many school systems adopted hierarchical structures to centrally control the educational process. Reflecting on this development, Tyack notes "the growth of vast and layered bureaucracies of specialized offices . . . byzantine organization charts, (and) tens of thousands of incumbents protected by tenure."[95] Such school organizations typically are top-down with limited flexibility for individual units in the system. In many school districts this pattern continues today. A study by *Education Week*, for example, found a pattern of bureaucratic inefficiencies in many urban school systems, leading to the conclusion that central administrations are often "perceived as sluggish and ineffective."[96] Reform advocates are particularly critical of school bureaucracies that fail to measure performance or create incentives for teaching excellence.[97] The movement to decentralize school systems is an example of reform efforts aimed, in large part, at altering this centralized bureaucracy.

Another variation of the school structure critique, however, argues that school systems are best characterized as "loosely coupled" rather than centralized bureaucracies.[98] From this perspective, a school system is viewed as a collection of actors who operate in a semiautonomous manner, although they are connected in a common educational endeavor. These actors—school board members, superintendents, central staff, principals, classroom teachers—have different roles and respond to different incentives.[99] They operate in different environments, and relationships among them tend to be "unpredictable, weak and intermittent." In this loosely coupled system, the diffusion of policy initiatives is "slow and erratic" and is likely to "sputter."[100] Administrative proclamations may have little, if any, impact in the classroom. The capacity of such a school system to extend and sustain educational reforms is problematic.

URBAN REGIMES AND EDUCATIONAL REFORM: EXTENDING CIVIC CAPACITY

Our survey of community power, urban regimes, and educational reform points to the common challenge of building cross-sector coalitions to address urban problems. In urban development, these coalitions combine government and business leaders in order to achieve economic goals. Downtown revitalization, for example, is a popular development goal in many cities. In educational reform, coalitions also play a central role. Joining school leaders with government officials, business leaders, and other community activists, school reform coalitions are key actors in supporting school choice programs, professional development, and other reform initiatives.

Civic capacity is the term we use to identify the presence of these community-wide coalitions and structures of support. Stone defines civic capacity as "the ability to build and maintain effective alliances among representatives from the governmental, business, nonprofit and community-based sectors to work toward a collective problem-solving goal."[101] Civic capacity entails creating both *civic* alliances across socioeconomic sectors as well as institutional *capacity* to implement policies and programs. Civic alliances operate at a governance level by combining key actors from different sectors of the community—government, business, education, and others—in support of jointly defined goals. Institutional capacity operates at a programmatic level to establish requisite authority and resources to achieve those goals. This process of building civic capacity has taken place in many American cities, albeit to varying degrees and principally to accomplish development projects.

The question we pose is whether an urban regime can effectively extend its scope and actions to include public education. More specifically, can civic capacity be created and activated that will support public education? The question poses a challenge similar to what the Annenberg Institute refers to as "public engagement: a purposeful effort, starting in either the school system or the community, to build a collaborative constituency for change and improvement in schools."[102]

In response to this challenge, doubts are expected. The isolation of many school districts, both structural and self-imposed, may cause potential allies to pause. The deep-seated poverty and current low achievement indicators in many urban schools also may make the problem appear too intractable, requiring a commitment more extensive than many actors, particularly business leaders, are willing to make. The growing minority populations of many urban districts also may deter action by white business leaders who often live outside the central city. Furthermore, school bureaucracies often are deemed weak and ineffectual, lacking the capacity to create and sustain educational reform. School districts have joined partnerships and embraced elements from the waves of reform, but few of these initiatives have taken root systemically.

Yet, some urban school systems have progressed further than others. In these cities, community-wide support for public education has made a difference by making available the tools and resources needed to support reform initiatives. Our task is to explain both the successes and failures of regime expansion into the field of public education. In the next chapter we set the stage by outlining two key explanatory variables: institutions and leadership. Institutions provide the platform for civic alliances and capacity building, while leadership is a key driving force in the creation of institutions and the pursuit of reform goals. Exploring this theoretical perspective is critical before turning to our case studies of educational politics in Pittsburgh, Boston, and St. Louis.

2

Building Civic Capacity:
Institutions and Leadership

Civic capacity is central to an active and effective urban regime. Building civic capacity entails a number of critical steps: articulating common goals, forming cross-sector alliances, creating program and policy resources, and establishing a platform for action. Many cities have been successful in building civic capacity to achieve economic development goals. Far fewer, however, have met success in the educational arena.

How can an urban regime extend its reach—create civic capacity—to include other policy areas, such as education? As noted in the previous chapter, the challenge is formidable. Civic alliances across socioeconomic sectors do not occur naturally. Goals and interests often differ among potential alliance members who interact at a governance level. Government officials, business leaders, and educators come to the civic table with different expectations. Educators, for example, may be supportive of a general development agenda, but their primary focus is educational achievement and, in many instances, institutional survival. Government and business leaders must be convinced that public education is critical to their political and economic interests. The resulting alliance is not easily formed and, when formed, is often tenuous.

Capacity building is equally problematic. Many cities have created redevelopment authorities to undertake economic development projects, but similar institutions dedicated to school reform represent new territory. Creating institutional capacity to foster and sustain educational reform raises a number of important questions and challenges. Alliance members, for example, must weigh the relative merits of creating new institutions to drive educational reform or turning to the existing school system to take the lead. For some members, an external agent outside the schools is viewed as central for successful educational reform. Others, however, emphasize a strategy of using the existing school system, albeit with a change in current practices. Both paths entail

21

important challenges at the programmatic level for the development of civic capacity.

There are two key elements to meeting these challenges and creating civic capacity: institutions and leadership. Institutions provide the foundation for civic capacity. Institutions, such as school departments, school-business partnerships, and cross-sector networks, are enduring parts of the urban setting that empower and constrain human actors. Institutions provide the empirical context in which collective civic actions are conceived and implemented. Creating a common set of interests as well as the capacity for collective action are critical elements in institution building. Furthermore, the development of different institutional forms —formal organizations, associations, and networks—takes place within a city's political culture that is itself shaped by past and present institutions. The political orientation within communities varies and establishes different environments for the development of civic capacity.

Leadership also is a critical element in building civic capacity. Leaders play a key role by creating a common vision and building institutions to help realize that vision. Our analysis focuses on leadership from both sides of the "double helix" of school reform. Educational leaders inside the school system, particularly super-intendents, are key actors, as are mayors and other community leaders outside the schools. Leaders play an important role by defining the problems and challenges that face a community and by building bridges across socioeconomic sectors in

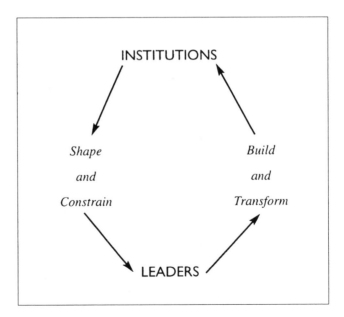

Figure 2-1. Development of Civic Capacity

the community. The effective use of resources is important, but equally important is the leader's ability to establish a definition of community needs that includes a strong educational system.

Our theoretical model is an interactive one. Regime formation through the
development of civic capacity is the result of a dynamic relationship between
institutions and leadership. In this model, institutions shape and constrain the interests, strategies, and actions of leaders. Institutions, and the political culture they
spawn, set the stage for discourse and political action. Leaders, however, are not
simply molded by institutional forces. Rather, they can play a key role in building
and transforming institutions. In fact, constructing a new institution is one of the
major accomplishments of an effective leader.

INSTITUTIONS

In 1996 a high school principal in Boston reflected on the debate in that city
over an elected versus appointed school board. His conclusion: debates over governance "mean nothing unless we *institutionalize* quality education for generations, not just for the moment."[1] In one sentence this principal pointed to a critical
challenge in public education—creating and sustaining opportunities for quality instruction and learning.

To institutionalize quality education is to create a structure of support that
will ensure the widespread adoption of effective educational practices as well as
their continuation over an extended period of time. As we noted earlier, the challenge of school reform is not generating new ideas and initiatives. Rather, the
challenges are ones of scale and duration. Can reform efforts be scaled up to extend district-wide? And are reform efforts of sufficient duration to have a lasting
impact on students and the school system? A positive response to these questions
rests on the ability to institutionalize reform efforts. In each of our cities, the development of institutional support for public education, or the lack of such support, plays a major role in explaining the success or failure of school reform efforts.

Institutional Theory

Institutional theory has captured widespread attention in recent years, but there
remains a diversity of perspectives on what is meant by "institution." W. Richard
Scott, a sociologist, writes that "institutions consist of cognitive, normative, and
regulative structures and activities that provide stability and meaning to social
behavior."[2] James March and Johan Olsen, emphasizing the role of "rules," define institutions as "routines, procedures, conventions, roles, strategies, organizational forms, and technologies around which political activity is constructed [as
well as] the beliefs, paradigms, codes, cultures, and knowledge that surround,
support, elaborate and contradict those roles and routines."[3] Institutions, clearly,

can be defined quite broadly to include a wide array of empirical, cognitive, and normative phenomena. The common element, however, is that institutions provide a basic context of established rules and procedures within which human actors develop strategies and pursue interests.

Institutions have two major characteristics. First, institutions shape human thoughts and behavior by empowering as well as constraining actors. A formal organization, network, or other institutional form (see below) creates an array of rules, incentives, and penalties that shape action. The rules of a formal organization, for example, empower some individuals to act in certain ways while constraining others. Individual actions are not guided simply by self-interest and rational strategies. Rather, they are shaped by and filtered through the complex surrounding environment. Thus, institutions shape how we think and how we act. Our conception of what is possible, and what is not possible, is influenced by the institutional environment within which we live and work. As March and Olsen note, "The individual personality and will of political actors is less important: historical traditions as they are recorded and interpreted within a complex of rules are more important."[4] Robert Putnam, in his study of civic traditions and institutions in Italy, makes a similar point, noting that "institutions influence outcomes because they shape actors' identities, power, and strategies."[5]

Second, institutions typically are self-perpetuating and long-standing. They are not dependent upon one person or group for their continued existence. Rather, they possess sufficient coherence and autonomy to endure for an extended period of time. Institutions are a relatively fixed aspect of the environment. Their influence on human actions is relatively constant, and they endure despite frequent changes in the political environment. Thus, school departments and city government agencies, for example, continue in existence for many years despite turnover in the superintendency and mayor's office or other political changes.

Institutions are important in educational reform because of these characteristics. They play a critical role in both scaling up and extending the longevity of reforms. Scaling up requires an institutional platform to expand reform efforts from a small-scale, pilot status to a district-wide or larger setting. A supportive school department structure, for example, can play an important institutional role in this regard. The school department provides numerous rules, incentives, and penalties that directly impact the scaling-up process. Extending the longevity of reforms also requires institutional support. Public-private partnerships, for example, can provide an important institutional platform for the assembly of resources necessary to extend the life of a reform. Not only does the partnership shape what is possible, but the durability and autonomy of the partnership are important in extending the reform effort beyond the support of the moment.

The study of institutions and institution building has a long history in the social sciences and has received widespread attention in recent years. Particularly in economics, sociology, and political science, institutional theory has emerged as an important perspective to help explain social phenomena.[6] In economics, for example, the role of governance systems in regulating and managing economic exchanges has received attention from many economists, although this perspective is clearly overshadowed by mainstream neoclassical economics. In sociology, attention focuses on the characteristics of institutions and organizations and on the effects of cultural belief systems on an environment of organizations.

In political science, two distinct schools have emerged.[7] The rational choice school, which includes such political scientists as Terry Moe and Kenneth Shepsle, focuses on individuals as interest-driven actors who operate within an institutional environment of rules. Institutions and the rules they entail are an important part of a strategic context that imposes constraints on the self-interested behavior of voters, politicians, and other actors. Importantly, the preferences of actors develop exogenously from the institutional environment. Interest maximization—in the form of votes, money, or another item of value—is the starting point of the rational choice school; institutions enter as environmental constraints in this world of interest maximization.

The historical institutionalist school, from which our analysis is drawn, gives greater weight to the role of institutions in shaping human behavior. Individuals are not simply self-interested maximizers. Rather, they often follow socially and institutionally defined roles. Human behavior cannot be understood without considering the institutional environment that both constrains and empowers individuals. Understanding the web of relations within which individuals operate is critical. The development of preferences is endogenous to the institutional environment. As Peter Hall, Theda Skocpol, March, Olsen, and others emphasize, the formal structures, rules, and procedures of an institutional world fundamentally shape the strategies as well as the actions of individuals.

Our institutional perspective also draws upon the concept of political culture. The beliefs, norms, and values that prevail in a particular community stem in part from its governmental structure and play a critical role in the development of different institutional forms. We treat political culture as an important characteristic that may, or may not, predispose individuals in a community to work together for collective purposes. In short, the creation of key institutions in a city to support educational reform depends in part upon the presence of a supportive political culture.

Institutional Forms

In our analysis we emphasize three institutional forms: networks, associations, and formal organizations. Each is a different means to coordinate actors from one or more sectors, such as business, government, and education. Networks achieve coordination through relatively informal arrangements among actors in different sectors; associations are more narrowly based with actors from a single sector; formal organizations coordinate actors through a system of rules, task specialization, and hierarchical controls. Each plays an important role in establishing the civic capacity of a city.

Networks. Networks are central to civic capacity. A network is a collection of organizations and individuals united by a common purpose or goal and joined together by established patterns of interaction and communication. These patterns of interaction serve to unite resources from network members and facilitate joint action. Network members "share a common ethic and outlook and can discuss and decide policy informally among themselves."[8] Central to a network is the relationship among actors, shaped around varying degrees of cooperation, trust, and loyalty. These relations help shape the "behavioral, perceptual, and attitudinal" nature of network members and have major consequences for the social system as a whole.[9]

Membership in a network is voluntary. Government does not mandate membership, nor are individuals and organizations compelled by others to join. Rather, network membership is driven primarily by self-interest and the desire to achieve the goals of the network. Given this voluntary nature, the intensity of network relations can vary depending upon the level of self-interest and commitment of the membership. One network of business and government leaders might be very tenuous and prone to dissolution, while another is well-established and enduring despite leadership changes among the parties.

The bonds that bind network members together can vary. In one network, mutual trust might be critical, while another network is based upon a quid-pro-quo relationship of economic transactions. In general, compliance within a network depends upon "shared norms, attitudes of trust, considerable knowledge about one another, and respect for each other's interests."[10] These bonds are crucial to the survival of a network, but their strength is sometimes tentative given the voluntary nature of networks. Exit from the network by disillusioned members is relatively easy. In addition, networks often have limited resources. Staff and financial resources can help to maintain coherence and purpose, but networks are often lacking in this area. Although a few networks possess significant, autonomous resources, most rely upon the resources of network members, which typically are provided in only a limited fashion.

Networks include members from different sectors in society, which is their distinguishing characteristic. Thus, a network might include individuals or organizations from business, education, government, and nonprofit sectors. In Boston, for example, signatories to the Boston Compact include representatives from business, government, and educational organizations. In Pittsburgh, the Council on Public Education is a network that includes members from education, business, government, and nonprofit sectors.

Given their multisector nature, the establishment and longevity of networks are problematic. The wide diversity of interests contained within a network makes it difficult to identify and maintain a common purpose. Network members continually are pulled to their own perspectives and interests. Business members, for example, typically approach problems with a cost-efficiency frame of reference, while nonprofit members are likely to be policy advocates. The former look for inefficiencies in the area of concern, while the later focus on achieving social results. Bridges must be constructed across these diverse perspectives, and brokers who can negotiate common ground must step in.

And yet, networks play a critical role in the development of civic capacity and educational reform. They provide a bridge that spans the parochial interests of individuals and organizations in the community. A network dedicated to excellence in education can provide a critical forum for discussion and action. The civic capacity of a community is dependent upon the development of networks that facilitate cross-sector communication and policy development. As we look closer at the institutional terrain in our three cities, the presence of networks—and the strength of those networks—is a characteristic that helps explain the city's success or failure in educational reform.

Associations. Associations have many similarities with networks. Like a network, an association is a collection of individuals or organizations united by a common purpose or goal and with established patterns of interaction and communication. Also like a network, an association typically develops long-standing communication channels and patterns of interaction that facilitate joint action.

Associations, however, differ from networks in that they are composed of members from the same sector. Thus, a business association, such as the National Alliance for Business, is composed of representatives from different corporations in the business community. In similar fashion, an educational association is composed of individuals and organizational representatives involved in various aspects of education. The newly formed Learning First Alliance, for example, is composed of the leaders of twelve educational organizations, including the American Federation of Teachers, National PTA, National School Boards Association, and National Education Association.[11] The Learning First Alliance is an association that is itself composed, in part, of other associations. In our three cities there are several associations that play important roles, particularly in the business community. The Allegheny Conference on Community Development in Pittsburgh, the Vault in Boston, and Civic Progress in St. Louis are three key business associations.

Associations vary in their resources. Some associations enjoy considerable resources in the form of staff and financial support. An executive director and cadre of policy analysts, for example, can provide an association with substantial capacity to play an active role in matters that come before the group. The Allegheny Conference on Community Development has an executive and support staff of more than ten individuals. Alternatively, some associations, like Civic Progress in St. Louis, possess very few resources. Lacking staff and financial resources, such associations are more circumscribed in their ability to engage in policy discussions and actions.

Associations rely upon different mechanisms to shape and influence the actions of their members. In some associations, a formal written agreement serves to outline expected behaviors of the various parties. A written contract could specify the rights and responsibilities of all parties as well as penalties for non-compliance. In contrast, other associations rely upon verbal agreements to coordinate action; an oral pledge of cooperation may be all that binds the parties.

Creating an association can be a formidable challenge, although typically less difficult than creating a network. Associations are at an advantage, since the relationship is established among actors within the same sector, whereas networks must span different sectors. Nevertheless, associations often struggle to maintain a common purpose and to forge and maintain strong communication channels. Participants often have goals that differ from those of the association, and their attention to the association is secondary to their primary role. As one observer of the Learning First Alliance noted, previous efforts to create similar associations faltered because of the "inherent rivalries between labor and management" among educational members.[12] Furthermore, an association usually does not have strong sanctions it can employ to require certain types of behavior. Rather, peer pressure, altruism, and access to the resources of other members are three of the more common means of achieving collective action. Thus, developing a common purpose and exercising collective action are problematic. When associations are successful, as we shall see, leadership usually plays a major role.

Formal organizations. Formal organizations constitute our third major institutional form. They are perhaps the most prominent and obvious type of institution. In a formal organization, behavior is shaped through a system of rules that include specialized position descriptions, authority structures, and various rewards and penalties that bind members of the organization. This system of rules establishes the basic operating procedures of the organization and outlines the roles and responsibilities of its members. Often hierarchical, formal organizations typically are built around an employment relationship that is bureaucratic in nature. School departments, city governments, and business corporations are examples of formal organizations.[13]

Formal organizations usually focus their efforts in one sector. A business corporation, for example, is organized around achieving success in its particular product markets. A government bureaucracy is focused in a particular area of public service. School departments are concerned with the education of students. Formal organizations in each of these sectors are structured to achieve their goals. Thus, the specialization of tasks—reading teacher and school principal, for example—is designed to achieve the goals of the organization. Similarly, authority systems outline the chain of command within a formal organization and thereby structure interactions and the pursuit of organizational goals. Authority systems can vary; a rigid and hierarchical authority system creates a much different environment than one that is flexible and collaborative.

Formal organizations are found throughout our three cities. In the "outside strand" of school reform, for example, city governments are large organizations with numerous properties that shape and influence actions. Strong-mayor systems in Boston and Pittsburgh create quite different constraints and opportunities than the weak-mayor system in St. Louis. The mayor in a strong-mayor system possesses considerably more authority and control over finances, appointments, and other aspects of city government.

On the private side, business corporations and nonprofit agencies are important organizations that can shape and influence the direction of educational reform. Banks, insurance companies, manufacturers, and other business corporations operate in a world of profits, sales, and markets that has an important impact on how members of each organization interact with the educational community. Nonprofit agencies, on the other hand, operate in a quite different world driven by the mission of the organization. Such goals as family support, early childhood services, and health care create a set of tasks and expectations that structure the actions of individuals within many nonprofit organizations.

Formal organizations also are important in the "inside strand" of school politics. School departments are very large organizations with numerous rules, policies, and procedures that influence the actions of teachers, administrators, and staff. Furthermore, school departments are complex organizations that often are bifurcated between the central office and individual schools. Administrators and staff in the central office are concerned primarily with district-wide activities that structure and support activities at the school level, while individual schools are focused on the classroom delivery of education. Each level has its own dynamic. Central offices are known for adherence to procedure and a focus on writing and enforcing rules that apply across the district. The organizational environment in individual schools often varies depending upon the style and authority of the principal. With union work rules and other contractual obligations added to the mix, school departments can be very structured and regulated environments.

Formal organizations are important building blocks for civic capacity. They provide the basic context within which most individuals work and attempt to achieve their goals. An individual's participation in a network or association typically is based upon the individual's position within a formal organization. City governments, school departments, and other organizations provide an array of incentives and penalties that shape the development as well as the pursuit of interests. When combined with a supportive political culture, organizations become the basis for the creation of associations and networks that link actors within and across sectors. In short, without a strong foundation of formal organizations, civic capacity in a city is unlikely to develop to any significant degree.

Political Culture

Political culture is another important element in our institutional analysis. It refers to beliefs, norms, values, and expectations held by individuals with respect to the proper role for politics and government. Political culture is part of the "framework within which politics takes place."[14] At the national level, American politi-

cal culture is heavily shaped by a capitalist economic system and democratic politics. These combine to give the business community a position of considerable
influence, what Charles Lindblom referred to as the "privileged position of business,"[15] and also to give deference to individuals rather than groups as the key
agents in economics and politics.[16]

There are, however, variations from this broad theme. In some regions and
cities of the United States, this national cultural orientation is tempered by local
values and norms. As James Q. Wilson notes, "Culture is to a group what personality is to an individual, a disposition that leads people to respond differently to
the same stimuli."[17] Local political cultures constitute different dispositions in
which politics and political action assume different dimensions and practices in
different parts of the country.[18] Some cities and regions, for example, have a political orientation in which traditional social elites tend to dominate the political
arena, while other parts of the country are characterized by a more competitive
environment among a broad range of individuals and groups. Also, some areas of
the country, such as the Northeast, are known for their openness to political innovations, while other regions are reluctant to venture down new political paths. As
developed in later chapters, Pittsburgh, Boston, and St. Louis possess local political cultures with important variations that affect each city's development of civic
capacity.

Regional variations in political culture develop through a historical interaction of race, ethnicity, religion, socioeconomics, geography, and political structures.
These various factors combine to produce different local values and expectations
over what is politically appropriate and acceptable. Political culture is akin to
organizational culture. It subtly shapes how issues are defined and how the roles
of various actors are viewed. Local history and past experiences play a particularly important role in shaping a local culture. Margaret Weir notes that "the conception of what problems are and how they are defined very often depends on
previous policies."[19]

The interaction between political culture and local political institutions is
particularly important. Each impacts the other: a community's political culture
influences what is possible and acceptable in the form of local government, while
government structures shape the development of local political culture. The Progressive movement in the early twentieth century, for example, spawned an efficiency focus that evolved hand in hand with changes to local political institutions.
Seeking a more professional and nonpolitical form of government, the city-manager
plan became the ideal governmental form. Nonpartisan and at-large elections also
became popular to reduce excessive partisanship and narrow electoral perspectives.
Thus, many local governments were recast in new organizational forms that fostered such preferred values as efficiency, economy, and nonpartisanship. Studies of
local government structure have identified biases in which certain governmental
forms, such as a reform structure, are more likely to promote particular values, such
as efficiency.[20]

Political culture is a critical building block in institutional analysis. For the development of civic capacity, the key question is the orientation in a community toward civic responsibility and collective action. Are individuals focused on broad community concerns, or are they concerned with issues more immediate to the neighborhood and self?[21] In the former case, political culture can combine with formal organizations to yield associations and networks that focus on collective action. Political culture, then, becomes an important prerequisite for institutional development in a city. As Putnam argues in his study of civic traditions, "Effective and responsive institutions depend, in the language of civic humanism, on republican virtues and practices."[22]

LEADERSHIP

Leadership is the second major piece in our analytical framework. If institutions represent the building blocks for civic capacity, leadership provides the catalyst for creating civic alliances and infusing institutions with the resources and purpose to address major policy concerns. Leaders play a critical role developing common interests and building an institutional platform to realize those interests. Leaders bring together individuals and organizations around common purposes, even as they strive to raise to a higher level those very goals and aspirations.

Leadership is defined in different ways by different writers.[23] While some focus on a "great person" approach that highlights the characteristics and attributes of individual leaders, others emphasize the relationship between leaders and followers. Our definition draws from both perspectives, although highlighting the latter. Using words penned by James MacGregor Burns, we define leadership as "leaders inducing followers to act for certain goals that represent the values and the motivations—the wants and needs, the aspirations and expectations—of both leaders and followers."[24]

The fundamental challenge for leaders is twofold: establish common purpose and execute a plan of action. The first task is critical. Crafting a common purpose or vision among leaders and followers sets the stage for subsequent actions. Followers, however, are likely to have diverse goals and motivations; the leader's task is to shape these around a common understanding of the issues, problems, and solutions that lie ahead. This is a challenge of issue or problem definition. Leaders must establish a definition—an understanding of the causes and solutions to a particular problem—that is shared by others in the community. As David Rochefort and Roger Cobb note, "The function of problem definition is at once to explain, to describe, to recommend, and above all, to persuade."[25] For leaders, persuading others to join in a common cause is critical. They must be prepared to craft a definition that incorporates the many perspectives of potential followers and at the same time convince other followers to accept a new perspective on the common challenge they face. Thus, extending civic capacity to include public education calls for a problem definition that rallies support from key community actors to put education at the center of the policy agenda.

The second key challenge for leaders is to establish and guide a plan of action. To achieve a common goal, leaders must be prepared to fight the battles of implementation and policy execution. A set of action steps are needed to bring together requisite resources and navigate the institutional environment. Leaders may employ existing policy tools and resources, or they may be required to create new ones. They also must be prepared to use existing organizations, associations, and networks—or create new ones—to achieve common goals. The potential obstacles are many, but the task is critical; leaders must design a policy and program strategy to realize common purposes. In our study of civic capacity, the leadership challenge is to put in place a set of policies and programs to support excellence in teaching and learning.

Conditions of Leadership

Successful leadership depends upon many factors. Three of the most important can be summarized as person, position, and setting. Jean Blondel makes a similar conclusion, noting that the "character of leadership" depends upon "the personal characteristics of the leaders, the instruments they have at their disposal, and the situations they face."[26] The first condition points to a leader's attributes. Leaders typically are persons of strong character, intelligence, vision, and self-confidence. Thomas Cronin emphasizes that "leaders have those indispensable qualities of contagious self-confidence, unwarranted optimism, and incurable idealism."[27] Personality, skills, and experience are important. Leaders are motivated to "make a difference," and they possess the capacity to analyze and interpret diverse situations that come before them.[28]

The position an individual holds also is an important condition of leadership. Mayors and superintendents, for example, have policy and management tools by virtue of their positions that greatly facilitate the tasks of leadership. Appointment and budget authority, for example, are important powers of an executive that relate to the leader-follower relationship. Thus, institutional position is important. The director or leader of a formal organization, association, or network enjoys certain authority that supports his or her strategies and actions. To be certain, a strong institutional position does not guarantee a strong leader—other factors come into play, such as the skills of the individual and the historical setting—but institutional position is not inconsequential. It represents an important platform of power and authority that can assist a leader in creating and realizing a common agenda.

The setting is the third key element to shape the nature of leadership. The historical setting provides constraints and opportunities for the exercise of leadership; it establishes the "chessboard on which leaders play and have to play."[29] The chessboard may include conditions favorable to leadership or quite unfavorable. The public mood, events in other communities and countries, economic changes, and a host of other environmental conditions can facilitate or hinder a leader. A mayor, for example, must contend with changing priorities at the national and state levels that directly impact the city. Leaders typically have little control over this changing scene. To lack control, however, does not mean leaders are passive recipients. Rather, leaders take advantage of changes to support their strategies and actions. An effective leader turns the setting into an opportunity rather than a constraint.

The nature of leadership, then, is dependent upon a complex mix involving personal attributes and skills, positional tools and resources, and the historical circumstances of the time. As Burns concludes, "leadership is fired in the forge of ambition and opportunity."[30] Personal ambitions carry a leader into a situation of opportunity created by position and setting. The leader-follower relationship is often difficult to predict, but it nevertheless represents a powerful force in shaping the course of events.

Leadership takes place in many different arenas. As noted in Chapter 1, educational reform requires support from both inside and outside the school system (what Hill et al. referred to as the "double helix" of school reform). Thus, our look at leadership considers both sides of the double helix. In the next section we focus on key characteristics of educational leadership followed by a discussion of leadership in the larger urban setting.

Educational Leadership

Urban school systems pose a host of leadership challenges. Within school districts, for example, different organizational structures call for different types of leadership. In school systems that retain a centralized bureaucratic structure, leadership often follows a command-and-control approach in which most power and authority is held by superintendents and, to a lesser degree, principals. In contrast, some school systems have moved toward a "loosely coupled" structure that decentralizes authority, such as in site-based management.[31] Leadership in this environment has quite different demands, requiring more communication, facilitation, and negotiation.

A rapidly changing environment has created economic, social, and political challenges for educational leaders. Schools, for example, must respond to the changing labor demands of a postindustrial, information-driven society, and at the same time they must accommodate changing demographics of both student and nonstudent populations. As schools increasingly become "open systems" to their surrounding environment, new actors—business leaders, mayors, social service providers, and others—enter the discussions on public education.[32] Educational leadership is needed to focus the debate, solicit resources from supporters, appease opponents, and construct a common agenda to guide all parties.

The demand for leadership is evident at all levels of a school system. Teachers are expected to be leaders in the classroom.[33] Principals are to exercise leadership at the school site, helping to define and communicate an educational mission.[34] School boards are to be policy-making bodies that provide system-wide leadership.[35] The primary leadership role, however, typically falls to the superintendent. As the chief executive of the district, the superintendent bears responsibility for the overall success of the system. The superintendent must "focus on the collective enterprise" rather than competing components of a school system.[36] As two students of the superintendency note, "There is the expectation that the superintendent should put the figurative noose around his/her neck and then adroitly work his/her way out of it. . . . This is part of being a real leader."[37]

The leadership role of a superintendent has three major dimensions: educational, managerial, and political.[38] An effective superintendent combines all three dimensions. As an educational leader, he or she develops and articulates an educational philosophy to guide the school district. The superintendent must rise above the day-to-day management of the system to develop a vision statement for educational excellence. This vision outlines a path for learning and achievement that can guide teachers and others in the school system. Lacking such a vision, a school system is likely to flounder as it attempts different pedagogies and reform strategies without any overall guidance.

A second leadership dimension is managerial. Educational leaders must be able to operate in the world of management, bringing order and consistency to an organization. They must ensure that resources are effectively and efficiently used. Managerial skills, however, must go beyond the efficient allocation of resources within a stable environment. Educational leaders operate in a dynamic setting in which the responsibilities of teachers, principals, and administrators are interrelated and changing. As Larry Cuban notes, managerial leadership takes place when administrative skills are "harnessed to goals that go beyond maintaining organizational stability."[39] School systems have become "fragmented and complex work settings [that] cultivate splintered, narrow, and incomplete framing of problems and their solutions."[40] In this setting, managerial leadership is often collaborative or empowering, allowing subordinates to become involved in framing problems as well as implementing solutions. Managerial leadership may become interactive and dynamic, "drawing members of an organization together to build a culture within which they feel secure enough to articulate and pursue what they want to become."[41]

The final dimension of leadership is political. Political leadership is concerned with the relationship between superintendents and the many actors outside the school building. The Progressive era image of superintendents as educational specialists separate from the political fray has been replaced by one in which superintendents are key actors in the community. Today, superintendents must interact with elected officials, business leaders, social service providers, community advocates, unions, taxpayer associations, and parent groups, among others. Incorporating these groups into the educational vision of the community can be a daunting task. As one study of four urban school systems concluded, public education and the community had become like a "giant dysfunctional family" in which "educational reform had fallen victim to division, factionalism and political gridlock."[42] Overcoming this division and gridlock is a political challenge faced by many superintendents.

Three primary constituencies that test the leadership of an urban superintendent are unions, local government, and school boards.[43] With unions, the adversarial nature of collective bargaining often dominates the superintendent-teacher relationship and focuses dialogue around wages and working conditions. Increasingly, however, superintendents are establishing union relationships that include not only collective bargaining but also incorporate the union into reform efforts. Teachers' unions can be valuable allies in school reform, or they can be major obstacles. An effective educational leader will ensure the former rather than the latter.

A superintendent also must forge alliances with local governments that provide both political and financial support for the school district. Increasingly, mayors in large cities—such as Boston, Chicago, and Baltimore—are taking a more proactive role in educational reform.[44] These mayors are appointing school board members and exercising financial control over school systems. Superintendents must extend their leadership role to work closely with these elected officials.

And finally, a superintendent's leadership role also extends to the school board. Susan Johnson notes the irony of this situation: "Although they are hired by school boards, superintendents are expected to lead them."[45] This situation is particularly true in the current era of dramatic school change. Increasingly, school board members bring to the board quite diverse views on educational reform. Superintendents must help forge a common agenda and vision for the board, then maintain board support during a lengthy period of implementation. The process, however, often turns conflictual and superintendents lose favor; the average tenure for urban superintendents is less than three years. Yet, as Michael Fullan argues, superintendents typically need ten years to implement real change.[46] This disparity points to the difficult nature of a superintendent's political leadership.

School leadership, then, is a complicated and challenging task for superintendents, principals, and other educators. Pedagogical skills of the classroom must be complemented by a wide range of leadership skills that span the institutional and political environments. As a recent Annenberg report notes, educational leadership requires a "new level of skill in listening, coaching, mentoring, encouraging, and supporting inclusion; forging consensus; and surfacing possibilities for action."[47] The skills of the educational expert are no longer sufficient. Educational leaders must operate in a complex political world that places a premium on skills and strategies involving consensus building, negotiations, and reciprocity. Says one former superintendent, "The expectations and constituencies are many, requiring a balancing act between internal and external forces over which [superintendents have] little control."[48]

Urban Leadership

In the outside strand of the double helix—government, business, and community—leadership is also critical for institution building and the development of civic capacity. An urban leader helps forge a set of common interests and goals (in our case, around educational reform) and then builds new institutions or reinvigorates existing ones to achieve those ends. This is a formidable task in which urban leaders create bridges across economic, political, and social sectors. As Clarence Stone argues, "Leadership is not solely a matter of policy making; it is also a matter of building, maintaining and modifying a governing regime."[49] An urban leader frames issues around a community-wide vision and agenda, then develops and sustains a coalition capable of realizing that agenda.

The ability of urban leaders to meet this challenge is contingent upon a number of factors. The basic political and cultural setting is perhaps the most important. Bryan Jones and Lynn Bachelor, for example, describe how the private control of business constrains the decision making of urban officials. In their study of three Michigan cities, they found that the automobile industry had significant control over the urban agenda. Although opportunities for leadership exist—what Jones and Bachelor refer to as "creative, albeit constrained, leadership"—the basic boundaries for action are shaped by the larger political economy.[50]

Political culture and the basic structures of the political system also shape the possibilities for leadership. Barbara Ferman, borrowing a phrase from Edward Banfield, concludes that Boston's "private-regarding" culture created opportunities for Mayor Kevin White to exercise a leadership style associated with partisan bosses, even though Boston had a nonpartisan ballot.[51] Relevant also is the nature of the local political system. A fragmented political system typically diminishes leadership opportunities, while a more centralized system often expands opportunities. A city with a weak-mayor system and separate finance board, for example, scatters key strategic resources among different actors, thereby diminishing leadership opportunities. Leadership in St. Louis, as we shall see, has been handicapped by such a political system.

The personal dimension also can be an important factor in shaping urban leadership. A mayor with strong political skills is able to "identify resource opportunities, select strategies, and choose the arena in which to operate."[52] A skillful mayor creates opportunities for leadership that build upon a city's political coalitions, history, and traditions. On the other hand, some mayors are focused more on short-term electoral concerns that can distract from institution building. Big-city mayors typically possess considerable resources, but their leadership potential may be diminished by "personal and career ambitions" in which they seek "quick successes [and] insulate themselves from citizen involvement."[53] A long-term perspective is critical for urban leaders who intend to build institutional capacity.

Mayors are not the only urban leaders. In many cities leadership is exercised by individuals from business corporations, religious organizations, universities, or community-based institutions. In fact, the central role of private businesses in the urban political economy places corporate executives in a position to play a critical part in urban leadership. Business organizations and associations possess considerable resources and can be major platforms for the exercise of leadership. Business leaders, like Richard King Mellon in Pittsburgh, can forge an agenda to significantly alter the urban landscape. As with mayors, their task is to unite a diverse community around a common set of interests and goals. Not surprisingly, business leadership is certainly evident in the development arena, where the interests of business are directly impacted. In the educational arena, however, the challenge to craft a common set of community interests around educational reform is more formidable.

The potential stumbling blocks to urban leadership are many. And yet, leaders do emerge. Similar to what John Mollenkopf referred to as political entrepreneurs, urban leaders "gather and risk political capital or support in order to reshape politics and create new sources of power by establishing new programs or products."[54] Leaders "reshape politics" by crafting a common agenda with followers and then implementing the programs and services to achieve that agenda. Leaders are architects in the urban setting; they serve as catalysts for creating and recreating the major institutions of the city.

INSTITUTIONS AND LEADERSHIP

The interaction between institutions and leaders is critical to our study. On the one hand, the institutional environment creates numerous constraints and boundaries on the exercise of leadership. Networks, associations, formal organizations, and political culture shape and define much of what a leader does. Institutions, however, also are empowering. They are critical mechanisms for achieving the goals of both leaders and followers. As Howard Gardner concludes, "If the tie is to endure, leaders and followers must work together to construct some kind of an institution or organization that embodies their common values."[55]

Both aspects of this relationship—constraining and empowering—are important. The constraining quality of institutions shapes much of everyday politics and policy making. As noted previously, the institutional environment often fragments and splits resources and otherwise restricts the ability of individuals to act. The American political system, for example, holds dearly the separation of powers as a principle to protect against the abuse of power. The additional effect, however, is to complicate the tasks of leadership. Furthermore, policy makers often become "institution-bound" whereby the "maintenance and survival of their organization" become the goal.[56] Gradual or incremental change becomes the standard operating procedure. Potential leaders focus more on issues of management and institutional survival than on matters of agenda building and goal setting.

Institutions, however, are also sources of opportunity and dynamic change. They represent a platform for leaders. The tools, resources, and vantage point of an institution offer important opportunities for policy and program development. In fact, to look beyond existing institutions to the creation of new forms of institutional expression is one of the most critical acts of leadership. As Burns concludes, "The most lasting tangible act of leadership is the creation of an institution —a nation, a social movement, a political party, a bureaucracy—that continues to exert moral leadership and foster needed social change long after the creative leaders are gone."[57] Institution building becomes the lasting contribution of leaders toward achieving collective goals.

How have Pittsburgh, Boston, and St. Louis fared in meeting this challenge? In the chapters that follow we answer this question by applying the theoretical framework outlined here. The next chapter introduces the three cities, then each city is presented in more detail in subsequent chapters. The three cities offer very different institution building and leadership experiences. Pittsburgh comes first and sets the example. Leadership both inside and outside the double helix of school reform plays a critical role in building networks and associations that support an agenda of educational innovation. A superintendent, school board president, and business community create a common set of interests and goals striving for educational excellence. Boston is presented second and represents our middle case. A long-standing governance battle among key actors—mayors, superintendents, and school board members—stymied many efforts for school reform. In the last few years, however, these same actors joined forces to take advantage of institutional opportunities that support educational improvement. St. Louis is our third case and demonstrates many of the frustrations of weak leadership and inadequate institutions. A fragmented political system and weak business sector provide little foundation for the leadership and institution building needed to create, support, and sustain an agenda of educational reform.

3

The Setting: Pittsburgh, Boston, and St. Louis

Pittsburgh, Boston, and St. Louis provide the setting for our comparative study of civic capacity and school reform. These cities are similar on some dimensions, such as population loss and deindustrialization, yet dissimilar on others, such as the structure of city government. These distinctions are central in our comparative case study research design. This research strategy allows us to focus on the dissimilarities among the three cities and the contribution these differences make in explaining variation in civic capacity and school reform efforts.

After World War II our three cities displayed remarkable similarities: they were comparable in population; each had a major manufacturing base; and each had a history of machine-style politics, with its individualistic reward structure. As the decades passed, the population in each city declined, and persons of color became an increasingly significant percentage of the population. Furthermore, school systems in each city faced similar challenges: a growing minority-dominated student body with many from poverty backgrounds; high drop-out rates and low student test scores; and growing dissatisfaction and exit by many parents and students, particularly whites.

Our three cities, however, are dissimilar in a number of ways. Modifications to local governmental structure allowed two of the cities—Pittsburgh and Boston—to centralize power in mayoral hands, while the third city—St. Louis—remained fragmented. Although each city saw a decline in its manufacturing base, the response in each followed a different path involving civic institutions and development policies. And, most important, each city developed its own school governance structure, which, in turn, supported a different form of civic capacity and school reform.

In this chapter we introduce both key similarities and differences among the three cities. We begin by looking at population trends, income levels, and demographic changes. The changing economies of each city are outlined, and the different governmental structures are described. The school systems of each city are introduced in terms of demographic changes, governance structures, and student achievement measures. We also use interview data to outline major problem perceptions in the cities. We conclude with three measures of local support for public education: financial support, programmatic innovation and effort, and interviewee perceptions of effort. These measures establish our ranking of the cities for their support of public education: Pittsburgh first, followed by Boston, and then St. Louis. The case studies that follow explain this variation using the language of institutions and leadership introduced in Chapter 2.

POPULATION, DEMOGRAPHICS, AND INCOME

Pittsburgh, Boston, and St. Louis reached their population zenith in 1950. Returning servicemen and their burgeoning families crowded into each city. The lack of housing construction during the Depression years and World War II caused considerable overcrowding. After 1950, however, the population in each city declined as the suburbs attracted many city residents (see table 3-1). In general, the postwar development of suburbia caused significant population declines in many American central cities, particularly in the Midwest and Northeast.

As the data in table 3-1 indicate, population losses have been severe in Boston, Pittsburgh, and St. Louis. The drop is sharpest in St. Louis; the city experienced a population loss of 54 percent between 1950 and 1990. Pittsburgh's population loss at 45 percent during this forty-year period was also steep. Although St. Louis started this period with almost 200,000 more people than Pittsburgh, by 1990 the city's population advantage was only 27,000. Boston's population dropped by 28 percent over the four decades. Interestingly, the city gained 11,000 people between 1980 and 1990, seemingly reversing the common trend.

Comparing central cities with respective metropolitan areas reveals very quickly the sharp movement to suburbia and the decreasing population share in the central city. As table 3-2 illustrates, all three metropolitan areas increased in

Table 3-1. City Population

	Pittsburgh	Boston	St. Louis
1950	676,806	801,444	856,796
1960	604,332	697,197	750,026
1970	520,117	641,071	622,236
1980	423,938	562,994	453,085
1990	369,879	574,283	396,685

Source: U.S. Bureau of the Census, *Census of Population* (Washington, D.C.: Government Printing Office, 1950; 1960; 1970; 1980; 1990).

Table 3-2. Metropolitan Area Population and City Share

		Pittsburgh	Boston	St. Louis
1950	Metro Area	1,532,953	2,333,448	1,400,058
	% City	44.2	35.9	61.2
1960	Metro Area	1,800,400	2,413,236	1,667,693
	% City	33.6	28.9	45.0
1970	Metro Area	2,401,245	2,753,7000	2,363,017
	% City	21.7	23.3	26.3
1980	Metro Area	2,263,894	2,763,757	2,356,460
	% City	18.7	20.4	19.2
1990	Metro Area	2,242,798	4,171,747	2,444,099
	% City	16.5	13.8	16.2

Source: U.S. Bureau of the Census, *Census of Population* (Washington, D.C.: Government Printing Office, 1950; 1960; 1970; 1980; 1990).

population over the past five decades. The sharpest growth occurred between 1960 and 1970. Overall, metropolitan Boston's population increased by 87 percent, Pittsburgh's by 46 percent, and St. Louis's by 75 percent. The Pittsburgh area actually lost population between 1970 and 1990, in part because of the entire area's dependence on heavy manufacturing. St. Louis's area population has grown only slightly since 1970. On the other hand, Boston's metropolitan population increased significantly between 1980 and 1990 as additional counties became part of its metropolitan statistical area. Each central city's share of regional population has declined significantly as would be expected.

A major demographic transformation in American central cities is the increasing representation of people of color, often African-American, in municipal populations. Because of changes in enumeration in census data from 1950 to 1990, we will look at the percentage of nonwhites in Pittsburgh, Boston, and St. Louis over time (see table 3-3). In the earlier decades, data were not kept on the number of Hispanics, who may be of any race. In any event, the number of Hispanics in Pittsburgh and St. Louis is negligible, although it is a growing component in Boston.

Table 3-3. Percentage of Nonwhites in City Populations

	Pittsburgh	Boston	St. Louis
1950	12.3	5.3	18.0
1960	17.2	9.8	28.8
1970	20.2	16.3	41.3
1980	24.9	29.5	46.4
1990	27.9	37.0	49.0

Source: U.S. Bureau of the Census, *Census of Population* (Washington, D.C.: Government Printing Office, 1950; 1960; 1970; 1980; 1990).

Each city began the period under examination as a predominantly white city. In keeping with national trends, the proportion of nonwhites has grown steadily in all three. St. Louis clearly is on the brink of becoming a majority nonwhite city. The nonwhite proportion of the population in Pittsburgh and Boston, however, is less than in many major American cities. Nonetheless, the general transformation of central cities into homes for people of color amidst predominantly white suburban areas holds for Boston, Pittsburgh, and St. Louis, although certainly to a lesser extent for Boston and Pittsburgh.

In addition, American central cities have experienced appreciable growth in the number of residents living in poverty. In 1970, the Census of Populations began to record the percentage of families and of children younger than eighteen living below the federally established poverty line. Table 3-4 arrays these figures for Pittsburgh, Boston, and St. Louis.

From the data in table 3-4, it is clear that St. Louis has the largest percentage of families and of children under eighteen living in poverty. This situation presents a dual problem for the city. First, its revenues may stagnate or decline since it has relatively fewer wealthy and middle-class taxpayers in its population. Second, its school-age population comes from areas of highly concentrated poverty with the concomitant social problems that affect the ability to learn. Boston and Pittsburgh fare better by this measure, but even in these cities there is a significant population living in poverty that poses a major challenge for educators and policy makers in each city.

A sizable poverty population could indicate a less well-educated population as well. The three cities show different patterns in regard to the percentage of their population completing high school or four years of college (see table 3-5). It should be noted that there will be a natural increase in the percentage of high school graduates over time, because new population cohorts are far more likely to finish elementary and secondary education.

Boston clearly has the most well-educated population, with twice the percentage of college graduates in 1990 as St. Louis. Since 1960, St. Louis has lagged consistently behind the other cities in educational attainment. Pittsburgh again takes

Table 3-4. Families and Children Below the Poverty Line

	Pittsburgh		Boston		St. Louis	
	% Families	% Children*	% Families	% Children*	% Families	% Children*
1970	11.2	34.9	11.7	37.9	14.4	41.5
1980	11.9	24.3	16.7	30.9	16.6	33.7
1990	16.6	32.2	15.0	28.0	20.6	39.3

*Children under eighteen.

Source: U.S. Bureau of the Census, *County and City Data Book* (Washington, D.C.: Government Printing Office, 1972; 1983; 1994).

Table 3-5. Education Level Percentage of High School and College Graduates in City Population

	Pittsburgh		Boston		St. Louis	
	High School Graduates	College Graduates	High School Graduates	College Graduates	High School Graduates	College Graduates
1950	21.3	3.5	28.9	6.4	15.1	4.4
1960	35.4	6.4	44.6	7.6	26.3	4.5
1970	46.0	9.0	53.5	10.3	33.1	5.6
1980	61.1	14.6	68.4	20.3	48.2	10.0
1990	72.4	20.1	75.7	30.3	62.8	15.3

Source: U.S. Bureau of the Census, *Census of Population* (Washington, D.C.: Government Printing Office, 1950; 1960; 1970; 1980; 1990).

a middle place, with almost as high a proportion of high school graduates as Boston in 1990 but considerably fewer college graduates. As the nation's economy becomes increasingly technological, locations with well-educated populations tend to fare better.

Median family income offers another measure of economic well-being. As table 3-6 indicates, in 1950 and 1960, the three cities had very similar median family incomes. By 1970, however, significant differences began to appear that became particularly marked by 1990. In that year, Boston's economic comeback was very evident in the data, as the city's median family income rose markedly. Pittsburgh seemed best positioned in 1980, but it had fallen back considerably ten years later and was closer to St. Louis in median family income than to the new leader, Boston. St. Louis trailed both cities in median family income, as it did on measures of poverty and educational achievement levels presented previously.

Table 3-6. Median Family Income

	Pittsburgh	Boston	St. Louis
1950	$3,314	$3,249	$3,205
1960	$5,605	$5,747	$5,355
1970	$8,787	$9,133	$8,173
1980	$17,499	$16,062	$15,265
1990	$27,484	$34,377	$24,274

Source: U.S. Bureau of the Census, *County and City Data Book* (Washington, D.C.: Government Printing Office, 1972; 1983; 1994).

ECONOMIC SHIFTS AND OCCUPATIONAL STRUCTURE

In Chapter 1, we outlined the general transformation from manufacturing to service economies that took place in most midwestern and eastern American cities after 1970. Pittsburgh, Boston, and St. Louis also experienced this change, although to different degrees. Boston and Pittsburgh witnessed the most dramatic increases in the services sector, while St. Louis experienced a smaller increase and continues to have the largest number of manufacturing employees among the three cities.

One measure that captures this economic transformation at the city level is the changing number of business establishments and employees in key sectors. Table 3-7 provides a historical account of the number of business establishments and employees in each city in the three major areas of manufacturing, services, and wholesale and retail trade. The overall trend is clear: all three cities experienced a sharp decline in manufacturing, as measured by both the number of establishments and employees. Wholesale and retail trade also declined in magnitude in all three cities. In contrast, the services sector expanded.[1] All three cities participated, albeit to varying degrees, in the overall economic transformation of the last thirty years.

A shrinking manufacturing base is evident also from employment data based on city residents rather than businesses located in the city. Table 3-8 presents the percentage of city residents in the civilian work force engaged in manufacturing. In 1960, in all three cities this percentage was sizable. St. Louis had the largest percentage of residents in manufacturing in each decade. This finding is consistent with the data regarding education and income: St. Louis clearly has been and continues to be more of a blue-collar community. Pittsburgh experienced the largest decline in the percentage of residents engaged in manufacturing, which is not surprising given Pittsburgh's heavy reliance on the steel industry and associated jobs. In Boston as well, manufacturing jobs are no longer a common option for city residents.

The key component in this economic transformation is the overall decline in the number of blue-collar workers and manufacturing firms and the subsequent shift to a service-based economy. This transformation has major implications for employee skill levels and educational systems. The limited skill requirements of traditional manufacturing jobs are being replaced, in large part, by service-related jobs, many of which require higher skill levels.[2] This trend does not bode well for individuals with a limited education or tied to a shrinking manufacturing base. St. Louis's continuing reliance on manufacturing, for example, augmented by its lower standing on income and education data, poses a major challenge for that city. Boston and Pittsburgh have adapted better to the new world economy, but they also have been buffeted by the winds of economic change. In all three cities, this changing economy represents a major test for school systems.

Table 3-7.
Business Establishments and Employment in Pittsburgh

Year	Manufacturing Establish.	Employees	Services Establish.	Employees	Wholesale and Retail Trade Establish.	Employees
1963	1,037	81,707	2,112	21,990	6,040	63,883
1982	671	52,300	3,286	41,384	3,779	53,261
1992	553	23,400	3,953	62,930	3,577	51,321
% Change in Employees 1963–1992	−71%			+186%		−20%

Business Establishments and Employment in Boston

Year	Manufacturing Establish.	Employees	Services Establish.	Employees	Wholesale and Retail Trade Establish.	Employees
1963	2,086	82,512	2,735	31,985	8,174	89,169
1982	1,032	47,400	5,039	87,785	4,716	67,869
1992	688	32,400	5,659	102,252	4,720	62,212
% Change in Employees 1963–1992	−61%			+220%		−30%

Business Establishments and Employment in St. Louis

Year	Manufacturing Establish.	Employees	Services Establish.	Employees	Wholesale and Retail Trade Establish.	Employees
1963	1,970	129,069	2,552	27,547	7,265	78,363
1982	1,107	68,900	2,397	31,413	3,633	47,989
1992	967	48,700	3,072	50,057	3,582	50,056
% Change in Employees 1963–1992	−62%			+82%		−36%

Note: Number of establishments and employment in services and retail trade data are based on paid employment.
Sources: For 1963 data, U.S. Bureau of the Census, *County and City Data Book* (Washington, D.C.: Government Printing Office, 1967); For 1982 and 1992 data, U.S. Bureau of the Census, *Economic Census: Census of Manufactures, Census of Service Industries, Census of Wholesale Trade, Census of Retail Trade* (Washington, D.C.: Government Printing Office, 1984, 1994).

CITY GOVERNMENT

The nature of a city's governmental institutions affects its policy making as well as the overall political culture, which in turn sanctions certain activities over others. In the realm of municipal governmental structure, our three cities share a number of common characteristics. Each has a heritage of machine-like politics. In Boston, James Michael Curley dominated local politics during much of the first

Table 3-8. Percentage of Civilian Work Force
Engaged in Manufacturing

	Pittsburgh	Boston	St. Louis
1960	26.1	24.3	31.2
1970	20.6	17.5	27.8
1980	14.8	14.3	21.6
1990	8.5	9.9	15.1

Source: U.S. Bureau of the Census, *County and City Data Book* (Washington, D.C.: Government Printing Office, 1962; 1972; 1983; 1994).

half of the twentieth century and often is portrayed as a quintessential machine politician.[3] Pittsburgh's legendary boss, David Lawrence, was not as well known for colorful escapades but was a formidable figure in city, state, and national politics for several decades.[4] St. Louis never had a centralized political machine, but ward factionalism created that city's own version of political patronage and machine-style politics.[5]

Although sharing a common heritage, governmental institutions in the three cities have evolved down different paths. Boston and Pittsburgh, for example, moved to strong-mayor forms of government, while St. Louis retained a weak-mayor form of government in which factional politics have continued unabated. Table 3-9 presents basic characteristics of the three city governments.

Boston's form of government shows the most evidence of reform. It has nonpartisan elections, and part of its city council is elected at-large. The position of mayor is strong but within a reformed system. Pittsburgh's system is more traditional; elections are partisan and the council is selected from districts, although the number is relatively small. The mayor shares citywide office with the comptroller, making the position less fiscally strong than in Boston. St. Louis's fragmentation is evident in this array. The mayor shares authority over city government

Table 3-9. Municipal Governmental Structure in Pittsburgh, Boston, and St. Louis

	Pittsburgh	Boston	St. Louis
Government Type	Strong Mayor	Strong Mayor	Weak Mayor
Mayoral Term	4 Years	4 Years	4 Years
Election Type	Partisan	Nonpartisan	Partisan
Council Size	9	13	28
District Councillors	9	9	28
At-Large Councillors	0	4	0
Council Term	4 Years, Staggered	2 Years	4 Years, Staggered
Other Citywide Elected Officials	Comptroller	None	Comptroller, Pres. of Bd. of Aldermen, 8 County Offices

with the comptroller and the president of the board of aldermen. In addition, St. Louis voters elect eight officeholders at-large, such as sheriff and recorder of deeds, to perform county functions, which further dilutes mayoral control and strengthens the city's ward-based politics. St. Louis also retains a relatively large legislative body, a twenty-eight-member board of aldermen, which is elected on a partisan ballot.

This brief outline of governmental structures provides certain clues to the likely nature of the regime structure in our three cities. St. Louis's fragmentation and plethora of wards point to less cohesive city politics and policy making. Boston, on the other hand, has a very strong mayoral system that could support more centralized policy initiatives. Pittsburgh lies in the middle, although its strong mayor-council system places it closer to Boston in political design. Our concern, however, is not only with city government but also with the relationship between municipal government and the local school system. In the next section we outline the nature of local school governance as well as student demographics and achievement levels.

LOCAL SCHOOL SYSTEMS

School governance in Pittsburgh, Boston, and St. Louis varies in a variety of ways (see table 3-10). In the Boston public schools the mayor has considerable authority: he or she appoints the seven-member school board, which then hires the superintendent, and the mayor also presents the total school budget to the city council for approval. Through these appointive and fiscal powers the mayor exerts considerable influence over administration and policy making in the school system. This governance system, however, has been in place only since 1992. Prior to that date, the school board was a thirteen-member elected body, although the school system was still fiscally dependent upon the city for its total budget allocation.

In Pittsburgh and St. Louis, on the other hand, there is no direct involvement by city government in school affairs. In both systems, the schools districts are fiscally independent from city government finances. The selection of school board members, however, does differ. Pittsburgh's school board follows the same sys-

Table 3-10. Local School District Structure

	Pittsburgh	Boston	St. Louis
Number on School Board	9	7	12
Board Selection	District Election	Mayor Appoints	At-Large Election
Type of Election	Partisan	—	Nonpartisan
Terms of Office	4 Years, Staggered	4 Years	6 Years, Staggered
Fiscally Independent	Yes*	No	Yes

*The city comptroller has some fiscal authority over the school district.

tem as the city council does: a nine-member school board elected in partisan elections on the basis of district representation. The similarity of city council and school board elections poses a potential link between the two, although the district lines are drawn differently.

In contrast, school governance in St. Louis deviates significantly from the pattern used for that city's board of aldermen. Whereas the board of aldermen is largely unreformed with district and partisan elections, the school board has adopted more reform elements, including at-large elections on a nonpartisan basis. The six-year term of office for school board members in St. Louis also differs from the board of aldermen's term and is longer than most elected local governing bodies. This difference between city and school governance structures further separated school politics from city government politics. Recent legislation at the state level, however, has ended this separation. Beginning with the 2001 elections, there will be a seven-member board elected from the districts. Each district will be made up of four city wards. This new arrangement may bring about a closer connection between city and school politics.

Whatever its form of governance, each school district has a student population that has become increasingly poor and predominantly nonwhite, most often in greater proportion than in the city itself. Table 3-11 presents key data on each school system.

School populations in both Boston and St. Louis are predominantly nonwhite. In St. Louis, almost 80 percent of students are African-American with few attendees from other minority groups. Boston, on the other hand, has many Asian and Hispanic students, although its student body is almost half African-American. Pittsburgh's student body remains nearly half white, reflecting the more heavily white city population. In all three districts, over half of the students qualify for the free or reduced-price lunch program. The student population in St. Louis is the most in need according to this measure, with 85 percent of students qualify-

Table 3-11. Student Characteristics for Pittsburgh, Boston, and St. Louis Public School Districts (1992–1993)

	Pittsburgh	Boston	St. Louis
Number of Students	41,160	62,407	42,278
% White	45.2	20.2	19.9
% African-American	53.0	47.6	78.3
% Asian/Pacific	1.4	9.1	1.3
% Hispanic	0.3	22.7	0.4
% Free or Reduced-Price Lunch	61.3	58.3	85.0
% Limited-English Proficiency	0.7	22.0	2.0

Source: Council of the Great City Schools, *National Urban Education Goals: 1992–93 Indicators Report* (Washington, D.C.: Council of the Great City Schools, 1994).

ing for lunch assistance. In general, the student bodies of the three districts are poorer and more likely to be minority than is true in the general city population; school populations, for example, are at least 25 percent more nonwhite than the population of their respective cities. And finally, Boston faces the most significant challenge in the area of bilingual education, reflecting its larger Asian and Hispanic populations as well as the large number of first-generation immigrants in that city.

Furthermore, large segments of the school-age population in each city do not attend the city's public schools. In Boston, 17,091 children attended private or parochial schools in 1993, representing 21 percent of the city's school-age children. In Pittsburgh, the figure is 14,062, or 25 percent of school-age children, and in St. Louis, 14,896, or 26 percent. Large Catholic populations that prefer parochial schools account for part of this trend, but dissatisfaction with the public schools is also an important factor. Voluntary transfer programs to public schools in nearby communities offer an avenue for students who decide not to attend the city's public schools. In Boston, approximately 3,000 African-American city youth attend suburban public schools, and an astonishing 13,500 African-American youth from St. Louis boarded buses in 1993 headed for schools in one of fourteen suburban districts. In St. Louis, then, approximately 50 percent of school-age children in the city attend private or parochial schools or public schools in the suburbs. Clearly, many parents of various backgrounds seek alternatives to city school systems.

On measures of academic achievement, each school system has shortcomings. Pittsburgh, however, has the strongest record, and St. Louis clearly has the lowest achievement levels (see table 3-12). On reading and math scores compared with national norms, Pittsburgh fares better than the other two school systems, although Boston is relatively close. Scores in St. Louis are considerably below the other two school systems. The annual dropout rate shows a similar pattern,

Table 3-12. Measures of Academic Achievement

	Pittsburgh	Boston	St. Louis
Reading:			
% of Students in Top Quartile	25.6	25.1	14.0
% of Students in Bottom Quartile	19.7	23.0	42.2
Math:			
% of Students in Top Quartile	35.9	25.1	18.0
% of Students in Bottom Quartile	17.4	18.8	36.7
Annual Dropout Rate	7.0	8.7	14.1
College: % of Graduates Enrolled			
in Four-Year Colleges	60.5	39.0	30.6

Source: Council of the Great City Schools, *National Urban Education Goals: 1992–93 Indicators Report* (Washington D.C.: Council of the Great City Schools, 1994).

with Pittsburgh having the lowest rate, followed by Boston and then St. Louis. In college attendance at four-year institutions, Pittsburgh graduates again demonstrate the strongest record, followed by Boston and St. Louis.

PROBLEM PERCEPTIONS

Another useful perspective on our three cities is elite perceptions of key problems and challenges facing each community. Despite some of the differences noted above, there are striking similarities among city officials and educators with respect to their perceptions of major problems. Whether in Pittsburgh, Boston, or St. Louis, elites in each community pointed to a common set of economic, educational, and social problems as constituting major challenges facing the city.[6]

To capture the range of public problems, a number of interviewees were asked, *What do you see as the major problems facing your city?* Each interviewee was allowed up to three responses. Similar responses about the three cities are evident in table 3-13. At the top of the problem list is inadequate economic resources, which is true when responses are averaged across all three cities as well as within each city. In Boston this problem received the highest frequency of mentions, 84 percent. One attorney involved in the education community described a "fundamental restructuring" in the economy that was having major impacts throughout the region, and a community advocate emphasized the importance of balanced economic growth to avoid dividing the city into "rich and poor." In Pittsburgh and St. Louis as well, the economy received the most mentions of all problems facing the city.

Education was clearly a major concern as well. Across all three cities, 56 percent of respondents mentioned inadequate education as a major problem. In Boston, for example, one editor of the *Boston Globe* emphasized that the quality of public education affects everything else that happens in the city. Beyond the economy and education, community elites identified a host of social problems as critical in their cities. The many social problems that individuals face—poverty, drugs, and broken families—received prominent mention. Also high on the list were race relations and crime. In Boston, one community advocate described rac-

Table 3-13. Elite Perceptions of Major Problems Facing the City (Rank)

	Pittsburgh	Boston	St. Louis	All Cities
Inadequate economic resources	74% (1)	84% (1)	61% (1)	73% (1)
Inadequate education	58% (2)	56% (2)	53% (3)	56% (2)
Social problems of individuals	26% (4)	31% (5)	58% (2)	39% (3)
Race Relations	32% (3)	38% (3)	31% (5)	33% (4)
Crime	16% (5)	38% (3)	44% (4)	33% (4)
No. of Interviewees	31	32	36	99

ism as an "umbrella over the city," and a school committee member noted that the "cultural clash" between white and minority groups overshadows other issues in the city.

The positioning of economic problems and educational concerns at the top of the problem list has important implications for school reform. To the degree that education is linked to the economy, school reform can become part of a city's economic agenda. A connection between economic concerns—job losses, wage stagnation, plant closings, corporate flight—and the classroom creates a powerful argument for school reform. As one corporate chief executive emphasized, "Education is the linchpin for economic improvement for all our citizens." Continuing the economic theme, this business leader argued that education must be seen as an "investment" rather than "consumption." As we shall see, the ability of city and community leaders to develop this connection varies among the three cities and is an important part of the school reform dynamic in each community.

Another question focused on education and also points to a common set of concerns across the three cities. Interviewees were asked, *What would enable your city to make a greater effort in the area of education?* In response, as outlined in table 3-14, addressing social problems ranked first in Pittsburgh and Boston and second in St. Louis. The other leading response in all three cities was to redistribute resources to schools and related services.

This emphasis on addressing social problems and redistributing resources highlights the broad context of school reform. Addressing social problems is viewed by many as a prerequisite to effective school reform. As one school principal commented, the problem of urban public education "doesn't come in pieces, it comes in one big chunk." Unless the "big chunk"—the environment of poverty—is part of the solution, schools will fall short in educating the youth of the city. As he concluded, the best response to the problems that face urban schools would be to "give every parent a job, and give every child a parent." In addition, a redistribution of power and resources to schools and related service providers is seen as critical. To address the problems faced in urban schools, a higher level of resources is needed. One interviewee described the need for "comparable resources" so urban youth can compete with youth in private and suburban school settings who benefit from either higher per student spending or a home environment that nurtures learning.

Table 3-14. Elite Perception of Preferred Actions to Enable a Greater Effort in Education (Rank)

	Pittsburgh	Boston	St. Louis	All Cities
Address social problems	40% (1)	42% (1)	38% (2)	40% (1)
Redistribute resources to schools and related services	35% (2)	27% (2)	45% (1)	36% (2)
No. of Interviewees	43	41	47	131

This comparison of problem perceptions, school systems, and cities high-lights both similarities and differences. Overall, our three cities have lost popula-tion, increased in the minority component of their citizenry, and become poorer with fewer blue-collar jobs. Of the three cities, Boston appears to have achieved some population and economic stability, while St. Louis has been most negatively affected by national and international economic shifts. They all have public school populations that reflect these changes and, in fact, often show these characteris-tics in greater numbers. It is clearly a daunting task to prepare the city's public school children for a very different work world than that of their grandparents. Students often come from homes with significant problems and neighborhoods with few workers.

Furthermore, the problem perceptions in each city pose a major challenge. There is widespread agreement across all three cities that a changing economy is a major concern along with developing an adequate educational system. The ob-stacles to addressing educational problems are formidable, including the social problems of an urban setting as well as the need for additional resources. Although there is general agreement on this agenda, our three cities have approached this challenge with quite different levels of effort and commitment to educational reform.

RANKING THE CITIES: INDICATORS OF CIVIC CAPACITY AT WORK FOR PUBLIC EDUCATION

Our central concern is the creation of civic capacity and its activation on behalf of public education. In this regard, Pittsburgh, Boston, and St. Louis offer quite different examples of civic capacity at work. Pittsburgh, we argue, ranks first among our three cities in supporting school reform, followed by Boston and then St. Louis. This ranking is based on three assessments of local effort on behalf of public education—financial support, programmatic innovation and effort, and interviewee perceptions of effort. Each is briefly presented below.

Financial Support

Public school districts receive financial support from all three levels—federal, state, and local—in the American political system. Since our focus, however, is on the development and application of a city's civic capacity, our central concern is sup-port from local sources. For dependent school districts, such as Boston's, this support comes through city government; for independent school districts, as in Pittsburgh and St. Louis, local support is derived directly from the taxpayers. In both instances, property tax receipts are the major source for local revenues.

The willingness and ability of a community to support its school district with local revenues are strong indications of that city's support for public education.

Our three cities differ on this financial indicator. Table 3-15 presents the split in revenue sources for each school district as well as two financial measures for local support. One measure focuses on local revenues per student provided in each city. Pittsburgh, with $5,155 in local revenues per student, is slightly higher than Boston's support level of $5,048 per student. St. Louis has a much lower level of local support at $3,055 per student. By this measure, Boston and Pittsburgh demonstrate a much higher level of local support for public education.

Table 3-15 provides a second measure that adjusts local financial support by the wealth of the community as determined by median family income. The last row of table 3-15 shows for each city the ratio of local revenues per student to median family income. Comparisons using this ratio compensate for the different levels of wealth in each city. With a possible range of 0 to 1, a ratio of 1 would indicate that local revenues per student equaled median family income in that city. In general, higher ratios indicate that more revenue is being raised from that particular city's wealth base. After including this component, Pittsburgh retains its first ranking as the city with the strongest revenue support for public education. Boston is still second, although its high income level moves it closer to St. Louis in this measure of wealth-adjusted local support for public education. St. Louis continues to show the lowest level of local financial support for public education.

Programmatic Innovation and Effort

The second measure we use to rank our cities is the level of educational innovation. Measuring and comparing innovation practices across school districts are difficult, but as a preliminary assessment each author analyzed the status of key

Table 3-15. Local Financial Support for School Systems (1993–1994)

	Pittsburgh		Boston		St. Louis	
Total Revenues	$365,632,000		$489,025,000		$312,624,000	
Federal	31,867,000	(9%)	49,588,000	(10%)	38,620,000	(12%)
State	127,011,000	(35%)	117,680,000	(24%)	148,080,000	(47%)
Local	206,754,000	(57%)	321,757,000	(66%)	125,924,000	(40%)
Enrollment	40,107		63,738		41,213	
Local Revenues Per Student	$5,155		$5,048		$3,055	
Median Family Income	$27,484		$34,377		$24,274	
Ratio of Local Revenues Per Student to Median Family Income	.19		.15		.13	

Source: U.S. Department of Education, National Center for Educational Statistics, *Digest of Educational Statistics, 1996* (Washington, D.C.: Government Printing Office, 1996), and U.S. Department of Commerce, Bureau of the Census, *1990 Census of the Population* (Washington, D.C.: Government Printing Office, 1990).

innovations in his or her hometown school district as of January 1995. Ten educational innovations were assessed. These innovations, such as school-based management, are indicative of the various reform efforts outlined in Chapter 1. The ten innovations are:

Preschool and early childhood development programs;

Postschool transition with school-to-work and school-to-college programs;

Support for parental involvement in the education of their children;

Administrative decentralization and site-based management;

Parent participation in school governance;

School-linked programs with community social services;

Evaluation research and its use by the district;

Choice programs;

Privatization programs; and

Innovation in pedagogy and student assessment.

For each innovation, a rating scale was established with three or four possible responses to measure its presence in a school district (see appendix 2 for a description of the responses and their respective point values). In general, higher numbers indicate a more system-wide adoption of an innovation. As presented in table 3-16, this ranking of our cities follows the already established pattern: Pittsburgh is first with 31 points, followed by Boston with 27.5 points and St. Louis with 19.5 points.

Table 3-16. Authors' Assessment of Educational Innovation in Each City*

	Pittsburgh	Boston	St. Louis
Preschool and early childhood	3.5	3.0	2.0
Postschool transition	3.5	4.0	3.0
Parental involvement	3.5	2.5	1.0
Administrative decentralization and school-based management	3.5	3.5	2.0
Parent participation in school governance	4.0	3.5	2.0
School-linked services	3.0	2.0	2.0
Evaluation research	3.0	2.0	1.5
Choice programs	3.0	3.5	3.0
Privatization	1.0	1.5	2.0
Pedagogy and assessment practices	3.0	2.0	1.0
Total Score	31.0	27.5	19.5

*Numerical responses correspond to different levels of educational innovation (see appendix 2 for more details).

INTERVIEWEE RESPONSES

A third measure of local support for school reform is drawn from the interviews conducted in each city. During these interviews many respondents were asked, *Recognizing that no city can do everything that it would like to do in education, how would you generally characterize the effort in your city?* Interviewees were then given four choices, which are listed in table 3-17.

Across all three cities, the dissatisfaction with current school reform efforts is very high. At least two-thirds of interviewees in each city cite a negative response of "not doing well at all" or "falling short of what we could be doing." In comparing the three cities, the responses generally are consistent with our ranking. Pittsburgh, for example, is ranked above Boston by respondents in the respective cities. In Pittsburgh, 32 percent of respondents gave relatively positive assessments, agreeing that their community was "doing everything that can be done" or "doing fairly well." In Boston, only 15 percent of respondents offered a similar assessment. Also consistent with this ranking, Pittsburgh receives a lower percentage than Boston of negative "not doing well at all" ratings.

Respondents in St. Louis, however, present a diversity of responses that deviate, in part, from our ranking. While some rate their city as supportive of education, a significant number find the city lacking in this area. Consistent with our ranking, St. Louis has the largest percentage of respondents—just over one-third—who state that the city is "not doing well at all" in supporting public education. Notwithstanding the more positive responses in St. Louis, this negative appraisal is more strongly supported by the other measures outlined above.

In summary, Pittsburgh, Boston, and St. Louis demonstrate different levels of support for public education. The economic and institutional differences among the three cities outlined in this chapter—wealth, economic fortunes, governmental structure, school governance—play a role in explaining this variation in effort. A more complete explanation, however, requires a closer look at the interaction of these and other variables in the political, economic, and social context of each city. In particular, our focus turns to the critical role of institutions and leadership in explaining different levels of civic capacity at work for public education. In the case studies that follow, we provide an in-depth analysis of each city.

Table 3-17. Elite Perceptions of City Effort in Public Education

Response Choices	Pittsburgh	Boston	St. Louis
• Doing everything that can be done	9%	0%	6%
• Doing fairly well	23%	15%	24%
• Falling short of what we could be doing	63%	70%	35%
• Not doing well at all	5%	15%	35%
No. of Interviewees	22	26	29

4

Pittsburgh's Public Schools: A Fragile Balance of Leadership and Institution Building

In 1990 the Pittsburgh Public Schools were heralded as "a national model of urban educational reform."[1] Far-reaching reforms in the central office and individual schools replaced more than a decade of deep divisions within the school system and the community. This period of school reform and educational achievement was built upon two key factors: Pittsburgh's civic leadership came to the support of the city's public school system, and strong leadership developed within the school system itself. In applying their "double helix" of school reform, Hill, Wise and Shapiro found that in Pittsburgh "the inside and outside strands [were] comparably complete and fully articulated."[2] In this chapter we describe how the simultaneous development of the two strands came to be, as well as the substance of the reforms that resulted from the opportunity presented. We also discover, however, that this "articulation" of inside and outside strands existed as a fragile balance, not an end state. The circumstances and issues facing the Pittsburgh Public Schools in the late 1990s show the dynamic and conditional nature of leadership and institutions.

THE GROWTH OF CIVIC CAPACITY IN PITTSBURGH

It is well known that the Pittsburgh region has suffered devastating economic decline in the past forty years. Almost as well known are the attempts to address the crisis through "public-private partnerships." The best-known example is Renaissance I, the redevelopment in the late 1940s and early 1950s of the Point area of Pittsburgh. Mayor David L. Lawrence and banker Richard K. Mellon forged a partnership that served as a model for cities across the country and laid the foundation for a pattern of public decision making in Pittsburgh that continues today.

56

Renaissance I reflected an earlier political history that included the simultaneous but separate development of political and civic-oriented institutions. During the last two decades of the nineteenth century, Pittsburgh politics was controlled by the Republican Magee/Flinn machine. Early in the twentieth century, however, reform-oriented Republicans implemented several structural changes in the city's political system, including a strong mayor-council form with no term limits and a nine-member, at-large city council. The Republican machine regained control, but these reforms and the rise of a new corporate economic elite profoundly changed how the machine functioned. New business interests, headed by the Mellon family, controlled mayoral elections, but their influence did not extend to the ward level. Therefore, to guarantee that elected leadership did not reestablish a grassroots base, Mellon would not support a mayor for more than a single term. In 1929, however, a mayor who had established independent relationships with the ward chairs defied Mellon and ran for a second term.

Having lost direct control of the public sector, Mellon and his fellow business leaders focused on establishing voluntary civic organizations as extragovernmental public policy vehicles. Thus, as early as the late 1930s, a parallel policy-making system was developing in Pittsburgh that included the political machine and private, civic-oriented organizations. The ward-based electoral machine existed separate from the public policy interest of the business elite. "Private civic nonprofit corporations provided [the business elites] with an organizational base beyond the control of the voting public."[3] These business-sponsored civic organizations produced development studies and plans, but little was accomplished. They were unwilling to cede to the public sector the authority to carry them out.[4]

In 1933, riding the New Deal wave, Pittsburgh Democrats won their first mayoral race in decades and began to establish their dominance in local politics. David Lawrence, as head of the state Democratic party, worked behind the scenes and used New Deal patronage to build a highly centralized machine in Pittsburgh. Fearing a Democratic defeat in the 1945 mayoral election, Lawrence threw his own hat into the ring. To broaden his base of support, Lawrence adopted the Republican downtown redevelopment agenda for Pittsburgh—an agenda articulated by Mellon's newest civic nonprofit, the Allegheny Conference on Community Development (ACCD).[5] Lawrence's victory and the subsequent joining of his public sector control with Mellon's private sector leadership resulted in the Renaissance I partnership that rebuilt the blighted Point, cleaned the air in the county, and ended the near annual flooding of the central business district.[6]

The partnership of Mellon and Lawrence brought together peak institutions that were themselves transformed. Unlike most business associations of the time, or since, the ACCD was established as a highly formalized institution, capable of garnering the authority, financial resources, and technical knowledge necessary to promote meaningful change. Its membership included the heads of many of the nation's industrial giants. The ACCD hired its own professional planning staff and partnered with major private planning and research organizations of the region. Complementary changes were made on the public sector side. Lawrence centralized the development function within the city bureaucracy by creating one of the nation's first urban redevelopment authorities. He named himself as the authority's chair and placed many ACCD supporters in key administrative posts.[7]

In combination, the two sectors were well positioned to make a significant impact on Pittsburgh's central business district. They provided leadership to initiate and implement key urban projects. Using corporate and foundation financial resources, the ACCD "underwrote the necessary expertise for planning and coordination and leveraged larger sums from private investors and public bodies for redevelopment."[8] Ferman describes these institutional changes as setting up a "corporatist decision making structure that insulated development policy from party control."[9] While private and quasi-private development organizations were able to define economic development in technical terms, the machine's need to reward electoral support was fulfilled through nondevelopment-related public services.

This pattern of decision making has dominated public problem solving in Pittsburgh in the post–WWII era. Except for one, each of Pittsburgh's five mayors since Lawrence has partnered with the ACCD in planning and executing central business district redevelopment. Exemplifying this was Renaissance II, a major reinvestment period during the 1980s.[10] Among the many projects during this period was the creation of a new performing arts center. An earlier arts center was conceived by Pittsburgh corporate leader Howard Heinz and funded through the Howard Heinz Endowment in the 1970s. In 1984, based on a consultant's report that it had commissioned, the ACCD launched the Pittsburgh Cultural Trust. This private nonprofit organization used public, private, and foundation funding to develop a second performing arts center, a smaller theater, a major office tower, and a small movie theater.

Foundation funding was important in this and other projects. Because of its industrial past, the Pittsburgh region is foundation-rich. In a 1994 ranking of cities, although fortieth in population and thirty-fourth in income, Pittsburgh was first in grants from independent foundations and seventh in grants from community foundations and the United Way.[11] Not only generous in financial terms, major philanthropies also are supportive by strategically addressing regional needs. Foundation staff work closely with one another and the staff of grant recipients to develop and implement innovative programs.

The Pittsburgh Cultural Trust exemplified several major themes in the city's approach to civic development: creation of autonomous implementing organizations, utilization of appropriate expertise, and reliance upon foundation funding to support projects. This pattern has been repeated even in policy areas usually defined as outside the purview of the business elite, such as employment for chronically unemployed, minority entrepreneurship, health, housing, and neighborhood development. Urban renewal is a good example. During the late 1950s the partnership of Lawrence and the ACCD used federal urban renewal funding to clear an African-American community bordering the central business district. As in most cities, the federally funded bulldozer prompted the creation of community-based opposition groups. Unlike most cities, however, Pittsburgh's public-private partnership attempted to integrate these demands into its agenda. It created a new nonprofit agency, ACTION-Housing, Inc., to construct affordable units as replacement housing for displaced urban renewal victims. Although the success of this initiative did not compare with Renaissance I, the pattern of community decision making remained the same—a new civic organization with policy expertise was created, insulated from the conflict-ridden electoral arena, and public, private, and foundation funding were combined to achieve desired goals. The result was another addition to an institutional landscape in which nonprofit implementing organizations share space with public and private organizations.[12]

The ACCD has played a central role in this tradition of public-private partnerships. The association has been instrumental in creating an environment of communication and collaboration across sectors. As the ACCD leadership said in 1984, the Conference "is more than a collection of business leaders. It has come to occupy a position at the heart of Pittsburgh's civic activity. As initiator, broker, supporter, monitor or facilitator, it touches nearly every major civic or development undertaking in the city."[13] A former ACCD director described the conference as a "state of mind" more than a real authority. Ferman adds a similar point, noting that "ACCD's early, and at the time quite spectacular, success added a strong dose of deference to the city's political culture."[14] Could this pattern of civic cooperation be applied to public education? It is to that question that we now turn.

CRISIS AND RESPONSE IN PUBLIC EDUCATION

Between the late 1960s and the early 1980s, public education in Pittsburgh faced a series of crises, both within the school system itself and in the external community. In the late 1960s, for example, parents were demanding more input in school policy making. In 1969, the Pittsburgh School Board responded by creating a pyramidal system of elected parent councils. Demands also came from teachers within the system. In 1968, in fact, teachers struck for union recognition. The Pittsburgh Federation of Teachers was recognized, and Al Fondy was elected president, a position he still held in 1999. Between 1968 and 1975, the PFT struck two more times over various contractual issues.[15]

But the most significant crisis came in 1968 when the Pennsylvania Human Relations Commission required the Pittsburgh Public Schools to submit a desegregation plan. Over the next decade four superintendents submitted plans.[16] None of the plans was accepted by the school board, and all four superintendents left office, voluntarily or involuntarily. In 1976, in the midst of this turmoil, the school board changed from a court-appointed, at-large board to an elected, district-based board with nine members. Districts were drawn in an attempt to guarantee at least two African-American representatives on the board. Early elections produced three prointegration members (two African-Americans and one white) who, ironically, often voted against the desegregation plans, arguing that the plans did not go far enough.

Neighborhood-based organizations vociferously advocated both sides of the issue—African-American communities demanded desegregation, while white ethnic neighborhoods called for preserving neighborhood schools. A citywide coalition, the Pittsburgh Neighborhood Alliance, struggled to find a compromise. Even the mayor entered the fray, writing letters to board members asking them to vote against the latest desegregation plan and arguing publicly that the Human Relations Commission's order could not be enforced.[17] The commission held steadfast in its demand and in 1980 issued an ultimatum: submit a desegregation plan within ninety days.

A Citizens Advisory Committee was appointed to bring the warring sides together. Robert Pease, executive director of the ACCD, agreed to serve as chair, and the ACCD granted him a leave with pay so that he could devote himself full-time to the development of an acceptable plan. The ACCD's assistant director, David Bergholz, became head of a subcommittee that ultimately developed the magnet school concept as a strategy of school desegregation.[18] The resulting plan utilized magnets, redrawn feeder patterns, and new middle schools to desegregate the system as much as possible. It also included "school improvement plans" to address achievement gaps in African-American schools that would remain segregated. Thus, the community dialogue spawned by the ACCD during the desegregation crisis forged a compromise between those who defined the issue as "quality education" and those who focused on the equal distribution of educational resources. The ACCD continued its involvement through the plan's implementation stage, conducting a series of public information and troubleshooting meetings in Pittsburgh's neighborhoods. A new mayor, Richard Caliguiri, while not openly endorsing the plan, called for its peaceful implementation.

The ACCD's interest in resolving the desegregation issue reflected a growing awareness that the public schools played a critical role in the community. This approach was the case despite the fact that the Pittsburgh Public Schools were becoming predominantly African-American. Unlike in many cities, where the civic leadership abandoned the public schools as the white population declined, Pittsburgh's leadership became engaged in a constructive way. Instead of criticizing the schools as being inferior or ill managed, they called for an open dialogue. As the ACCD's assistant director noted, "The problems of desegregation, the financial and political climate that faced the schools, and a general insularity of school leadership had created a less than favorable public perception of the schools' administration and on the schools' side, a feeling that the community lacked the understanding and willingness to assist it with its problems."[19]

In consultation with the superintendent, teachers' union, businesses, and foundations, the ACCD established a Public Information Advisory Committee to promote the accomplishments of the public schools. Thus, when the desegregation issue reached crisis proportions, the ACCD had already gained legitimacy in the educational arena and had done so in collaboration with major actors within the school system.

Furthermore, the ACCD created the Allegheny Conference Education Fund (ACEF) in 1978 to provide ongoing dialogue among actors and financial resources to the public schools for innovative projects. The ACEF funded a variety of projects designed to bolster the school staff's confidence that the larger community supported their work. Under the umbrella of the ACEF, the Education-in-Residence program brought national education experts to Pittsburgh to work with education, business, foundation, and community leaders, and the Partnerships-in-Education program fostered partnerships between schools and individual businesses. Also, the Mini-Grants for Teachers and the Grants-for-Principals programs funded innovative school-based projects.[20]

These grants and programs built small yet symbolic linkages between civic leaders and front-line educational professionals—teachers and principals. The ACCD wanted to make sure that the existence of these linkages was quickly communicated to the larger public. It funded a national search for a new position within the Pittsburgh Public Schools—director of public relations—who would answer directly to the superintendent. The candidate selected had public relations experience both in corporate and educational settings.[21]

Thus, by 1980 the Pittsburgh Public Schools had survived a tumultuous decade and a half. The school system had taken initial steps in responding to an onslaught of demands emanating both from within itself and from a wide range of external actors. It was making progress in the formulation of a desegregation plan. In the process, civic leadership had been activated and fragile partnerships established. But much more needed to be done, and the new reform-minded school board lacked confidence in the current superintendent. In March the board voted not to renew his contract, and the ACCD assisted in a national search for a successor.

SUPERINTENDENT RICHARD WALLACE AND AN "EXCELLENCE AGENDA," 1980–1992

Dr. Richard C. Wallace Jr., with impressive academic as well as administrative credentials, was hired in 1980 by the Pittsburgh School Board to implement its new desegregation plan, respond to union and parental pressures, and improve the quality of public education. Wallace quickly developed working relationships with the business community represented by the ACCD, the school board, community organizations, and the educational research community. In forging these relationships he demonstrated leadership skills that extended both inside and outside the school system.

Reform Initiatives

Wallace focused his early efforts on strengthening the school system. As he wrote later, "There is no substitute for constant reinforcement of a vision and an excellence agenda; it is critical to successful leadership."[22] Shortly after arriving in Pittsburgh, he engaged the assistance of the Learning Research and Development Corporation (LRDC) at the University of Pittsburgh to conduct a needs assessment survey of stakeholders within the school system and in the broader community.[23] Using these data he presented the school board with six priority areas: achievement in basic skills, personnel performance, management of enrollment decline (i.e., school closings), enrollment retention and attraction, discipline, and the performance of individual schools, especially African-American segregated schools. The board gave him six months to present a specific program in each priority area. His initiatives in each area represented a willingness to reform the system in significant ways as well as to form partnerships with other stakeholders.

Achievement in basic skills. The first step in supporting student achievement was an effective monitoring system. Wallace developed a student testing program to help teachers monitor progress in such a way that timely corrections could be made. Tests would be administered frequently and also would be "curriculum based" rather than "standardized." The system, known as Monitoring Achievement in Pittsburgh (MAP), was developed in 1981 and implemented in 1982. Curriculum-based objectives were tested in various subject areas every six weeks, and results were returned quickly to teachers and parents for corrective action.[24] This immediate feedback and corrective action led to improvements in basic skills performance among all students, including African-American students. In fact, Pittsburgh became one of the first urban schools to publicize the size of the "gap" between African-American and white students' performance on standardized tests.[25] Between 1979 and 1984 this gap was halved.

With the assistance of the ACCD, Wallace obtained a $200,000 grant from the R. K. Mellon Foundation to establish the MAP testing system, which provided computer-based testing information systems at individual schools as well as at the district level. This approach allowed for more efficient maintenance of student records and implementation of data-based decision making. Wallace enlarged the testing office of the central administration and "changed its orientation to include a strong research emphasis."[26] Teachers, students, and parents showed a high degree of satisfaction with the program.[27] One author stated that MAP was "arguably the most comprehensive internal assessment program in any U.S. school district."[28]

Personnel performance. A second major priority was to improve staff training and development. Superintendent Wallace established a personnel system that trained principals both to encourage teachers to become better teachers (known

as PRISM I) and to become more effective instructional leaders themselves (PRISM II). The initiatives that received the most attention concerned teacher training. Over the course of the next several years, all teachers—secondary (PRISM III), elementary (PRISM IV), and middle (PRISM V)—were pulled out of their regular classrooms for six to eight weeks of intensive training at district teachers centers. In an interview with one of the authors, Wallace argued that "firing teachers was the easy way out. The more difficult issue was to make marginal teachers good, good teachers better, and better teachers excellent."

At first, teachers viewed this approach with skepticism. In the same interview Wallace recalled the first group of teachers to attend the Schenley Teachers Center. They were department heads in their schools and were skeptical of Wallace's motives. "They sat there with their arms folded, staring in a hostile way. It took five weeks for them to unfold their arms and to begin to realize that [they were] being treated like professionals and [were] learning something." According to Wallace, among the things teachers were taught was how to get beyond the basic skills tested in MAP and into "higher-order thinking."

This undertaking was expensive. Staffing the training centers and replacing teachers as they took sabbaticals to attend the centers were very costly. Wallace again went to the ACCD for help in raising the money. The ACCD assisted in arranging local and national foundation support for planning and initial costs, but it would not provide ongoing fund-raising services. Mellon Bank Foundation, however, gave Wallace funds to hire a development officer for six months, who succeeded in raising $1.5 million for the teachers centers.[29] The school board was so pleased that they retained the development officer beyond the foundation-funded period.[30]

Wallace's treatment of teachers as professionals formed the basis of a partnership with the Pittsburgh Federation of Teachers. This partnership, which lasted throughout his tenure, resulted in what Kerchner and Caufman call "professional unionism." Under this model, teachers viewed themselves as professional educators rather than technicians, and bargaining became more of a "continuous problem-solving process and less of a periodic tournament."[31]

Management of enrollment decline. Responding to a declining student population posed a major challenge for Wallace and other supporters of the school system. The population of the Pittsburgh Public Schools had dropped 50 percent in the decades before Wallace's arrival, and it was projected to drop another several thousand students by 1990. There was no alternative but to close schools. In a city with strong neighborhood ties, Wallace knew that objections to school closings would be strong.

The successful response that followed attests to Wallace's political skills. He closed nearly a dozen schools and sold several school buildings, but he spread the closings across all nine districts of the school board. Every board member lost a school, but each gained something as well. In one district, for example, South High

was closed as a traditional high school but reopened as a vocational-technical magnet, something the community had long wanted. Thus, Wallace succeeded in garnering support from board members while enlisting their assistance to soothe relations between schools and neighborhoods.

Enrollment retention and attraction. Wallace used the magnet concept to desegregate schools as well as attract enrollment. In addition to creating quality magnet programs, an extensive marketing campaign brought schools to the attention of parents. Within a few years, many programs had become so successful that parents camped out overnight to reserve slots for their children. Noting the class bias of such overnight waits—the expense of down parkas and recreational vehicles, not to mention the ability to take a day off from work—the reservation process changed to a lottery system.

A second strategy to enhance enrollment was to emphasize gifted programs. At the elementary and middle school levels, gifted students attended scholars centers one day a week. At the high school level, gifted students attended separate Center for Advanced Studies classes. Treated as "special education" in Pennsylvania, state funding was essential for the maintenance of these programs. State officials challenged Wallace's extensive use of state funding for gifted programs, but he successfully met their objections.

By 1985 not only had the decline in enrollment stopped, but students were entering the system from parochial and private schools at the rate of nearly one thousand per year. Ironically, enrollment retention and attraction policies were so successful that by the time Wallace retired, every school that was closed earlier in the decade had been reopened and the system was buying parochial schools.

Discipline. Wallace's initiatives to address discipline concerns were straight-forward—develop a student code of conduct and establish a discipline committee at each school. Although simple, these initiatives addressed the priority in such a manner as to promote other goals, in this case, school-based decision making. Although discipline was not a major problem during the early 1980s, by 1989 gang activity was on the rise in and around schools. Wallace anticipated this problem and was among the first to formulate a response. By the early 1990s, he was concerned that educational excellence had taken a back seat to safe schools.

Performance of individual schools. The final initiative specifically targeted those African-American students who attended schools that, despite the desegregation plan, remained predominantly African-American. Wallace again turned to the concept of personnel training. This time, however, it was peer training among African-American administrators. He selected an African-American principal, who had ten years of success in producing high-achieving students in a predominantly African-American school, to mentor principals from six other minority segregated

schools. This "lead principal" was also charged with authoring a model school improvement plan that could be used by any school in the system.

Although this initiative focused on educational equity, quality was the thrust of most of Wallace's reforms. The MAP testing system and the personnel training programs benefited all students, including African-American students. This focus on overall quality was successful, as noted earlier, in narrowing the achievement gap between white and African-American students during the early years of Wallace's tenure.

National Recognition

Wallace began his tenure as a reform superintendent and promoted his "excellence agenda" throughout his twelve years.[32] The reforms he initiated focused on the school system's primary mission—teaching and learning. Most of the reforms, such as the achievement monitoring system and teachers centers, were aimed at directly improving the instructional process. Others, such as data-based decision making and central office positions in public relations and development, were aimed at changing the school system as an organization so that it could better achieve its instructional mission. In recognition of these reforms and his success in Pittsburgh, in 1990 Wallace became the first school superintendent to win the Harold W. McGraw Jr. Prize in Education.[33]

Extending Educational Leadership

Wallace's success depended upon the relationships he nurtured with other educators as well as leaders in the public and private sectors. For most of his tenure, he enjoyed a supportive school board and teachers' union. With the school board, Wallace received strong support for most of the 1980s. The president of the board from 1983 until 1989 was Jake Milliones, an African-American who was an assistant professor of psychiatry and psychology at the University of Pittsburgh. Milliones provided the leadership necessary to bring the disparate board members together, shepherding through much of the Wallace reform agenda. One informant said that under Milliones's leadership most school board votes were 9 to 0. At the same time, Milliones was a strong and informed advocate for the African-American community. He kept Wallace and the board focused on the performance gap between white and African-American students. If it were not for Milliones, the Wallace agenda might have focused exclusively on issues of quality and efficiency in education.

Wallace also established a strong working relationship with the teachers' union. Again, stable leadership was critical. Throughout Wallace's superintendency Al Fondy served as president of the Pittsburgh Federation of Teachers. Wallace recognized the critical role played by the teachers' union, noting that "pro-

fessional unions are in a powerful position to mobilize their members to embrace and support educational reform; they can also pull the plug on reform."[34] Wallace's reforms that emphasized teacher professionalism elevated teachers and the union to a partnership role in the "excellence agenda." Fondy, a strong and progressive union leader, reciprocated, stating that "if there are problems in the school system, and the union is strong, then the union is responsible either for the fact that the problems exist in the first place, or at least responsible for the fact that they are not being addressed."[35]

Cross-sector Collaboration

Wallace's primary strengths were in leadership within the school system. His focus on educational expertise and achievement fit comfortably with the corporate leadership style of Pittsburgh, characterized by one observer as an "old-style 1960s technocrat, in the Robert McNamara mold."[36] He did, however, venture outside the school system in a number of cross-sector initiatives. In 1991, for example, Wallace, who served on the board of Blue Cross of Western Pennsylvania, brought together a group of health care and foundation leaders to form a School Health Partnership Blue Ribbon Committee. The Blue Ribbon Committee helped Wallace develop broad policy and a funding strategy for the creation of school-based health centers. At the same time, a foundation provided financial support to hire consultants, the Health Education Center, to assist in building relationships between major health providers and individual schools. As a result, in 1992, policy guidelines were approved for the establishment of school health partnerships. These partnerships utilized school facilities and school personnel, a unique integration into the school administration.[37]

Another important cross-sector initiative was the New Futures Project supported by the Annie E. Casey Foundation. In 1987 the staff at the Allegheny Conference Education Fund presented Wallace with an opportunity to participate in the foundation-funded New Futures Project.[38] New Futures would provide multimillion-dollar support to communities to "make long-term changes in the operation, principles, and policies by which education, employment, and other youth services are administered, financed, and delivered at both the local and state levels of government as well as in the private sector."[39]

A proposal planning committee was formed representing, among others, the school district, city and county operating agencies, the Pittsburgh Foundation, and the United Way. Although the program represented a multiagency approach, the proposal had to be written quickly, and the school system's director of development and strategic planning took the lead. The proposal targeted two high schools and their feeder elementary and middle schools, representing one-third of the public school population and four of the city's eleven at-risk neighborhoods. Wallace's administration recognized that the in-school performance of children in these neighborhoods was affected by more than what happened in the classroom.

Wallace's director of research, testing, and evaluation had cautioned that the school reforms of the "excellence agenda" had limits. As he noted, "To the degree that those reforms don't pay any attention to multicultural influences or any of the other environmental influences on achievement, there will be clear limits to what you can accomplish. Some of the achievement gap is because schools aren't doing the job well with respect to minority students. Much of it is a consequence of social and economic conditions."[40] Addressing these issues required the cross-sector collaborations anticipated in New Futures.

The proposal was funded, and over the next five years more than ten million foundation dollars were spent for a vast array of programs aimed at building school-to-work relationships, reducing teenage pregnancy, improving attendance, reducing drop-out rates, enhancing achievement, forging community-school relationships, strengthening school building management, and encouraging team teaching.

Educational Challenges and Changing Times

Superintendent Wallace was widely acclaimed as one of the best urban superintendents in the country. His focus on teaching and learning helped raise academic achievement in the schools, and he garnered support and praise from many business and community leaders outside the schools for his educational leadership. By the early 1990s, however, times were changing, and pressures mounted for a different leadership style. Old actors in the education arena—parents, community activists, and board members—were demanding more participation in decision making. New approaches to serving at-risk youth necessitated collaboration with other youth-serving agencies. Wallace was less successful in meeting these challenges to his leadership than in implementing his "excellence agenda."

The first challenge involved participation in decision making. The growing pressure to widen participation in educational decision making did not match well with Wallace's leadership style. Wallace sought the advice of a broad range of interests, but under his leadership task forces and committees were tightly controlled. As he has written, "The superintendent needs to remind [advisory committees] of their proper, yet important, role as advisers; it needs to be made clear from the outset that the superintendent is the final decision maker. Advisory groups sometimes have a tendency to view themselves as decision-making groups."[41] Wallace promoted teacher professionalization and principal leadership, but he resisted decentralization of authority. He very cautiously explored site-based management in 1991, requesting proposals from teachers for two "restructured" elementary schools.

Wallace's relationship with the school board was another important challenge. In 1989 Milliones left the board to join the city council and was replaced in the presidency by Barbara Burns, a community activist first elected to the board in 1983. During the early years of Burns's presidency, conflict developed between the board and Wallace. Several board representatives, also with community activist roots, pressed their individual agendas within the board. One informant described the board during this period as "populist," with individual members attempting to "micro-manage all the way down to the staff level." Indicative of the increased level of involvement was the expansion of board committees: between 1986 and 1992, the number of school board committees expanded from two to eight and the number of subcommittees from eight to twelve.[42]

Individual board members, including the president, hurled a variety of criticisms at Wallace and his agenda—overcentralization, spending too much money, too concerned with his national reputation. The most outspoken critic was Valerie McDonald, an African-American female elected to the board in 1989. Charging that there were improprieties in the district's purchasing and bidding systems, she said that she was "trying to do away with the 'good old boy' system."[43] She objected to spending $150,000 of school funds for a three-year membership in the National Alliance for Restructuring Education (a group the Pittsburgh Public Schools helped to create), describing the alliance as "a lot of fluff and a way to build Wallace's reputation."[44] When Wallace proposed replacing three retiring African-American principals with African-Americans from outside the city, bypassing local African-American educators, McDonald called his actions "racist and elitist."[45] Wallace threatened to sue her for slander, but the dispute died down.

Finally, New Futures provided a significant challenge to Wallace's leadership capacity. Although the project produced a number of important programmatic changes in school operations, it was less successful in reaching its primary goal: to permanently alter the way in which policies for disadvantaged youth were made, financed, and implemented. Midgrant evaluations concluded that such change was not occurring. Several major stakeholders—city and county executives, the corporate sector, public sector workforce agencies—were not at the table. In addition, data generated by the programs under the New Futures umbrella were not being utilized to formulate comprehensive policy initiatives, and service-delivery integration had not been accomplished. Perhaps the single most critical factor was the lack of active involvement by the ACCD. Robert Pease, the longtime director who had guided the ACCD's involvement in a variety of social issues, resigned in 1990 while New Futures was still in a formative stage.[46] The New Futures Board dissolved, and some of the programs were folded into a new regional collaborative, the Allegheny Policy Council for Youth and Workforce Development.

There are many reasons for the failure of New Futures in Pittsburgh—too much money spent too fast, the overly prescriptive agenda of a national foundation, the focus on programs rather than directly on systemic change, and the lack of commitment on the part of major community actors, including the ACCD. Particularly significant is the lack of cross-sector collaboration to address the problems of at-risk youth. The Casey Foundation recognized the need for systemic change through collaboration, but in Pittsburgh the leaders of key institutions were not participating in the effort, and others were only halfheartedly involved. Millions of dollars were spent on add-on, pilot programs in a limited number of schools with no plans for how they would be continued, let alone expanded district-wide, after the New Futures money left the city.

The New Futures Project threw Wallace into a leadership position that he did not seek. The unreasonable time constraints imposed by the Casey Foundation required that a proposal be written quickly, without sufficient time for broad collaborative planning.[47] Wallace's staff stepped forward, and, not surprisingly, the proposal focused on the school system. Sixty percent of the Pittsburgh grant was spent on school programs, leading to unreasonable reliance on the schools to solve complex problems. Yet, New Futures funding accounted for just 1.2 percent of the school system's budget, allowing for only marginal change. Because the collaborative planning body was weak, Wallace approached the New Futures grant as he did other grants from outside funders rather than as an exercise in multi-institutional collaboration. Wallace, while more than willing to lead the school district in dramatic change in its instructional mission, was frustrated by the inability of the New Futures Project to bring other key actors to the table for a more comprehensive strategy to address the problems of at-risk urban youth.[48]

After twelve years as superintendent, Wallace could point to many accomplishments, but he also recognized that new challenges faced the school system. In 1992, he resigned as superintendent and accepted a joint appointment at the University of Pittsburgh's Learning Research and Development Corporation and its School of Education.

SUPERINTENDENT LOUISE BRENNEN AND RESTRUCTURING, 1992–1997

In 1992, the board voted 6 to 3 to hire Louise Brennen, a forty-two-year veteran of the Pittsburgh Public Schools, as the system's first female superintendent. Unlike her predecessor, she had neither an advanced degree nor a national reputation. However, she had the respect of those within the system, including Wallace, for whom she had served first as associate, then as deputy, superintendent.

Most board members who voted against her favored an African-American female who came with a doctorate and administrative experience elsewhere. The board meeting at which Brennen was hired was uncharacteristically contentious. "Brennen's supporters were booed as they entered the large, crowded room where the vote was being taken. When the vote was final, a group of African-American students in one part of the room stood and chanted, 'No justice, no peace,' loudly and passionately."[49] Brennen, however, later gained the support of dissenting board members and won over many representatives of the African-American community, although one group continued to oppose her appointment and filed a complaint with the Pennsylvania Human Relations Commission.

Although she was a "place bound" as opposed to "career bound" superintendent, Brennen did not present herself to the board as a candidate who would merely "stay the course."[50] She gained the support of several members during her interview when she presented an aggressive plan for restructuring the Pittsburgh Public Schools by decentralizing decision making and working more closely with nonschool providers of key services. Based upon her experiences in the school system, she was convinced that the problems of the city's youth reached well beyond the school walls, and, thus, solutions must involve more than educational professionals. Further, she saw a special need to involve parents and communities in school building decisions and in utilizing schools to address problems beyond education.

As Wallace had done in his first year, Brennen developed with the school board a set of priorities for the system. Unlike Wallace, however, who went to a university research center for his list of priorities, Brennen held a retreat with the school board and solicited her list from its members. The five priorities were achievement, assessment, partnerships, sound management, and safe and caring schools. Brennen proposed to use her restructuring plan as the means for addressing these five priorities.

First, however, she had to address a financial crisis. While the Pittsburgh Public Schools were gaining a national reputation during the 1980s, the costs were escalating, and in 1992 they faced a $40 million deficit. Brennen's first budget called for cutting 250 positions and passing the largest property tax increase in the school's history. The next year the board passed an austere but balanced budget that avoided another tax increase by, among other actions, eliminating another 141 positions. A large portion of the personnel savings came from a dramatic shrinking of the central administration.

In addition to the downsizing, the central administration was reorganized to reflect the decentralization theme—new roles were defined, old roles were downgraded, and entire decision hierarchies were altered. As Brennen described it, the "central office has been reorganized to serve rather than regulate the schools."[51] She also reached out to the African-American community by appointing African-Americans to several high-ranking positions, including that of deputy superintendent. As one African-American board member who had originally opposed Brennen's appointment put it, "She's done a good job of closing the communication gap and she's addressing the concerns in the way they should be addressed."[52]

SCHOOL RESTRUCTURING

Restructuring actually had begun under Wallace, albeit in a limited fashion. Wallace asked a citywide advocacy group, the Pittsburgh Council on Public Education, to oversee a "community conversation" on the topic, and he secured foundation funding for the process. Foundation funding also was obtained to develop two pilot restructuring elementary schools. The two schools, which had been closed in the mid-1980s, opened in September 1992 as laboratories for the restructuring plan—school-based management, curriculum integration, hands-on learning, team teaching, parental involvement, and portfolio evaluation.[53]

Brennen took the restructuring plan system-wide by making it the linchpin of the school system's strategic plan, a document required by the state.[54] During the 1992–1993 school year, school restructuring task forces developed the "visionary" component of the plan, and the following year implementation task forces recommended specific strategies. Over five hundred parents, students, teachers, administrators, board members, and civic and business leaders participated in the open and well-publicized process.[55] The plan focused on five areas: high standards for all students, effective schools, dynamic parent/guardian and community partnerships, highly qualified staff and effective volunteer partnerships, and school-based decision making.

The document outlined major changes in what students would learn, how they would be tested, and how teachers would teach. Pittsburgh's plan adopted the fifty-three state-mandated learning outcomes and added nine of its own, focusing on the preparation of students as productive citizens and workers. To accommodate the learning outcomes, the school district pledged to spend the next six years redesigning its curriculum and assessment tools, citing some of the most current thinking in educational reform, including new standards testing, community service, portfolios, and flexible scheduling.

The strategic plan also established school-based decision making in all schools. Each school would establish a Parent-School-Community Council to represent major stakeholders—students, teachers, administrators, staff, parents, and community members. Each council was charged with developing an annual comprehensive educational improvement plan. The scope of authority for the councils would evolve over time, but it was clear that it was not envisioned to include staffing decisions or full budget control.

Superintendent Brennen argued that the success of the school councils rested not so much on their initial grant of authority but upon the level of participation, particularly by parents. Brennen realized that meaningful parental involvement would not follow automatically from the creation of a new structure, so staff were hired to train and support parental involvement on the councils.[56] Just as significant as parent training was guaranteeing that school professionals—teachers and principals—would be receptive to parental input. A major issue was the amount of time these new relationships would require of teachers. The 1994 negotiations between the Pittsburgh Federation of Teachers and the district hinged as much on this issue as on salaries.

Parents began to utilize their newly acquired power late in the summer of 1995. The school administration announced that fifty-one principals, vice principals, and school-based administrators were being transferred to new schools for the upcoming school year. Parents at several of the schools mounted protests. Reassignments had been made in previous years but without incident. This year, however, school councils began to voice their opinions. As Brennen admitted, "There's been this bonding that has occurred, and I think what we're hearing now is from stakeholders who feel that they were left out of the process."[57] A placard carried by one parent at a school meeting agreed: "You asked for parental involvement—you got it."[58] Although the transfers were ultimately carried out, the district did agree to change the process to minimize objections in the coming years. Transfers in 1996 did not elicit vocal protests.

DECLINE IN CIVIC SUPPORT

Another problem Brennen faced was a decline in support from corporate and other city leaders. As noted earlier, the faltering New Futures program was subsumed under a new regional initiative called the Allegheny Policy Council on Youth and Workforce Development (Policy Council). Also brought under this umbrella were the county's Private Industry Council and the Allegheny Conference Education Fund (ACEF) programs. The ACEF, in particular, had supported a number of partnerships with the Pittsburgh Public Schools.

The Policy Council, which continues today, is an important initiative. Its board includes chief executive officers from several of Pittsburgh's major corporations, the mayor, an Allegheny County Commissioner, the superintendent of the Pittsburgh Public Schools, staff from several major Pittsburgh foundations, and a representative of the University of Pittsburgh's Learning Research and Development Corporation. The Policy Council is unique in its breadth of membership and focus. As its first director notes, "This type of partnership isn't being done by any other region across the nation. It speaks volumes for the Pittsburgh region to dig in and aggressively set out to change how we educate our children. Pittsburgh was so successful in its Renaissance efforts that upgraded the buildings and skyline. The next logical step is making sure those buildings are filled with productive, successful, skilled employees. We see our effort as a human resource renaissance to bring vitality to the region."[59]

The Policy Council has the potential to be a major regional network in the education and workforce areas. It offers a forum for cross-sector issue definition and program development as originally envisioned by New Futures, and it provides a regional advocacy group to address funding inequalities facing public education. The Policy Council, however, has not realized this potential. Meetings are infrequent, and little initiative has been demonstrated.

Publications from the ACCD continue to list education as one of its issue areas and name the Policy Council as the implementing agency, but the organization's attention has shifted from social issues to regional economic decline (described below) since the retirement of Bob Pease. In this new focus there is no indication that human capital development, through the public school system, is seen as an essential part of the strategy. Furthermore, the Policy Council has a regional mandate that shifts attention away from Pittsburgh's schools, and the problems of city schools compete with those of other communities in the area.

For the Pittsburgh Public Schools in general, and Louise Brennen in particular, the Policy Council represents not only lost potential but also the demise of the partnerships sponsored by the ACEF. Once the ACEF was absorbed into the Policy Council, individual programs were eliminated. The first director stated that the Policy Council could not be bogged down in program administration. Thus, the school system lost the action-oriented linkages the ACEF had fostered between educational professionals and community organizations.

LAME DUCK STATUS FOR SUPERINTENDENT BRENNEN

After her first three years as superintendent, it seemed questionable that the school board would renew Brennen's contract. The Human Relations Commission investigations still hung over her, and restructuring, as shown above, created new demands and challenges that left some in the community dissatisfied with the schools. Ultimately, the board voted 9 to 0 to extend her contract for two years with the condition that she retire in 1997. The board did not want to change leadership during the extensive restructuring process, but this was a clear statement by the board that new leadership was needed for the long-term development of the school system.[60]

In many ways, Louise Brennen had been as strong a leader as her predecessor, Richard Wallace. She initiated dramatic changes in the operation of the school bureaucracy. She led a broad-based planning process that highlighted a major shift in the way schools related to students and their communities. Wallace's leadership style relied on a strong personal vision, while Brennen's style was more process oriented. New stakeholders—parents, community-based organizations, and nonprofit service providers—found her much more approachable than Wallace. As one interviewee reported, "Unlike Wallace, you feel she is really listening."

Brennen, however, was not able to continue the instructional reform agenda begun under Wallace. The budget problems she inherited in 1992 grew even worse (discussed below), and she was forced to drop or alter many of the institutional reforms initiated by Wallace. For example, the teachers centers, student testing and tracking research system, and multicultural focus proved to be too expensive to maintain and were either eliminated or dramatically reduced. Furthermore, much of her own agenda as expressed in the strategic plan was slow getting off the drawing board.

THE SCHOOL BOARD FACES NEW CRISES, 1995–1997

During the first half of the 1990s, Pittsburgh's educational policy-making arena changed markedly. The demise of the Allegheny Conference Education Fund lessened the civic leadership's attention to the Pittsburgh Public Schools. Within the school system, the leadership role of the superintendent was weakened. By 1995, the focus of decision making had shifted to the school board.

The Pittsburgh School Board always had been an important decision-making actor. When Richard Wallace arrived in 1980, he recognized the importance of the board and quickly won support for his reform agenda, retaining it through most of his tenure. By the late 1980s, however, he faced mounting board criticism. The populist nature of much of the criticism formed the basis of the decentralization reforms of Brennen who, in turn, enjoyed board support during the first two years of her superintendency.

Between 1995 and 1997, however, the school board rather than the superintendent directed educational policy making in Pittsburgh, which was partially due to Brennen's lame duck status. But perhaps of more significance were two highly controversial issues that confronted the board: first, a call by some segments of the community for neighborhood schools along with an end to busing, and second, a severe fiscal crisis, precipitated by stagnant local revenues and cuts in state funding. Both issues caused divisions within the broader community and, consequently, within the board.[61]

Neighborhood Schools

The call for neighborhood schools could be traced back to the desegregation crisis of the 1970s. Particularly from residents of white, south Pittsburgh neighborhoods, there was strong objection to the forced busing element of the desegregation plan of 1980. These neighborhood school advocates organized in 1995 when the school administration released enrollment figures showing a decline for two consecutive years after three years of increases. Although the decline was small, approximately three hundred in 1993–1994 and four hundred in 1994–1995, the district acted swiftly. A study revealed that the largest drop occurred among students entering sixth grade, the first of the middle school years. Further, non–public school enrollments were remaining steady, leading the administration to conclude that families were shunning the public schools.[62]

To discover the reasons for student withdrawal and to propose a strategy to curb it, the school board appointed an Attract and Hold Steering Committee. Over the next several months, the latent neighborhood school advocates were activated, and a number of city and state elected officials joined their cause. Two members of the Pennsylvania State Assembly who represented south Pittsburgh neighborhoods cosponsored a neighborhood schools bill in Harrisburg. The premise of the bill was that an end to busing would build stronger communities around individual schools as well as save city taxpayers' money.[63] In Pittsburgh, the mayor and three city council members expressed their support.[64]

In December 1995, the board voted unanimously to adopt an attract and hold strategy that would, among other things, "assign all children to full-day kindergarten through grade twelve in schools close to home, keeping neighborhoods intact and maintaining racially-balanced schools, to the extent possible." The changes would be implemented by the following school year, but they sparked immediate debate.[65] The *Pittsburgh Post-Gazette,* in an editorial entitled "Disintegration?" expressed "skepticism" about the plan.[66] The NAACP and the Urban League called the plan "resegregation," citing school administration estimates that under the plan the percentage of students who attended racially balanced schools would drop from 58 percent to 45 percent.[67]

Over the course of the next four months the board's unanimity dissolved as it heard the testimony of hundreds of speakers at numerous hearings. Joining the race-based organizations in opposing the move to neighborhood schools were the supporters of the district's extensive magnet school system. In April the board approved a significantly modified version of the original plan, opening three new neighborhood schools in the areas of the most vocal neighborhood school advocates but leaving intact the magnet system and much of the existing feeder pattern.

The school board agreed that more needed to be done to balance the demands for neighborhood schools, desegregation, and equity. They anticipated other plans that would be phased in during subsequent years. Board President Ron Suber saw a silver lining in the long, tumultuous battle over redistricting, saying, "Our proposal has produced a sorely-needed and long overdue reawakening of interest in public education in Pittsburgh."[68] But with the reawakening came additional pressure on the school board to fashion new compromises.

The neighborhood school issue was important in the primary elections in the spring of 1997. An advisory referendum posed the following question to voters, "Do you favor the neighborhood school concept as a necessary part of our public school system?" Voters agreed 3 to 1.[69] It was left to the school board, however, to interpret the meaning of the referendum. Neighborhood school advocates hoped to influence that interpretation by winning a fifth vote on the school board, thus becoming a majority. To do this they needed to defeat incumbent Maggie Schmidt.[70] Schmidt, however, was reelected, and the compromise plan remained in effect. School enrollment increased for the 1997–1998 school year, partially defusing the neighborhood school debate.[71]

Fiscal Crisis

The second major challenge that faced the Pittsburgh Public Schools in the mid-1990s was a severe fiscal crisis. This problem had been brewing for some time. Although expenditure increases averaged only 3 percent, the district faced huge deficits in each of the years between 1991 and 1996, due primarily to a combination of flat local revenues and decreased state funding. As described above, a projected $40 million deficit was averted in 1992 by a combination of major staff cuts and the largest tax increase in the district's history. The school board continued to make deep cuts in order to balance the budget without tax increases. As part of this process, in 1995 the teachers union agreed to a salary freeze, and in 1996 the district borrowed needed funds from its fire damage, unemployment compensation, comprehensive general liability, and capital improvement funds.[72]

Yet, the crisis continued. By 1997 the school board faced a $35 million deficit.[73] Projected savings from eliminating busing for desegregation faded when the attract and hold strategy described earlier was scaled back. Between May and October 1996, the $35 million deficit was whittled to $7.1 million, primarily through the sale of delinquent tax liens and cuts in central administration. School principals were asked to make the remaining cuts. Parents, particularly those of the prestigious Taylor Allderdice High School, took to the streets to protest these cuts. The central administration responded, agreeing to reduce individual school cuts by bearing an even greater share of the burden in the central office.[74] Again, the board passed a balanced budget by reducing expenditures and without a tax increase.

The scenario for the 1998 budget was the same as those for the previous years. During the summer of 1997, the projected deficit was $26 million. Another round of personnel cuts enabled the board to pass a balanced budget without a tax increase. This time the cuts were so deep that the resulting total budget was more than $1 million less than the year before.

Political Battles with City Hall

The challenges that faced the school board, particularly in the fiscal area, prompted a number of political skirmishes with city hall. City government officials, fearing that the school board would raise taxes and thereby absorb any unused tax potential, began questioning the wisdom of an independent school district. In 1995, the city council authorized the city comptroller to conduct a "performance audit" of the school district.[75] Legally, the comptroller could conduct a fiscal audit, but there were serious questions as to whether he had the authority, or competency, to review the programmatic outcomes of the school district. Two dissenting council members, one a former school board president, wondered "why the council was meddling in the district's business when the city itself was facing a $15 million to $22.5 million budget shortfall."[76] In an editorial, the *Post-Gazette* chastised the city council and the comptroller for "stepping over the line" and advised the mayor to veto the audit bill.[77] Although he voiced doubts about the legality of the audit, the mayor did not veto the bill.[78] School officials did not cooperate; they charged the comptroller with political motives and challenged the legality of the audit. They preferred an independent audit of school performance.

In early 1997, a city councillor who had supported the neighborhood school concept and who had instructed the comptroller to "Go get them!" with the audit, floated a proposal that would replace the elected board with one appointed by the mayor.[79] He also recommended that the mayor appoint a chief executive officer to administer the schools as a department of the city. The mayor found the proposal "thoughtful and timely" and proposed a series of public forums.[80] There was an outcry by sitting school board members. Even one member who had welcomed council involvement in the neighborhood school issue and the call for an audit described this proposal as a "slap in the face."[81] A former board member pointed out that Pittsburgh's schools were not like those in Chicago, Washington, or Baltimore. Those cities, she argued, "have school systems that are so far gone that making a governance change to cure their problems is like putting a smoke detector in a building after it's been gutted by fire!"[82] This move to mayoral appointment received little support, representing a skirmish between the elected leaders of two taxing bodies rather than a broader frustration with the school system.

Challenges and Compromises

These issues—neighborhood schools and the fiscal crisis—activated conflicts within the community, between city officials and the school district, and between the district's central administration and individual schools. The conflicts found expression on the school board, raising the level of discord among board members to a degree not seen in Pittsburgh for a decade and a half. Highlighting this level of conflict, the 1996 and 1997 elections for the board presidency were three-way races, the final selection reflecting a compromise rather than a vote of confidence in the leadership abilities of a single candidate.

In this environment the school board deserves credit for fashioning acceptable compromises on both issues. But the compromises represented short-run answers rather than long-term solutions. In fact, the two solutions were on a collision course. In search of budget cuts, the board commissioned a long-term facilities plan that recommended numerous school closures. The implementation of the plan would result in millions of dollars of savings for the district. School closures, however, would reduce the number of neighborhood schools, a policy direction opposed by neighborhood school advocates.[83]

NEW LEADERSHIP AND RENEWED CIVIC ATTENTION

During the early 1990s, the discussion of educational issues had revolved around race and taxation rather than quality of education. By 1996, however, some were voicing concern that Pittsburgh might lose its reputation as a high-performing urban school system. The school board president warned that while Pittsburgh still had one of the best urban school systems in the country, without financial assistance it could not retain that position. "We're not in the same situation as Chicago, Detroit, or Washington, D.C., but we could get there."[84] A *Post-Gazette* editorial predicted that a "tax increase could be needed in 1998," arguing that "Pittsburgh can't afford to let the quality of its education system drop. The health of city schools is one of the most important considerations for any potential business or resident looking to settle here."[85]

The challenges facing public education in Pittsburgh had become formidable. Proponents of neighborhood schools remained active and vocal, and a tight fiscal environment continued to put pressure on the school budget. Within the schools, a weakened superintendency and very active school board complicated the tasks of governance. Although the private and nonprofit sectors had a long legacy of support for the school system, this support had fragmented in recent years. Meeting these challenges in the broader community and within the school system would be critical to the future of public education in Pittsburgh.

Renewing Business Support for Public Education

One important step would be a renewal of business support for the school system. Since the 1980s the Pittsburgh region had been experiencing an economic restructuring that captured, indeed demanded, the attention of many corporate leaders. Economic decline and its variable impact across race, class, and geography were reshaping the region.[86] The restructuring of the steel industry, the decline of mill towns, the rise of the service industry, and the globalization of business interests drew the corporate attention of the ACCD and other business leaders away from many community concerns.

In this context, regional economic decline became a central concern of the ACCD. This challenge, however, was much different from what was faced in Renaissance I and II; economic dislocations could not be solved by the "engineering, construction, and money" that characterized those earlier efforts.[87] The ACCD formulated a response in the early 1980s by sponsoring a series of broad community task forces charged with articulating a new economic vision. The vision, not surprisingly, was one of economic diversification.[88] But the report, while an impressive compilation of current conditions and recommendations, lacked an implementation strategy.

This scenario of analysis without action was repeated time and again over the next ten years, with two notable exceptions, Strategy 21 and the Regional Asset District. In both cases, regional leadership, private as well as public, presented a united front in the state capital for either state funding or the ability to raise local taxes.[89] The monies were used to fund discrete projects or for existing organizations, but a comprehensive strategy of economic diversification eluded policy makers. In 1993 a white paper commissioned by the ACCD presented a surprisingly frank, and bleak, analysis of regional economic trends over the past two decades. The region had not only suffered greater job losses than other northern industrial cities, but it was replacing those jobs with service sector employment at a slower rate. The report also documented that the annual average wage of the Pittsburgh worker had declined.[90]

The next year the ACCD sponsored the Regional Economic Revitalization Initiative, a planning process that presented a group of "flagship initiatives" which promised the creation of 100,000 jobs.[91] The initiatives were diverse, including infrastructure, tax reform, new industry support, and downtown development. Quick action was promised under each, but downtown development received the most attention. Corporate leaders turned to downtown development as a generator of regional economic growth. Yet another ACCD-sponsored civic organization—the Regional Renaissance Partnership—was created to promote $1 billion in downtown development projects, including two new stadiums, an expanded convention center, and further development in the cultural district. To fund the projects the partnership recommended a regional sales tax. Despite a well-funded public relations campaign, the voters of southwestern Pennsylvania soundly rejected the plan in November 1997. The civic leadership regrouped to come up with an acceptable "Plan B" for funding the projects.

Corporate leadership did turn its attention to other areas of the community. In 1996, for example, the mayor created a Competitive Pittsburgh Task Force to focus on the delivery of city services. The chair of the ACCD served as the head of the task force and helped produce a report that recommended seventy-nine steps to deliver city services more efficiently.[92] The ACCD, however, continued to be challenged. In a February 24, 1998, editorial, the *Post-Gazette,* historically a supporter of ACCD recommendations, criticized the "cheerleading" and "boosterism" of recent ACCD proposals, arguing that they were based on biased research and favored the business community at the expense of "neighborhoods, minority groups and other disparate interests in the region." The editorial called for more objective economic analysis of the region's problems.[93] The editorial, while strongly critical of corporate leadership, was asking that the ACCD broaden its focus.

School Leadership

Developing leadership within the school system is a second key challenge. As noted above, the nature of issues before the board in the mid-1990s as well as the weakened superintendency have encouraged board-dominated decision making. In 1997, the question was whether a new superintendent could reestablish control over policy making. As one columnist asked, "Will Louise Brennen's successor be able to overcome the board's penchant for intervening in daily operations and protecting their own turf?" While many thought a new superintendent was the answer, others argued that board activism was too entrenched. Someone who worked closely with the board lamented, "It doesn't matter who the superintendent is. Nine people are running this district."[94]

The hiring of a new superintendent would be a critical step. The board appeared initially to relinquish some of its control when it appointed a very broad-based Community Input Committee to screen applicants for the position. The committee would make recommendations to the board and "help the board in maintaining contact with the community throughout the search process."[95] Eight of the sixteen members on the committee were individuals or representatives from groups involved in issues currently facing the Pittsburgh Public Schools: four parent leaders, a school principal, the director of a citywide public education advocacy group, the head of the neighborhood schools movement, and the director of the Urban League. The remaining members consisted of representatives from the foundation, university, neighborhood, and religious sectors. Interestingly, only one member represented the private sector, but even she was a longtime civic activist who ran unsuccessfully as a Republican candidate for county commissioner in 1995.[96]

The editor of the *Post-Gazette* had a strong set of directives for the committee and the board. He encouraged them not to passively wait for candidates to come to them but to actively seek applications from "star educators." Furthermore, the school district "should be prepared to pay whatever was necessary."[97] The school board, however, tightly controlled the process. They did not allow the committee to seek candidates, nor did they allow them to interview, or even call, applicants. Their role was to review the resumes and make recommendations.

The candidate ultimately chosen—Dale E. Frederick—was not among those ranked by the committee but was, at the insistence of one of the members, on the list of finalists turned over to the school board.[98] The board, however, was so favorably impressed with Frederick that they voted unanimously to hire him. They praised him for being "first and foremost a teacher" and for "putting children first."[99] They also were impressed with his "in-the-trenches style of management"[100] and his reputation as a community "peacemaker."[101] Finally, they could not help but be attracted to a candidate who had quickly restored the fiscal health of his previous district in Warren, Ohio.

There are indications that Frederick may be able to provide the leadership needed if the district is to face the current crises and return to the instructional reform processes begun under Wallace and Brennen. He appears to have school board support to begin that process. In an article entitled "New City School Superintendent Is off to a Promising Start," the *Post-Gazette*'s education reporter described how his "charm," "enthusiasm," and "down-to-earth style" were winning the support of central as well as school building administrators.[102] A year later, however, the question of whether he can calm the board and solve recurring fiscal crises so that he can become an education leader is still unanswered. Frederick described his first year: "What I was doing was bailing water out of the ship to keep it afloat. I needed to be bailing the water, but I wasn't sailing the ship."[103]

Reviving Civic Capacity

Steps to revive civic capacity are being taken. In 1997, school board member Maggie Schmidt recommended creation of a broad-based, blue-ribbon committee to address the audit concerns noted earlier and to focus on issues of educational quality. This committee, the Financial and Education Program Assessment Panel, brought civic leadership back into the dialogue on school issues. The panel was headed by the dean of the School of Business at Duquesne University, staffed by the ACCD's research arm, the Pennsylvania Economy League, funded by a local foundation, and included membership from the public, private, and nonprofit sectors. Although the panel recognized that the Pittsburgh schools have "not gone into serious decline," it saw the system as "at the edge." The panel noted in their report that "what happens in the next five to ten years will determine whether or not the District survives as a viable urban school system. The Assessment Panel's recommendations may be the last attempt to fix the system before more dramatic approaches are needed"[104] The panel's recommendations were very specific, calling for additional state financial support, a doubling of expenditures for professional development, stronger superintendent leadership in principal selection, and a return of the school board to a broad policy-making role. But the panel also made it clear that none of this was possible without significant and ongoing community support.

The Pittsburgh public school system is at a crossroads. Pittsburgh has a history of civic support for public education, but sustaining that support is an ongoing challenge. New events and pressures continually test the resolve of civic leaders to support public education. If civic leadership refocuses on public education and if school leadership is reestablished, the district can resume its reform agenda. Hopefully, this leadership can move beyond school reform and plan collaboratively to address the special needs of at-risk youth. If new leadership cannot be established, the accomplishments of the past decade and a half could unravel.

5
Boston's Public Schools:
Emerging Institutions and Leadership

Boston occupies a middle position among our three cities. Pittsburgh's decade of successful educational reform and civic support surpasses the Boston experience, and St. Louis lags behind as it struggles to improve its educational system. In this middle position Boston is poised, however, to make significant strides to improve public education. Key elements in the educational support structure are in place: Boston Compact III provides an umbrella for civic support; an innovative labor contract involves the teachers' union in educational reform; a new superintendent is directing the school department; a restructured, appointed school committee provides policy oversight; and the mayor is publicly committed to improvement in the schools.

Yet, this institutional support structure with strong leadership was slow to develop. Boston struggled for many years to create and activate a structure of civic support for public education. In the 1970s and 1980s, racial tensions, court-ordered desegregation, and political divisions overshadowed efforts to improve the school system. Even the withdrawal of the federal court from desegregation oversight did not end the struggle. A debate ensued over governance roles among the mayor, superintendent, and school committee. This debate occupied the attention of community leaders for a number of years. With this debate settled, however, Boston has emerged with a significant structure of civic support for public education. To understand this current system of support, however, we first must examine the past, including a closer look at development politics in Boston.

DEVELOPMENT POLITICS AND CIVIC CAPACITY

After World War II, Boston was a city of political divisions and economic stagnation. Political divisions were fueled by a long-standing split between Yankee business leaders and Irish politicians who controlled city hall. James Michael Curley, four-time mayor of Boston, was the principal protagonist on the city side. Curley was known for his patronage-style politics and abrasive way with business. High property taxes and the trading of tax abatements for favors prompted the business community to turn their backs on investment in Boston.[1] The decline of textiles and other industries, along with business reluctance to invest in the city, left Boston by the wayside as the American postwar economy began its resurgence.

The late 1950s, however, witnessed a renewal of interest in the development of Boston. Curley's defeat at the polls in 1949 by John Hynes, along with a change in the city charter to provide more mayoral authority, pointed to a new political environment. In 1954 Boston College started a series of citizen seminars in which political and economic leaders met to discuss major issues before the city. Among key concerns raised by the business community were high property tax burdens and excessive government spending.[2] In 1955, a group traveled to Pittsburgh to study Renaissance I to see how progress was made in that city to address urban problems.

The Vault was the culmination of this process of business involvement. Known officially as the Coordinating Committee, the Vault (which first met at a bank) was launched in 1959 by fourteen leading businessmen in banking, retail, industry, law, and insurance. The Vault channeled support to the mayoral race of John Collins and touted a strategy of urban revival through investment in the downtown area and more business-friendly government policies. In institutional terms, the Vault represented an association of business leaders held together by a common interest in economic investment in the city. Reforming the city's tax policies and supporting a more responsive city government were themes that united the members of the Vault.

As an institution, however, the Vault did not develop an infrastructure of staff and programs as did the Allegheny Conference in Pittsburgh. Rather, the Vault relied upon a more informal network of support from among its members. Its meetings were held out of the public eye, and its identity was never widely touted or advertised. Membership expansion to include nonbusiness players, such as educational institutions, brought this association closer to a network, but business members always dominated the Vault and kept its focus on economic and fiscal issues central to the business community.

The mayoral victory of John Collins and his subsequent tenure (1960–1968) marked a period of close collaboration between business leaders and city hall. Mayor Collins met with the Vault at least once a month, and he delivered on his promise to make Boston more conducive to business investment. He cut the city budget, reduced the city workforce, and sponsored a small reduction in the property tax rate. Equally important, the mayor lured Edward Logue from New Haven, Connecticut, to direct the Boston Redevelopment Authority as the primary development arm of the city, and he received state approval for a new property tax tool, known as 121A, that allowed the city and businesses to enter into negotiated reductions in property taxes. The $200 million Prudential development, previously stalled, was the first investment to take advantage of this new tax tool.[3]

The 1960s were boom years for investment in Boston. The Prudential project was joined by Government Center ($217 million), the Waterfront ($131 million), central business district developments ($314 million), and a number of major residential renewal projects. To direct this expansion, the Boston Redevelopment Authority grew between 1957 and 1968 from a staff of seventeen to seven hundred and increased its annual cash flow from $250,000 to $25 million.[4] The Redevelopment Authority became a formal organization with considerable responsibility and clout in shaping Boston's future. Redevelopment, however, carried with it numerous tensions. In particular, a number of residential renewal projects were opposed by large segments of the affected communities. Such opposition eventually led to a scaling back or halt in some projects.

The Redevelopment Authority, Vault, and other major business groups, such as the Greater Boston Chamber of Commerce, had become major actors in the redevelopment and fiscal stability of Boston. These associations and organizations created a strong institutional environment for urban development. Business and mayoral leadership provided the other critical ingredient. Although Collins's successor, Kevin White (1968–1984), enjoyed a less cordial relationship with the Vault, the business community continued to support new investment in the city. Furthermore, when the city faced major fiscal troubles, as it did in 1976 and 1981, the Vault provided critical support to help city officials meet financial targets.[5] The business community was clearly vested in Boston's economic and fiscal future.

THE BOSTON PUBLIC SCHOOLS AND
EMERGING CIVIC SUPPORT, 1974–1989

The Vault, however, was much less visible in the area of education. The Boston Public Schools were outside the control of city hall, and many business leaders had limited, if any, personal or professional contact with the schools. Furthermore, the school system had a negative image and reputation as a conservative institution adverse to change.[6] One critic noted, "From the very top to somewhere near the very bottom, the Boston system is steeped in conservative ideas and traditional practices, in a patronizing outlook, and in subtle prejudice."[7] One superintendent described the system as an "Irish-dominated, patronage-ridden, job-security-oriented institution."[8] Islands of excellence and innovation existed, but the system as a whole was noted for mismanagement and political corruption.

Furthermore, the problems of the schools—racial divisions, declining enrollments, dilapidated buildings—were not in the normal domain of interest and competence for the business community. Many business leaders saw little connection between these issues and matters of more direct concern, such as economic and fiscal stability. In short, the schools operated in a world largely apart from that of the business community. As one observer noted, "John Collins, Ed Logue, the Vault and federal money had saved corporate Boston . . . but they could not cope with social Boston, and they were getting the messages of discontent."[9]

Desegregation and the Courts

In the 1970s and 1980s, racial desegregation was the most prominent issue facing the Boston schools. Between 1974 and the late 1980s, Boston was the site of a desegregation experience that captured national attention while fundamentally changing the city's public school system. Court-ordered busing attracted the most media attention, but court involvement in public education went far beyond busing. Federal District Judge W. Arthur Garrity issued over four hundred court orders involving school closings, student assignment, personnel hires, textbook adoption, community partnerships, and a host of other school matters.[10] For much of this period the federal district court governed the Boston public school system.

School officials had been opposed to desegregation demands for a number of years. The Massachusetts Racial Imbalance Act, enacted in 1965, established state desegregation guidelines for all schools, but the Boston Public Schools failed to meet these criteria. In 1971, for example, only 5 of the system's 140 elementary schools had a racial composition within 10 percent of the citywide ratio; schools were either predominantly white or predominantly black.[11] The five-member Boston School Committee refused to consider or implement desegregation strategies. Opposed to state intervention and possessing what one observer described as an "authoritarian" style, the Boston School Committee was ill disposed toward flexibility in meeting a changing racial environment.[12] State authorities threatened legal action, and a lawsuit was filed by black parents. The desegregation battle moved to the courtroom.

On June 21, 1974, Judge Garrity issued the first of his many desegregation orders. The judge concluded that the Boston School Committee and the school department "had knowingly carried out a systematic program of segregation affecting all of the city's students, teachers and school facilities, and had intentionally brought about or maintained a dual school system."[13] In phase one of the court's order, a state-designed desegregation plan was adapted for use during the 1974–1975 school year. Busing was required for approximately 17,000 students, and, in a move that would prove most controversial, South Boston High School, a white school, and Roxbury High School, a black school, were paired for busing.[14] The judge also created school-level and district-level Citywide Parents' Advisory Councils.

During the 1974–1975 school year, Judge Garrity and the school committee worked separately to create a long-term desegregation plan. Judge Garrity hired two educational experts to advise the court and established a four-member panel of masters to work with the educational experts in designing a desegregation plan. After the school committee failed to produce a plan acceptable to the judge, the court-appointed experts and panel of masters solicited public input and designed a comprehensive plan. Using parts of this plan, in June 1975 Judge Garrity announced the next phase of desegregation.[15] Phase two involved more extensive busing under an assignment plan organized around eight community school districts and one magnet district. An administrative structure of community superintendents was established to manage the system. In addition, the judge ordered the closure of twenty-two schools.

Judge Garrity also established a number of community support structures for the public schools. A forty-member Citywide Coordinating Council was created to monitor school compliance with desegregation orders; district advisory councils were established in each community school district; and racial-ethnic parent councils were established for each school. Borrowing from the plan created by the panel of masters, phase two established twenty partnerships between area colleges and individual schools; phase two also outlined twenty business-school partnerships.[16] The latter were initiated during 1974 by the Boston Trilateral Council for Quality Education, an organization created that year by the Boston Chamber of Commerce and the National Alliance of Businessmen.[17]

Court orders continued. In 1977, for example, Judge Garrity stipulated creation of a unified facilities plan to address the deteriorating school infrastructure. In total, the court ordered the closure of thirty-two schools, construction of eight, renovation of ten, and repair of fifty.[18] Not until 1982 did Judge Garrity remove himself from compliance monitoring, giving this authority to the state Department of Education. In 1985 the judge issued his "final orders," yet he retained jurisdiction over a number of critical areas, including student assignment, faculty composition, condition of school buildings, parental involvement, and vocational education.[19] The final court ruling was made in 1989 when the judge approved a voluntary "controlled choice" assignment process as an acceptable desegregation plan.

Institution Building: Networks and Civic Capacity

This was a difficult period for Boston. Controversies over desegregation, busing, and court orders dominated the educational arena. One participant described the 1970s as the "war years," while another likened this period to the "battle of Boston."[20] The environment was problematic for the development of networks and associations that could support public education, particularly from the business community. Yet, amidst the controversy and struggle, three networks emerged with a specific focus on improving public education. Although subject to growing pains, these cross-sector alliances offer our first look at how Boston's civic capacity can be directed toward public education.

Boston Compact. The Boston Compact was most prominent among these networks. Established in 1982, the compact was a partnership between the business community and the public schools. In 1983 higher education joined the compact, and in 1984 the Boston building and trades unions joined. The essence of the compact was an agreement whereby the Boston Public Schools would improve the education and learning outcomes for its students, and in return, businesses, colleges, and labor organizations would provide jobs and postsecondary educational opportunities for school graduates.

The formation of the compact in 1982 was a reflection of changing times. Prior to this date, during the most controversial days of busing in the 1970s, many in the business community were reluctant to join the fray. Business chief executive officers, who often lived in the suburbs, were hesitant to pass judgment on the busing of children within the city. As one business leader told a civil rights commission, the business community did not see itself as a "major actor in this situation."[21] Business leaders supported quality education and the development of school-business partnerships, but in the areas of desegregation and busing, their role was, as the same leader noted, "supplemental."[22] Desegregation was an issue best left to the residents of Boston.

By the early 1980s the passions around busing had subsided, and several key ingredients came together to support creation of the Boston Compact. Leadership, both inside and outside the school system, was one important piece. Outside the schools, the chairman of the Vault, William Edgerly, adopted public education as an important concern for the business community.[23] Edgerly, chairman of State Street Bank, appealed to the corporate citizenship role of his peers as well as the economic link between successful public school students and employees of the future. He convinced the members of the Vault to be the first signatories to the compact.

On the schools' side, a new superintendent was hired, Robert Spillane, who was willing to work with businesses and other community institutions. As one participant in the process was quoted, "It's not that Spillane is such a brilliant educator. It's that he's perceived as a strong leader—someone you can deal with. He's someone who handles himself extremely well with a sophisticated crowd."[24] Spillane improved the financial reporting of the schools and agreed to have the school system held accountable for the education it provided. He viewed the compact as an opportunity to increase the support structure for the schools. As he noted, "The major achievement of the Compact is a sense that everyone has a responsibility to this city and the schools."[25]

Another critical ingredient was the existence of several organizations that could provide an institutional platform for the Boston Compact. Most important of these was the Boston Private Industry Council (PIC). Created in 1979, the PIC involved the business community in the design and implementation of government-funded training programs. It was a forum for key business leaders and also provided staff capacity to implement new programs. Like other private industry councils around the country, the Boston PIC played a central role in implementing federal labor-training grants. However, it went much further. It was incorporated as a nonprofit agency and assumed a major role in the overall development of job programs within the city. In 1981, with support from the city, the PIC de-veloped a summer youth jobs program as well as job counseling services at sev-eral high schools. Both programs brought the business community as well as other community actors together with the school department. This early collaboration became a building block for the compact.

Most important, the PIC provided an independent umbrella for the develop-ment of business-school programs. This independence was important to many in the business community. Given the school department's reputation for patronage, politics, and poor management practices, many business leaders were reluctant to grant school officials authority to oversee programs and to monitor the flow of funds.[26] The PIC was a more reliable and dependable institution and became the institutional home of the compact as well as the business-school partnerships begun in the 1970s.

Furthermore, the concrete and explicit provisions of the Boston Compact ap-pealed to the business community.[27] The school department would improve daily attendance by 5 percent each year, reduce the high school drop-out rate by 5 per-cent each year, and improve math and reading scores of graduates. Boston busi-nesses, in turn, would increase their hiring of Boston public school graduates by 5 percent each year. Colleges and universities would improve college placement rates by 5 percent each year. Boston building and trades unions would actively re-cruit school graduates into apprenticeship programs.[28] To implement this agreement, a steering committee, executive committee, and eleven work groups were created.

The Boston Compact was an important first step in cross-sector collabora-tion and network building, but it was fairly limited in its educational focus. In particular, the emphasis on employment and college opportunities for public school graduates left elementary and middle schools untouched. This focus on jobs and employment reflected the dominant role of business leaders in drafting the com-pact. Similarly, the premise of the compact—that job opportunities for students would foster improved learning—was a relatively narrow view of educational reform. A more comprehensive and systemic approach to school reform would develop in later years.

Furthermore, support for the Boston Compact fluctuated. Spillane's departure from the superintendency in 1985 removed one of its strongest advocates, and grow-ing awareness that schools were not improving left nonschool parties to the agree-ment frustrated and disillusioned. During renewal negotiations in 1987 and 1988, business leaders insisted on a number of changes in how schools operated, includ-ing a new student assignment plan and greater decentralization in school operations. The compact was becoming an instrument for more comprehensive educational reform, but reaching that status was a very slow and often frustrating process.

Boston Plan for Excellence in the Public Schools.   A second network—the Bos-ton Plan for Excellence in the Public Schools—was a spinoff of the compact. The plan was created in 1984 by leaders in the business community. The Bank of

Boston, celebrating its 200th anniversary, established a $1.5 million endowment fund to create a grants program supporting innovative teaching and curriculum in elementary and high schools.[29] This competitive grants program would be operated through the newly created Boston Plan for Excellence in the Public Schools. The nonprofit organization soon became the recipient of other corporate contributions, including $1 million from John Hancock Financial Services for middle school programs and $1 million from a law firm for professional teacher development.[30] By 1988, the plan had over $10 million in endowments to support programs in the public schools.[31]

The Boston Plan for Excellence in the Public Schools, like the Private Industry Council, provided a safe and reliable avenue for business involvement with the schools. Staff at the plan were independent of the school department and not subject to the political ventures of the school committee. Furthermore, the organization provided a platform for corporate visibility and leadership. Although the plan included university and community-based leaders on its boards of trustees and overseers, the business community clearly set the agenda.

Citywide Educational Coalition. A third network created during this period was the Citywide Educational Coalition (CWEC). Formed in 1973, the CWEC grew out of a human services collaborative that focused on the needs of city youth as well as desegregation issues. In addition, this network coalesced around efforts to introduce more public input into the 1973 search for a new superintendent. In 1974, the CWEC was incorporated as a nonprofit organization with its primary membership coming from parents, educators, and community organizations.

The CWEC established parent councils at each school and became an early advocate for more community involvement in educational decision making. The membership expanded to include local businesses, foundations, banks, and institutions for higher education, and the organization began to assume a role as a major information clearinghouse. The CWEC sponsored public forums and disseminated information on the school system.

Networks and the Federal District Court

The Citywide Educational Coalition, Boston Plan for Excellence in the Public Schools, and Boston Compact were important steps in the development of civic capacity and its application to public education. These steps, however, were limited. All three networks were new and seeking an identity and base of support. Most important, they operated in the shadow of a court-directed desegregation plan that had two quite different impacts on the development of civic capacity. First, many people credit the courts with forcing change in the school system. Court intervention was critical in moving the system toward a desegregation plan. Furthermore, the court pressured businesses, higher education institutions, community organizations, and parents to become more involved in the Boston Public

Schools. The first executive director of the compact noted, for example, that businesses, colleges, and the schools would not have joined forces without "the six or seven years of working together under the court order."[32] In a more pointed comment, one participant in the process wrote that a number of community institutions, such as colleges and businesses, were "dragged into the arena by court order."[33] Another observer confided to one of the authors that "there have been no genuine efforts to improve the schools without a court order."

In forcing this type of change, however, the courts had a second impact of displacing or truncating a more community-based development of civic capacity. Interested parties often did battle in the courts instead of engaging in the more deliberative process of coalition building. The federal courthouse, rather than business boardrooms, city hall, or the school department, set much of the agenda for educational change. Community and school leaders were certainly involved in educational reform, but many of their strategies and actions were in reaction to court orders. Even when the role of the courts was reduced in the 1980s, coalition building was still done in an environment created by court orders. As two participants in the process noted, "The side effects of [court] intervention—of doing that which elected leaders refused to do—have clouded the image in the mirror. Many Bostonians can no longer perceive the situation of their city."[34]

To borrow Clarence Stone's phrase once again, the federal district court exercised "power over" rather than "power to."[35] That is, court orders displayed considerable power over the community, but the court's power to create civic capacity was limited. Courts are arenas for the adjudication of disputes and the exercise of rights; they are less adept at building new institutions. Creating associations and networks to address the long-term problems of public education is a more organic process of independently identifying common interests and building a platform for action. Court orders can serve a useful role in bringing different parties together, but they cannot mandate the trust, consensus, and voluntary compliance that are critical to associations and networks. In Boston, the federal district court sparked considerable collaboration, but its long duration cast a lengthy shadow over the development of civic capacity.

GOVERNANCE BATTLES AND STALLED REFORM EFFORTS, 1989–1992

The federal district court's return of educational responsibility to local actors raised a key question: Would the civic organizations of the city step forward in support of public education? In particular, would the city's civic capacity, as developed in the previous decade, be strong enough to build and sustain a citywide structure of support for education? An answer depended not only on the success of existing institutions, particularly the Boston Compact, but also on leadership both inside and outside the school system.

Failure of Leadership

It was in this area of leadership, where Pittsburgh was so strong, that Boston fell short. Key coalition actors—the Boston School Committee, the superintendent, and the mayor—became embroiled in a governance battle that undermined, at least temporarily, the exercise of civic capacity on behalf of public education. Without strong leadership, the institutions created in the 1970s and 1980s lacked the direction and resources needed to sustain educational reform initiatives.

Boston School Committee. The Boston School Committee was at the center of the governance battle. The thirteen-member elected committee, which replaced a five-member committee in 1984, consisted of nine members elected by district and four at-large.[36] All committee members served two-year terms and chose a president from among their ranks. Salary compensation to committee members was small, only $7,500 per year, but each member received $52,000 to hire staff and operate an office.[37] The staff hired by committee members often served a constituent relations function and also provided a base of knowledge for each committee member that facilitated extensive committee involvement in school policies and programs.

The committee often was criticized for political infighting and discord. Battles over school closures, for example, were commonplace. In the late 1980s the superintendent recommended three years in a row that a secondary school be closed, but each time the committee rebuffed the superintendent without acting on an alternative to address space issues.[38] Racial divisions also were prominent. In 1989, for example, the committee approved a controlled-choice busing plan by a 9 to 4 vote with all four black members in opposition. In the following year, the committee voted 7 to 1 to fire black superintendent Laval Wilson; prior to the vote the four black members of the committee walked out in protest.

Fiscal irresponsibility was another frequent charge, which, in part, was a reflection of the structural division of financial power between the school committee and city hall. The school committee controlled the allocation of resources within the school budget, but the mayor and city council set the total appropriation for the school department. Not surprisingly, the school committee often decried city hall for offering inadequate financial resources to operate the school system. The committee typically refused to make expenditure cuts equal to those requested by city hall and would end the year in a deficit, requiring a last-minute appropriation from the mayor and city council. Between fiscal years 1986 and 1990, the school department ended each year with a deficit.[39] Newspaper stories would capture the ensuing debate as the mayor and school committee traded accusations of fiscal mismanagement and failure to adequately support education for the youth of the city.

The media were frequent critics of the school committee. A *Boston Globe* editorial, for example, described the school committee as "a disaster." The editorial continued: "Infighting, grandstanding, aspirations for higher political office, and incompetence have become mainstays of the 13–member committee. The system is floundering."[40] In 1991, the *Globe* presented a five-part series—"Boston Schools on the Brink"—that traced the plight of the schools as well as the dysfunctional nature of the school committee.[41]

Similarly, several blue-ribbon commissions recommended major changes. In 1989, for example, a commission appointed by the mayor declared that "frustration with school performance had reached an historic high" and that changes in governance were critical to the future of the system.[42] After reviewing the governance system for the schools, the study concluded that "Boston is unique. The buck does not appear to stop anywhere."[43] A study by the Boston Municipal Research Bureau, a business-sponsored municipal watchdog agency, decried the poor performance of the school committee. As the director of the bureau noted in a committee hearing, "The inherent flaw of the current school governance structure is that it does not insure accountability, especially fiscal accountability."[44]

Pressures to change the makeup of the committee mounted. Mayor Raymond L. Flynn (1984–1993) was a leading proponent of abolishing the elected committee and replacing it with an appointed body, even though some cautioned the mayor about the perceived futility of trying to improve the school system. Many others in the community, including business leaders, joined in opposition to the elected body. The elected committee, however, did have supporters. Particularly in the minority community, the elected committee was seen as an important means of enfranchisement for the residents of Boston. Furthermore, granting power to the mayor to appoint a school committee was seen by many as affording one individual too much power over education. Thus, Flynn's support for an appointed committee carried considerable risks. Some saw an appointed committee as a loss of voting rights, while others perceived it as a power play by the mayor.

In November 1989, a citywide advisory referendum on the issue yielded mixed results: 37 percent in favor of an appointed committee, 36 percent opposed, and 26 percent not voting. The movement to an appointed committee was temporarily shelved, but in late 1990 efforts resumed and resulted in an April 1991 vote by the city council in favor of a seven-member appointed committee. The city council's measure was presented as a home rule petition to the state legislature and governor, where approval also was received. Under the new system, a thirteen-member nominating committee was appointed by the mayor to review applications and recommend three individuals for each open committee position. After receiving the nominations, Mayor Flynn appointed seven individuals to begin terms in January 1992. A new committee was on board, but it had been a long and difficult period for public education in Boston.

School superintendent. A second key leadership position, the superintendency, also was mired in the governance debate. In comparison to Pittsburgh, Boston has a history of high turnover in the superintendency. Between 1972 and 1992, Boston had six different superintendents and four periods under an acting superintendent.[45]

Laval Wilson, the city's first black superintendent, was hired in 1985 when Robert Spillane left Boston. By 1988 Wilson was under frequent attack for his reluctance to adopt school-based management, which was viewed favorably in the business community, and for educational initiatives that failed to take root. The Boston Education Plan was Wilson's major planning effort that involved over three hundred staff and community members in developing a three-year improvement plan for the school system. The education plan was approved by the school committee but proved generally ineffective in sparking substantial change in individual schools. In April 1989, by only a one-vote margin, Wilson received a two-year contract but was subject to a six-month review. In February 1990 the racially divided committee fired Wilson, appointed an interim superintendent, and initiated a search process. As the state education commissioner noted, there was a "leadership crisis" in the Boston public schools: "There is great turmoil over the management of the Boston school system. It is quite clear we have a problem."[46]

The process of choosing a new superintendent became controversial, particularly when the first list of finalists included no women or Latinos. Furthermore, one nationally known candidate withdrew from the process, complaining that local politics had become more important than educational policy.[47] The search process was repeated, and Lois Harrison-Jones, a black female with experience in Virginia and Texas, was hired in May 1991. Although a new superintendent was finally in place, governance issues were hardly settled. Within six months the committee that hired Harrison-Jones was replaced by the appointed committee, none of whom had been involved in hiring the new superintendent. She now faced the task of establishing a working relationship with a new set of educational policy makers.

City mayor. A third actor, the mayor, also was part of the governance debate. As noted in Chapter 3, Boston is a strong-mayor city, but by institutional design the mayor has a very limited role in the schools. As Mayor White noted, the school department is "probably the only branch of city government in which the mayor has virtually no authority or influence, except budgetary."[48] Administrative control of the schools rested with the superintendent and school committee, and as noted earlier, the allocation of funds within the school budget was outside the formal power of the mayor.

Boston's mayors, then, have historically kept an arm's-length distance from the public schools. Mayor White played a cautious role in the desegregation debates and other discussions of school policy. White was a coalition builder who attempted to adopt a neutral role in school politics.[49] Mayor Flynn, during the early years of his tenure, was also hesitant to become involved in school politics. As Flynn admitted in remarks prepared for the business community, "Public education is an area that can swallow up the most promising career, and politicians are counseled at every step to 'stay away from the schools.'"[50] The complexity and volatility of school politics created dangerous ground for a mayor.

By 1989, however, Mayor Flynn began to exercise more leadership with respect to the school system. He was openly critical of the school committee and failures in the school system. He criticized the elected committee for budget deficits and an inability to act on major education issues, and he was a leader in the move to an appointed committee. Although still tentative at times, Mayor Flynn pointed to changes in school governance as critical to the future of Boston's schools.

The battle over governance was a major preoccupation of civic leaders during this period. In our elite interviews, issues of leadership and governance received the single largest number of mentions as "challenges" or "obstacles" facing public education in Boston.[51] Business, political, and community leaders frequently cited the need for stronger leadership and a better working relationship among the school committee, superintendent, and mayor. The media presented a similar concern. Based on an analysis of reporting in the *Boston Globe,* governance as a topic was most prominent among all educational articles from 1989 through 1991 and was the most frequent topic of educational editorials by *Globe* editors between July 1990 and June 1992.[52] The *Globe*'s call in January 1991 to replace the elected school committee with an appointed committee capped the steady media criticism of school governance.[53]

Other Obstacles to School Reform

In addition to failures in leadership, there were a number of other obstacles to school reform, of which several—public cynicism and racial discord—were part of the city's underlying cultural orientation. Public cynicism toward the school system had been widespread for a number of years. This negativism was prominent in our elite interviews. One business leader described the public schools as a fiscal "black hole," while a former school administrator emphasized the "mean spirit" and lack of trust toward the schools. Two other school administrators commented on the "cynicism about the school system" and the fact that the "general public has little faith in [it]."[54] A survey of public opinion found similar sentiments. In a 1989 poll, 62 percent of registered voters thought the schools had "lost ground" in the past two or three years; only 9 percent believed the schools had "made progress."[55]

This cynicism was rooted, in part, in a growing split between users of the school system and the overall city population. By one estimate, only 20 percent of households had children in the public schools.[56] Many city households did not include school-age children, and a significant number of families with children did not use the Boston Public Schools. In fact, one-fourth of school-age students in Boston attended either private schools or public schools outside the city. For these families and households, the Boston Public Schools had little direct relevance to their lives. Indeed, there was a pattern of disownership of the public schools.

Public cynicism included a widely held belief that the school system was a rigid, inflexible organization incapable of providing adequate educational programs. Labeled an "entrenched bureaucracy" by one civic leader, a former area educational administrator called the school department the "worst planning organization" he had seen. A former school administrator commented that the "system drains energy" as innovations die. A government official noted the presence of entrepreneurial skills only at the school level; in the rest of the system, "people don't feel empowered." Mayor Flynn also pointed to the educational bureaucracy as a major obstacle to reform: "We have got to take on—and take apart—the educational bureaucracy if we are going to provide quality public education for our children."[57]

Racial discord was a second important obstacle to building and sustaining support for school reform. Boston was a community divided, in many respects, along racial lines. One community activist noted that race is an "umbrella over the city," while another declared that the "tough issues are all tinged with race." Another local activist and writer concluded that the "fundamental reality is the city is torn by racism and elitism."[58] In this context, the Boston Public Schools were increasingly seen as the educational home for minority youth. White flight from the city, a growing minority population, and the controversy over desegregation and busing resulted in a student population dominated by minorities, even though the city remained predominantly white. As noted in Chapter 3, 80 percent of students in the Boston Public Schools were of African-American, Asian, or Hispanic heritage, yet persons of color accounted for only 37 percent of the city's overall population. Furthermore, children of color were more likely to be in the public schools: 90 percent of African-American, Asian, and Hispanic elementary and high school students in Boston attended public schools, whereas the comparable measure for white school-age children was approximately 50 percent.

This racial cleavage had important political implications. While public school students came predominantly from communities of color, the largest voting blocs in the city were primarily white areas. Boston was becoming a city split between adult white neighborhoods—politically active but with limited involvement in the public schools—and neighborhoods of color—with children in the schools but limited political involvement. Building a constituency of support for educational reform within this environment was indeed a challenge. As one community activist commented, "It's going to take a lot of going out and convincing people that the future of the city is grounded in the future of the schools."[59]

Stalled Efforts to Activate Civic Support for Public Education

In the business community there was a growing skepticism that the public schools in their present form were capable of improvement. Leadership skills were lacking, and the school bureaucracy seemed incapable of change. In 1987, the five-year Boston Compact was up for renewal, but business leaders were dissatisfied with the lack of progress in the schools. In 1987 and 1988 a compact committee noted the increase in jobs for graduates and postsecondary educational opportunities but less success on the part of the schools in lowering the drop-out rate and improving academic achievement. The business community called for "fundamental change" in how the schools were run, emphasizing the need for more parental control in student assignment and the need for school-based management to increase the power of site-based professionals, particularly the principal.[60]

After lengthy negotiations, Boston Compact II was signed in 1989. Major elements of the agreement included the adoption of school-based management, an increase in parental involvement, implementation of the new controlled-choice assignment plan, expansion of postgraduate job search and college assistance programs, an increase in the high school completion rate, and an improvement in overall academic performance. Each major party to the compact—the business community, higher education, the mayor, and the school department—had a role to play in meeting these goals.

Compact II represented a step forward in civic support for public education, but it was soon derailed by other forces.[61] In particular, the governance problems already cited involving the superintendent and school committee undermined the structure of support for the agreement. Furthermore, an economic downturn that began in late 1988 removed the fiscal underpinnings of not only the compact but also the recently negotiated teachers' contract that included a number of the compact's initiatives. City funding for the Boston Public Schools declined by 2 percent in fiscal year 1992 and another 2 percent in fiscal year 1993.[62] The cutbacks were relatively modest, but they effectively curtailed most new initiatives, such as school-based management as well as negotiated salary increases for teachers.

The economic downturn also took a toll on the ability of the business community to focus on public education. Many business leaders turned their attention to economic survival and their own balance sheets. Even when economic recovery arrived, a number of major businesses in Boston found themselves purchased by corporations outside the city.[63] With Boston no longer the headquarters, city connections and community affairs were demoted. As one business leader noted, the loss of headquarters' operations in Boston meant local chief executive officers were being replaced with "surrogates" less likely to provide leadership on community issues.[64]

This was a period of instability in educational politics in Boston. The Boston Compact was renewed in 1989, but progress was limited. An embattled school committee provided limited leadership and was finally replaced; controversy and turnover in the superintendent's office weakened leadership of the school system; and the mayor challenged both the school committee and the superintendent but lacked direct authority over the schools. Some in the business community were prepared to abandon the public schools, advocating instead a school choice policy to bring the marketplace to public education. The civic capacity of the city was still substantial, but it was not being activated on behalf of public education. It would take a new combination of events and individuals to activate broad-based support for public education in Boston.

THE EMERGENCE OF LEADERSHIP AND INSTITUTIONAL SUPPORT, 1993–1998

The appointment of a new school committee in 1992 marked the beginning of a transition period for Boston. Over the next few years a structure of support for public education developed in two critical arenas. First, strong leadership emerged as new individuals assumed positions on the school committee and in the offices of superintendent and mayor. And second, considerable progress was made in institution building when the Boston Compact was strengthened and the Boston Teachers' Union became partners with the school system in a wide range of educational reforms. By the end of this period, Boston was poised for a substantial effort in improving public education.

New Leadership

Strong leadership, however, did not come easily. Even with an appointed school committee, governance battles continued, only now they often took a more personal tone. Mayor Flynn and Superintendent Harrison-Jones, in particular, were at odds, and the executive secretary of the new school committee, hired at the prompting of the mayor, was also in frequent disagreement with the superintendent. These clashes touched on personal political styles as well as educational philosophies. Furthermore, as noted earlier, the new appointed school committee had to develop a working relationship with a superintendent not of its own choosing.

Resolution to these disputes came slowly. Tensions between the superintendent and school committee's executive secretary continued until the executive secretary resigned in early 1993. Disagreements between the mayor and superintendent became increasingly public. In mid-1993, however, Mayor Flynn left Boston to join the Clinton administration as ambassador to the Vatican. City Council president Thomas Menino became acting mayor, then won the special election in November 1993. With a new mayor in city hall, the relationship between the superintendent, school committee, and mayor was less volatile, but tensions continued.

Superintendent Harrison-Jones was at the center of the leadership debate. From her perspective, the problem was the intervention of Boston politics into public education and the city's persistent criticism of her role as superintendent. As Harrison-Jones noted in a *Globe* interview, the key difference between Boston and other cities is that "Boston will not respect the agenda or the plan or the vision put forth by the superintendent. It has happened here for the past two decades."[65] On the other side, however, was mounting criticism of the superintendent's performance. Mayor Menino and some business leaders were increasingly critical of the superintendent, and the *Globe* editorial staff produced a report card on the superintendent that included such comments as "limited vision," "poor management skills," "strained relationship with outside parties," and "meager overall progress in academic achievement." The *Globe* concluded that it "is time for new leadership" in the schools.[66]

The final step came in early 1995 when Superintendent Harrison-Jones was informed that her contract, due to expire in July, would not be renewed. A search process was initiated by the school committee. Mayor Menino made it clear that he would take a central, albeit less public, role in the process. In July and August three finalists were interviewed, and an offer was extended to Thomas Payzant, assistant secretary in the U.S. Department of Education and former superintendent in San Diego and Oklahoma City.

The search process for a new superintendent sparked the creation of another network, known as Critical Friends, that would add a strong voice to school reform. Critical Friends brought together in monthly meetings approximately twenty individuals from a broad range of organizations, associations, and other networks involved with the public schools, including the Boston Plan for Excellence in the Public Schools, the Private Industry Council, and the Citywide Educational Coalition. With foundation funding to support one staff person, Critical Friends became a watchdog of the school system. Its goal was to push and prod the system down a path of educational reform. It had access to the mayor and superintendent and placed collective bargaining and reform within the school bureaucracy as first on its agenda.

With the hiring of Payzant in September, the stage was set. As one school principal commented in an earlier interview, successful school reform requires that the mayor, superintendent, school committee, and school administrators be in accord, or as he put it, "All the planets have to be lined up." Finally, after many years of policy disagreements and personal clashes, leadership on the public side of the civic ledger was in place.[67] Commented one business leader, "For the first time we have a mayor, a superintendent and a school committee singing from the same sheet of music."[68]

Institution Building

Leadership is important and essential, but equally critical is an institutional platform upon which leadership can be exercised. That is, the planets may be lined up, but unless the requisite resources and institutional support are available, community leaders are destined to fall short in their efforts. Fortunately for Boston, at the same time that governance battles were being resolved, key actors were expanding and strengthening existing institutional arrangements to support public education. This process was most apparent in two areas—the Boston Compact and negotiations with the teachers' union.

As noted earlier, Boston Compact II, signed in 1989, fell victim to an economic downswing as well as ongoing governance disputes. The compact had a number of important innovations, such as school-based management, but it received limited attention during this volatile time; by mid-1992 negotiations were begun for the next version of the agreement. Compact III, signed in January 1994, brought together all the key educational actors. The compact actually was completed earlier in 1993, but the formal launching of the new agreement was postponed until the new mayor, Thomas Menino, was inaugurated. Compact III offered an aggressive agenda for reform, emphasizing the need for better educational preparation of students and expanded opportunity for graduates of the system.

Five major goals were outlined in the agreement. The first goal emphasized initiatives to increase access to employment and higher education for school graduates. The second goal was a commitment to innovation within the school system, including the extension of school-based management to all schools and the establishment of at least six "pilot" schools (within-district charter schools). Goal three included comprehensive review and revision of the school curriculum and the development of new assessment standards. The fourth goal called for the creation of a Center for Leadership Development to strengthen professional development. The final goal highlighted greater support for parents and families, including an expansion of early childhood opportunities.[69]

The signing of the new compact was an important event for the city and an important step in strengthening this network to support public education. Signatories included the mayor and superintendent as well as representatives from the school committee, Vault, the Higher Education Partnership, the Private Industry Council, and the Boston Teachers' Union. In addition, plans were made to include representatives from parents, cultural institutions, and human service providers. Three committees—a working group, steering committee, and measurement committee—were established to handle the ongoing activities of the compact, and staff support would continue to be provided by one person in the superintendent's office and staff at the Private Industry Council. In addition, one of the three subcommittees of the school committee—the compact implementation subcommittee—would focus on the work of the compact.

Institution building also focused on the school bureaucracy as an organization. Central to any school organization is the role of teachers, which in the case of Boston and most large cities involves a teachers' union. Adoption of Compact III in early 1994 coincided with an intense period of collective bargaining negotiations between the Boston Teachers' Union and the school committee. This period began when a proposed contract was rejected by the school committee in September 1993, with Acting Mayor Menino playing a decisive role in the rejection.[70] To avoid school disruptions during the year, a one-year agreement authorizing

3 percent raises was signed in November. Union and school committee representatives met at the bargaining table throughout the school year along with an outside party that helped develop a collaborative rather than adversarial environment.

In June 1994, the new contract was signed and applauded by parties throughout the city. Along with salary increases for teachers, the contract included many of the reform initiatives outlined in the Boston Compact: school-based management, pilot schools, learning standards, and a professional development center. The contract also included a career ladder for teachers, a new teacher evaluation system, and school improvement awards. It was clear that the union was prepared to play a major role in reform. As Mayor Menino was widely quoted in announcing the new contract, "We have no more excuses."[71]

Sustaining Reform Efforts

Indeed, the pieces were falling into place. By 1996, an impressive structure of support was in position for public education in Boston. Mayor Menino, in an unprecedented move, held his January "state of the city" speech in the Jeremiah Burke High School, a school that had just lost its accreditation. Menino described public education as the "hub" of the urban "wheel," with economic security, good jobs, safe streets, quality of life, and public health as "spokes" in the wheel. The mayor outlined recent accomplishments of educational reform—school-based management, new teachers' contract, new superintendent, and appointed school committee—and highlighted the agenda for the next five years, including more extended-day programs, better curriculum and assessment standards, more computers, and improved school buildings. In closing, Mayor Menino declared: "I want to be judged as your mayor by what happens now in the Boston public schools. I expect you to hold me accountable to what I have said tonight. If I fail, . . . judge me harshly."[72]

Superintendent Payzant also has taken a strong and visible stand in a number of areas. To exercise managerial leadership, in February 1996 the superintendent initiated a major reorganization of the school department.[73] The existing three-level structure of high schools, middle schools, and elementary schools was replaced by ten clusters with approximately eleven schools from all grades in each. Among the principals in each cluster, one serves as cluster leader to work collaboratively with other principals as a "leader, coach and peer counselor" and to represent cluster schools on the superintendent's new "leadership team."[74] Other changes in the central office shifted more responsibility to individual schools, and a personnel evaluation review resulted in the removal of six school principals. In 1998, recognizing the need for additional changes, Payzant reorganized positions in senior-level management to strengthen support for and evaluation of principals and also provide greater oversight of human resources functions.[75]

Payzant's educational leadership is embodied in a five-year plan called *Focus on Children*. Approved by the school committee in July 1996, this plan outlines four major goals to guide the school system:

Improve teaching and learning to enable all students to achieve high standards of performance;

Change the structure of the Boston Public Schools to focus on student performance and to serve the community;

Provide safe, nurturing, healthy schools where students receive the support they need to succeed in school; and

Engage parents and the community in school improvement through a unified, collaborative structure and effective communication.[76]

Focus on Children describes Boston as a "community ready for change." The "essential elements" for reform are in place, which include a supportive mayor, a school committee committed to reform, an experienced superintendent, a partnership with the Boston Teachers' Union, and community support through the Boston Compact. With this "structure for collaboration," the forty-four-page plan outlines a series of steps and actions focused on the primary goal of improving teaching and learning.

The guiding educational philosophy is referred to as "whole-school change."[77] The key is to focus all reform efforts on teaching and learning. As noted in the plan, "schools do not need to add more new programs." Rather, all efforts should be targeted to a common mission. Specifically, students must be prepared to meet the citywide learning standards established in mid-1996. High standards and curricula must be put in place; leadership development is needed for all staff; and each school must develop its own comprehensive reform plan. As the superintendent notes in a later memo, "Whole-school change occurs when the structure, organization, expectations, activities and practices in a school are connected to improve student achievement. Separate projects, disjointed activities, fragmented practices will not result in the comprehensive overhaul schools need."[78]

Whole-school change is supported by a collaborative effort involving the school department and the Boston Plan for Excellence in the Public Schools. In early 1996, the plan replaced its ten-year practice of funding distinct programs with a new initiative called the Twenty-first Century School Grants Program. Henceforth, the plan would no longer sponsor targeted grant programs identified with individual corporate sponsors. Rather, grants of $25,000 for each of four years would be made to individual schools to support a process of self-assessment, planning, and implementation of whole-school reform.[79] Each school would look at the totality of its needs when designing a program of change and improvement. In the first year, a "coach" would work with staff in each Twenty-first Century School to assess instructional needs.

Support from the Annenberg Foundation was sought to extend the whole-school change model to all schools. Extensive collaboration on this grant application among the Boston Compact partners yielded positive results in October 1996, when Boston received a $10 million award.[80] Since that time, the Annenberg grant has been matched by $12 million from the private sector and a $10 million commitment from the public sector. The plan serves as fiscal agent for the grant, and a governing board and executive committee have been established to oversee the award. By the fall of 1998, 94 of Boston's 128 schools had received support for whole-school change. Funds from the Annenberg grant also have helped support the Center for Leadership Development and pilot schools.[81]

Raising expectations for students and strengthening the accountability of teachers have received special attention. In 1998, the school committee adopted a rigorous promotion policy that requires students in the third, fifth, and eighth grades to pass citywide or state tests to be promoted. Those failing the test will be required to attend summer school. The policy includes a number of other requirements, including a new attendance standard, that are intended to end social promotions.[82] Adoption of the policy was controversial, passing on a 3 to 2 vote. Many argued that the weight of accountability should be on the school system first rather than on the students.[83] To that end, Superintendent Payzant emphasized changes within the system to improve teaching in the classroom. The new reorganization, for example, will provide additional support to instructional staff, and principals will receive intensive training on evaluating and supporting teachers.[84]

This overall reform path and governance arrangement received a vote of confidence in the 1996 and 1997 elections. On the ballot in November 1996 was a binding referendum question to return to the thirteen-member elected school committee. (The referendum vote was required by the state legislature when it approved the change to an appointed committee in 1991.) Mayor Menino, business leaders, and the *Boston Globe* came out as strong advocates to retain the appointed committee. Arguing for stability and continuity as well as accountability through the mayor, the defenders of an appointed committee launched an extensive campaign to sway the voters. Proponents of an elected committee, including former superintendent Harrison-Jones and many members of past elected committees in Boston, emphasized the importance of parental involvement through the ballot box. In the end, however, the vote to return to an elected committee was defeated decisively by a 70 to 30 percent margin. Said Menino, "The message was clear throughout Boston that we should continue the progress we've made in the schools."[85] In 1997 the voters delivered another vote of confidence when Mayor Menino was reelected to a new four-year term. Menino ran unopposed, the first time in recent decades that a Boston mayor had not faced an opponent.

Challenges Remain

These are important steps down the path of educational reform, but challenges remain, apparent both inside and outside the double helix of school reform. Inside the schools, there is impatience on the part of some that change is taking hold and that students will be ready for state-mandated graduation tests. In the broader community, issues of poverty and race persist, and the collaborative spirit is sometimes found lacking.

Inside the school system. Changing the organizational culture of the Boston Public Schools is a long-term challenge for the superintendent and other educational leaders. As Critical Friends concluded in a recent assessment, the culture of the school system is one "in which attention is more often paid to the politics of survival than to the performance of duties."[86] This watchdog group identified a host of issues—general cynicism about change, inequities among schools, racial divisions, persistence of patronage appointments, and distrust of outsiders—that must be addressed before reforms can take root in the Boston schools. The reform approach of Superintendent Payzant includes some steps to address this organizational culture, including the reorganization plan and whole-school change reform model. The teachers' collective bargaining contract also is a critical piece to change the organization and remains a major challenge for the superintendent's leadership.

The general pace of reform also is under criticism. The Municipal Research Bureau, for example, recognized progress in a number of areas but noted that "educational reform efforts are still very much a work-in-progress."[87] The research bureau identified a number of areas for priority action, including professional development, remedial instruction opportunities, and enforcement of the teachers' union contract.

Critical Friends issued a two-year assessment of reform efforts that concluded with a call for an "immediate shift from rhetoric to radical action."[88] The report emphasized the need for risk taking if reform was to be "significant, long-term and systemic." The superintendent and school system received high marks for some efforts—the Annenberg grant, for example—but overall implementation of reform had not met expectations. Of sixty-one "grades" given to Payzant and the school system, twenty-two were "unsatisfactory" and twenty-four were "must improve." In general, student academic performance was not satisfactory, and the school system needed to be more open and aggressive about seeking community support. Of particular concern was personnel management. The performance evaluation system was found lacking, and "few building blocks to improve the performance of BPS personnel exist currently." The report concluded with an offer of assistance from Critical Friends and an emphasis on the need for a "sense of urgency, a willingness to take some risks, and widespread community involvement and support."

The report by Critical Friends sparked a sharp retort from Mayor Menino and the school committee. Both disagreed with the report and praised Superintendent Payzant for his work. Superintendent Payzant acknowledged some areas that require improvement but took exception to the overall conclusions of the report. Several members of Critical Friends, including the executive director of the Boston Plan for Excellence in the Public Schools, resigned in protest over the report. Still, a founder of Critical Friends defended the report: "You are not going to change the Boston public school system unless you are prepared to go for broke. This is a wake-up call."[89]

Student test scores are of particular concern, and a looming, state-mandated "high stakes" test for graduation poses a major challenge. Superintendent Payzant replaced the Metropolitan Achievement Test with the more difficult Stanford 9

Achievement Test as one step to raise the standard of expectations for Boston students. In 1996, the first year of the Stanford 9, students fared poorly, particularly in the high schools. Among eleventh grade students taking the exam, 81 percent scored below basic levels on the math portion, and 41 percent fared similarly on reading skills. Elementary students performed better, but Payzant admitted that "this is a tough reality check" for the school system.[90] This "reality check" is particularly important, since in 2001 all tenth grade students in Massachusetts must pass a state-mandated test in order to graduate. Students who fail the test have until the end of their senior year to score a passing grade. By one estimate approximately one-half of Boston high school students currently would not pass such a test.[91]

Test scores in 1998 showed improvement at the lower elementary level, but among middle and high school students there was little progress. As Superintendent Payzant commented, "We still have a long way to go."[92] Furthermore, the racial gap in achievement scores pointed to another major issue facing the school system. Test scores for black and Hispanic students continued to lag behind those of white students, particularly in math. Since the mid-1980s, this gap has been widening.[93] Superintendent Payzant, in response, set a goal of bringing the average test scores of all racial groups to within five percentage points of the top group's average by 2003, which will indeed be a major challenge.[94]

Outside the schools.   Major challenges also exist outside the school system. Persistent poverty in parts of the city continues to pose an obstacle to effective school participation by many students. As noted in Chapter 3, the public school system in Boston, as in many other cities, has a high proportion of students in poverty. Recent economic growth has not changed this fact. As one recent study noted, "The city's economy still primarily benefits the long-standing business structure and a workforce that does not live in the city."[95] High poverty is correlated with family structures that provide less support for student learning. As one teacher commented, "We are asked to do so much, be everything, everybody. You need dedicated parents."[96]

Race is a related issue that continues to pose a challenge for the school system and the broader community. As Critical Friends noted, "Issues of racial diversity are not openly discussed or dealt with. They linger beneath the surface."[97] From the school committee to the classroom, racial diversity is a fact of the Boston schools. Yet, as the number of minority students in the school population increases, many whites in the city distance themselves from the school system. As one columnist noted, race is the "killer virus of Boston politics."[98] It is often unspoken, yet it affects many of the actions and policies of the city. Mayor Menino admitted that "race is *the* issue in this city. People talk about crime, but that's just a smokescreen. They say crime, but they mean race. It's the most important issue we face as a city."[99]

A changing economy, along with racial divisions and other changes in the city, affects the ability to construct long-term and sustainable collaborative efforts. The work of such networks as the Boston Compact and the Boston Plan for Excellence in the Public Schools is laudatory, but the underlying infrastructure of collaboration in the city has been brought into question.[100] The business community, for example, is much more diverse and fragmented today than during the 1960s and 1970s. The rise in services has brought new actors to the forefront and diminished the role of older associations like the Vault. Writing in 1988, one *Globe* reporter noted that "the Vault is not the close-knit group dominated by bank, insurance, and utility company chairmen it once was."[101] By 1997, the Vault was no longer a player. The new chief executive officer of BankBoston, rated by one magazine as "Mr. Boston" for his influence in the city, noted that he has yet to attend a meeting of the Vault. "Obviously," this business leader noted, "if I thought it was vital I'd make time."[102] Instead, this individual joined seven other business leaders—and former Vault members—to meet informally to discuss issues of common concern.

Broad collaboration is more complicated in this environment. Forty community leaders traveled to Atlanta to see and hear how that city fosters collaboration in a variety of areas, particularly development. The lesson: Boston needs a "civic culture" that promotes dynamic leadership and a more open dialogue on racial issues.[103] In Atlanta, collaboration among business and community leaders is expected and is critical to that city's support for urban development policies. As in Atlanta, Boston must develop more "civic will and optimism." As one study of the greater Boston area concluded, the "infrastructure for collaboration is ad hoc, fragmented, and poorly developed." There are many "magnets" in the region but too little "glue—mechanisms to help organizations work together to build the future and solve current problems."[104]

These challenges are formidable, although by many accounts Boston has the institutional infrastructure and leadership to meet them. Institutional capacity in the form of the Boston Compact and other networks provides support and resources for school reform. The superintendent, school committee, and mayor are providing leadership on both strands of the double helix. Success is far from guaranteed, however, and there are some in the city who see current efforts as the last, best shot for successful reform. Said one longtime observer of the schools, "If we lose Payzant, or if he is not successful, the ball game is over. The business community is about to go south on the schools, as will a lot of other people. We're about at the end of the line here."[105] Recognizing the importance of Payzant's leadership, the school committee extended his five-year contract by three years, ensuring his role as educational leader through 2003.[106]

The key pieces—institutions and leadership—are present to forestall an abandonment of the schools. The challenge is to translate reform ideas into real actions in the school system and broader community. As Mayor Menino stated in his 1998 inaugural address: "We know that our schools *can* operate differently. We know that they *must*. It takes innovation. It takes discipline. It take teamwork."[107] For Boston, bringing these pieces together is the critical task.

6

St. Louis's Public Schools:
Weak Sectors and Low Cohesion

By most contemporary standards, the St. Louis Public Schools are failing to provide adequate education to many of their students. Test scores are low, drop-out rates are high, and the parents of numerous city children choose to send them on long bus rides to schools in neighboring St. Louis County or opt for private or parochial alternatives. St. Louis's present educational predicament stems in part from its geography, history, and political culture. Its current problems are similar to those of districts in many large cities, but, as we shall see, it has been difficult to create a cross-sector alliance to address the system's failings.

St. Louis's court-ordered desegregation program, which began in 1981, has absorbed the energies of many civic leaders and school personnel at the expense of concern about educational quality. Desegregation, however, has made possible certain highly regarded magnet schools, and public education in St. Louis is not an unmitigated failure. Yet, the pressures for reform evident in Boston and Pittsburgh have not manifested themselves in the same fashion in the Gateway City. In this chapter we examine the various factors that have molded the St. Louis school system, and how educational reform has been addressed by educators, political figures, and corporate leaders. Before discussing the schools, however, we begin with an introduction to development politics in St. Louis.

URBAN DEVELOPMENT IN ST. LOUIS

In development politics, Civic Progress is St. Louis's counterpart to the Vault in Boston and the Allegheny Conference in Pittsburgh. Civic Progress is an association composed of chief executive officers of major firms headquartered in the St. Louis area. Throughout the association's history, it has concentrated on brick-and-mortar projects in the downtown area, such as a new stadium or hockey arena.

Although it has had numerous successes, Civic Progress has not sustained a long-term partnership with political leaders. In regime terms, St. Louis's is one of low cohesion between elected officials and business leaders, marked by intermittent project-specific cooperation.

Mayor Joseph Darst (1949–1953) founded Civic Progress in 1953, and his successor, Raymond Tucker (1953–1965), expanded it the following year. The early days of Civic Progress coincided with the federally financed urban renewal program. At that time, Civic Progress held weekly meetings for which the mayor's office drew up the agendas. Mayor Tucker, an engineering professor elected to three terms—and not a typical ward politician—interacted well with the men of business, and they mutually developed strategies to rebuild downtown St. Louis. Civic Progress also brought aldermen on board with periodic receptions and trips to the nation's capital.

The tight collaboration of the Tucker years, however, faded under his successor, A. J. Cervantes (1965–1973). Cervantes owned a taxicab company and an insurance firm and was more of a professional politician than Tucker. The city's daily newspapers considered some of his allies to be unsavory. Although Civic Progress continued to interact with Mayor Cervantes on certain projects, the regime became less cohesive after his election in 1965. Later mayors also experienced intermittent involvement with top business executives regarding specific projects. At times, the mayors encouraged business leaders to support certain development projects, generally in the central business district.

Civic Progress has been a loose association over most of the past thirty years. Unlike the Allegheny Conference in Pittsburgh, it has never had its own office space or staff. Instead, it has utilized a staff member of the Fleishman-Hillard public relations firm as spokesperson. Members meet monthly at the exclusive Bogey Club in St. Louis County. Ex-officio members—the mayor of St. Louis, the St. Louis County executive, and the leaders of three major universities[1]—attend these meetings. The corporate members of Civic Progress pay annual dues, but for most of them, involvement in this association is not a high priority.

DESEGREGATION AND WEAK INSTITUTIONS, 1954–1985

In 1954, the U.S. Supreme Court, in its desegregation ruling of *Brown v. Board of Education,* launched a major chapter in American history. For St. Louis and its school system, the issues of race and desegregation would dominate much of the public agenda for the next forty years. This was a policy area, however, that did not match well with the bricks-and-mortar approach and downtown focus of Civic Progress. Some businesses pursued individual school partnerships, and there were limited forays into school governance, but the business community was not a major player in desegregation debates that shaped the school system. Unfortunately, other institutions in the city, including city government, also were not well equipped to play a positive role in desegregation. Yet, desegregation would be the major force shaping the St. Louis Public Schools.

A Legacy of Segregation

St. Louis has a culture and history in which race and segregation have played a major role. Located in a former slave state, St. Louis displays a southern heritage as well as certain midwestern features. The city's hospitality is highly touted, and many consider it to be a small town inside a big city. However, its legacy of systemic racism is a very real one, and residents often describe St. Louis as a racist city.

Similar to other border states as well as the eleven states that joined the Confederacy, Missouri adopted various forms of de jure segregation at the close of the nineteenth century. Its 1865 constitution specified that "separate schools may be established for all children of African descent."[2] That stipulation was maintained when subsequent constitutions were adopted, and separate schools for blacks and whites existed throughout the state. Until 1954, St. Louis's public schools were completely segregated. In fact, the state directed that any African-American children residing in St. Louis County be bused to the city's all-black schools. Segregation also affected the private and parochial schools and colleges until the late 1940s. St. Louis University, a Jesuit institution, integrated its student body in 1947. Nonsectarian Washington University followed suit in 1949, and the primary and secondary schools of the archdiocese ended segregation shortly thereafter.

Missouri also segregated public accommodations. Restaurants and other entertainment venues excluded blacks or, in the case of some theaters and movie houses, confined them to remote balconies. African-Americans were not permitted to try on clothing in department stores, although their money was welcome at cash registers. Unlike the deep South, however, streetcars and buses did not have a "blacks-to-the-back" regulation.

Many barriers for nonwhites existed in both housing and employment. Although the percentage of nonwhites in the city's population was less than 10 percent in 1910, St. Louis joined other border-state cities such as Baltimore and Louisville in passing a segregation ordinance in 1916, designed to prevent blacks from moving into white neighborhoods.[3] The U.S. Supreme Court declared such ordinances constitutionally unenforceable in 1919. St. Louis continued to rely on the establishment of private streets for the wealthy and restrictive covenants to keep the races living apart. In fact, the landmark 1948 Supreme Court decision that outlawed such covenants, *Shelley v. Kramer,* originated in the city of St. Louis. Today, the city is largely residentially segregated, with most of the northern portion predominantly black and its southern reaches predominantly white. The city's central corridor has been integrated for several decades, and areas of near south St. Louis have become both black and white in the past several years. In fact, several St. Louis neighborhoods in the central corridor are predominantly black but have maintained a sizable white minority as well.

Despite the legacy of de jure segregation, St. Louis accepted the U.S. Supreme Court's 1954 decision mandating desegregation. School board members and staff met immediately after the decision was rendered to plan a formal end to racial barriers when school resumed in the fall. As a first step, the district desegregated its schools devoted to special education. The following February, it integrated five of its nine high schools and in the fall of 1955, its elementary schools.[4]

Although de jure segregation ended, a significant degree of integration did not immediately occur. Residential patterns kept the races separate, and school attendance areas allowed students to attend the schools closest to where they lived. Except for those living in a few transitional sections, white children continued to go to school with whites and blacks with blacks. When the school board attempted to ease overcrowding at certain black schools, it bused students to underutilized schools in white areas. However, the black children were kept on a different schedule and did not sit in the same classrooms with white youth.[5] The busing of black children from St. Louis County school districts to the city ended with the *Brown* decision, although segregation at some county schools did not cease completely until 1975. The considerable disparities in resources and facilities between schools in black and white city neighborhoods continued unabated.

Desegregation Moves to the Courts

In 1972, Minnie Liddell filed suit in federal district court against the St. Louis Public Schools. She charged that her son was receiving an inferior education in inadequate facilities at his all-black school. She and other plaintiffs who joined her pushed for integration as the only way to end this dual education. The court, however, did not immediately rule on the case. Instead, the school system began to work with the court to create additional integrated educational opportunities. In September 1972, for example, the district opened a specialized high school, Metro High, to provide alternative education to talented youngsters. Metro High soon became the leading college preparatory school in St. Louis and a model for future magnet schools. In 1975, a federal judge ruled that St. Louis schools were indeed segregated and directed school officials to end racial imbalance by creating magnet schools at the elementary, middle, and high school levels. Magnet schools were intended to create high-caliber public schools that would stem white flight from the city as well as a growing black middle class exodus.

In 1981, the court case entered a new phase when a federal judge mandated the creation of a city-to-suburb busing program. The court order created the Voluntary Transfer Program, a bold departure from court decisions in other cities. Whereas other court-ordered busing programs involved only the central city, this program included as key participants suburban school districts and state government. According to the courts, both parties shared liability for the current situation: suburban school districts because they bused their black students to the city's black schools, and the state of Missouri because it sanctioned de jure segregation in all of its school systems.

Under this busing program seventeen school districts in St. Louis County agreed to accept up to 15,000 voluntary transfer students from the city. These students could be from any grade level. The suburban districts ranged from the most affluent—Clayton and Ladue—to others with working-class populations. In fact, several of the latter districts gained in black population in the years after 1981. For that reason, the Ferguson-Florissant district was dropped from the court order, and when the student bodies in the Hazelwood and Ritenour districts became 25 percent black, they no longer accepted new transfer students. The Voluntary Transfer Program also permitted white children in participating county districts to ride buses to city magnet schools. To fund the program, the federal district court required the state of Missouri to cover most costs. The Voluntary Transfer Program, its magnitude and particularly its suburbs-to-city component, made St. Louis's desegregation order unique.[6]

As in Boston, federal district court judges came to possess substantial powers over the local school district. Judges held the power to open and close individual schools, supervised physical renovations on existing structures, and decided the locations of any new facilities. The judges participated actively in all forms of educational decision making previously within the sole purview of school district administrators. Prominent citizens worked very hard to prevent any disturbances when the buses rolled out in earnest. They wanted to protect the city's image by avoiding the violence that had marred desegregation efforts in Pontiac and Boston several years before. On this level, they were successful. As we shall see, however, resistance did develop in parts of St. Louis and became most evident in school board elections.

The Failure of Institutions

The intervention of the federal courts to address the city's segregated school system points to the failure of other institutions to resolve this situation. Institutional failure was evident at a number of levels, including the state, city government, and the school department itself.

State of Missouri. Missouri has a low-tax, low-service approach to governance, which is particularly evident in the limited support it provides for local schools as well as the overall tax burden in the state. In 1959, Missouri ranked eighteenth in per capita income but only thirty-eighth in per capita expenditures for schools. If public school revenue was depicted as a percentage of per capita income, Missouri ranked a dismal forty-ninth when compared with other states.[7] By 1992, the pattern had not changed. Missouri slipped to twenty-third in per capita income, while it continued to rank thirty-eighth in per capita expenditures for schools. In 1997, it again ranked forty-ninth on the measure of school revenue per capita.

This low ranking in support for public education came despite the funds required by the federal courts to support desegregation programs in St. Louis and Kansas City. As a more general indicator of state support for public services, by 1992 Missouri ranked last among all fifty states in its overall tax burden, a ranking it continues to hold.

Missouri's parsimonious nature certainly limited the amount of state funding made available to the St. Louis public schools. The situation has not been improved by the traditional out-state antipathy toward the big city. As local revenue sources declined, the Missouri legislature was not one to take up the slack. Many St. Louis schools had been built close to the turn of the century, and their physical condition deteriorated because of inadequate funding. Even in this area of capital construction, state officials historically provided only limited assistance.

City government. St. Louis city government also has provided only limited support for innovation and reform in the city's school system. Since the latter years of the nineteenth century, St. Louis has been a machine-politics city with a system of personal rewards counting more than policy outcomes. However, it never had a hierarchical machine dominating its political activity. Rather, the politics has been factional, and the form of government has worked to maintain its decentralized nature. The city's unreformed character is evident in its partisan elections, its use of districts or wards to elect council members, and the large number of wards (twenty-eight) from which to elect aldermen. The wards elect party committeemen and committeewomen as well as aldermen. St. Louis's mayor has limited statutory powers and shares budgetary and contractual responsibility with the comptroller and president of the board of aldermen on a Board of Estimate and Apportionment. The comptroller and board president also are elected citywide.

This pattern of fragmentation began early in the city's history. In 1876, St. Louis chose to separate itself from the county of which it was a part. In so doing, it became the nation's first home rule city. It also permanently sealed its borders, preventing further annexation and hastening the growth of suburban municipalities in the area. When the state allowed the city to separate from St. Louis County, it mandated that residents elect a number of "county" officials on an at-large basis to administer so-called county affairs. These officials, such as the sheriff, recorder of deeds, and license collector, administer offices staffed by patronage workers who are referred by the ward committeemen and committeewomen. Many of these offices are no longer elective in other Missouri counties (or no longer exist) but remain in St. Louis by state statute. Ward disposition of patronage and the election of so many county officials, who are often committee people as well, contribute significantly to St. Louis's decentralized politics.

Many American cities resembled the St. Louis model at the beginning of the twentieth century. However, most changed all or part of their structure as a reaction to the Progressive reform movement that tried to eliminate incompetence, inefficiency, and venality at all governmental levels. Especially at the local level,

Progressives tried to curb the influence of the political party, their particular bête noire. They also favored a strong mayor–council system originally and then became advocates of the depoliticized city manager form of government. Progressives, however, enjoyed little success in St. Louis. After an experiment under the 1914 charter with at-large elections of aldermen who would represent individual wards, St. Louis in 1941 returned to a district format with only ward voters choosing their aldermen. The city also failed to adopt a civil service system until 1941. Its system of employee selection has never been free of some form of political influence, and the county offices, governed by state rather than local statutes, have continued to be bastions of patronage.[8] The machine nature of city government, then, fostered more concern with the provision of favors, particularly in jobs and contracting, than in responding to such policy problems as school achievement.

St. Louis Public Schools. The school department and the school board also have provided little institutional support for proactive educational initiatives. Despite elements of reform in its board structure and support for reform from some board members, the system as a whole has been unable to institute change and educational innovations. To a significant degree, the school system has reflected the machine-politics nature of city government.

Turn-of-the-century reformers successfully separated the school district from municipal government and set up a system governed by a board of twelve members elected at-large on a nonpartisan ballot. Interestingly though, selection of board members for staggered six-year terms has occurred on the same date as municipal general elections, in April of odd-numbered years. Despite this reform structure, state law governing the St. Louis Public Schools provided for a Division of Building and Maintenance with its own director, separate from the instructional component of the system. This division hired employees for its principally blue-collar positions based on the recommendation of ward committeemen, who often were state legislators or heads of the county offices. The committeemen in turn took a keen interest in elections to the school board. Most school board members were considered part of an old guard, part and parcel of the patronage system.

Beginning in 1953, voters started to elect members of a "blue-ribbon" faction to the board. Led by businessman Daniel Schlafly, the blue-ribbon faction sought to expose corruption endemic in the school district. By 1961, they commanded a majority and were able to see that the Division of Building and Maintenance lost its independent status. A variant of civil service became the rule for the hiring of noninstructional personnel. The exposure of a number of scandals, such as district maintenance workers performing tasks at board members' and administrators' homes, aided the work of the blue-ribbon group.

These changes to district operations were made possible in part because many city politicians decided that patronage and other benefits available to them from the public schools were no longer worth a continual fight with the board's new majority, the newspapers, and other good government types.[9] Elected officials' concerns had never been pedagogical. Ending the direct link between committee-men and the school system increasingly meant little overt involvement of any kind with the public schools by the majority of elected officials. As the school population and the teaching staff became increasingly black, black officeholders began to look to them as a base of support and influence. In keeping with the city's machine tradition, black politicians, no less than whites, looked at favors as the chief business of politics, school or otherwise.

The school department was generally incapable of responding to new educational demands. The school bureaucracy could best be described as calcified, inbred, and resistant to change. St. Louis's system is far from alone in this respect. In many cities, local elites and educational professionals separated public schools from local governance and turned over the decision making to experts.[10] Public school systems often became autonomous bureaus or, in Theodore Lowi's terminology, "islands of functional power."[11] Similar to experts in other professions, educators used their particular knowledge to protect their prerogatives. According to Philip Meranto, "Educators have been notably successful in developing and selling others a set of ideological doctrines which have given them considerable autonomy of operation and insulation from public inspection."[12] The end result has been that change occurs slowly, and autonomy is carefully guarded.[13]

In St. Louis, a top-heavy administration and inbred personnel system have strengthened this reluctance to change. Daniel Monti found that "a high percentage of candidates for teaching positions in the district had been reared in the city and had attended the local teachers' college. Many had eventually become part of the director's administrative staff."[14] In fact, in 1976, 156 of 160 principals had graduated from Harris-Stowe, the local teachers' college made up of the formerly all-white Harris and its black counterpart, Stowe. Monti also discovered that "spouses, cousins, and friends were all securely nestled" in the city's public schools.[15] More than one observer has commented on the inbred nature of the institution and on the influence of Harris-Stowe's sororities and fraternities in the administration of the public schools.

For many African-Americans, employment in the school system historically has represented one of the few professional opportunities open to them. Even after other possibilities emerged following the passage of civil rights legislation in the 1960s, education has remained a frequent career choice. As a bastion of the city's black middle class, the school system enjoyed ties with black elected officials. Some close to the system felt that the city's leading African-American politician, Congressman William L. Clay Sr., had a special influence at school district headquarters. White politicians, on the other hand, have not exercised much clout for some time. Most white elected officials were Catholic and the product of archdiocese schools. Many of their constituents had historically used the parochial system as well. Separate budgets, separate revenues, and especially decreasing patronage opportunities allowed the public schools their autonomy but also left them relatively isolated. This isolation as well as the district's desire for autonomy combined to create a rigid bureaucracy with a cadre of administrators sensitive to any boundary violations.

In general, St. Louis was ill prepared to respond to the demands for desegregation and educational equality. State government officials were reluctant to provide financial support to the city's school system, and both the city government and school system were dominated by a patronage system that focused more on jobs than educational policy. Furthermore, general public support also declined. In the 1970s, as the St. Louis Public Schools began to experience severe fiscal problems, public support for school bond issues waned. According to Missouri law, bond issues require a two-thirds majority vote. None were passed by the voters for two decades. By 1981, increases to the property tax rate, which required only a simple majority, began to go down to defeat as well. Lack of electoral support was most evident in white south St. Louis. There, an increasingly elderly population in a heavily Catholic area failed to provide electoral support for a school system that they or their children had not utilized. At that time, St. Louis's population was over 40 percent Catholic.[16] State funding continued to be anemic, and local sources no longer were able to fill the breach.

Opposition to desegregation and busing also entered the electoral arena. In south St. Louis, a white citizens' council formed in opposition to the busing program. Beginning with the 1985 school board elections, the group supported candidates for seats on the school board. They met with some initial success and added to their numbers on the board in the 1987 and 1989 elections. Their presence at school board meetings immediately became divisive. Shouting matches were not infrequent occurrences, and often little board business could be accomplished. The presence of this white antibusing group helped to continue the community's focus on the yellow buses that took children away from their neighborhoods every weekday. The academic strengths or weaknesses of the public schools were rarely the subject of attention, although they were generally assessed poorly. A former municipal elected official commented that St. Louis's leadership focused on keeping this supremacist group from taking over the schools, thereby missing an opportunity to address academic concerns.

DESEGREGATION, INSTITUTIONAL INERTIA, AND WEAK LEADERSHIP, 1985–1998

For over a decade, the desegregation court order has dominated the agenda for the St. Louis schools. Academic achievement has taken a back seat to debates over busing as community leaders focused on the costs and inconvenience of one of the largest busing programs in the country. The Voluntary Transfer Program has overshadowed and stymied other reform efforts in the city. At the same time, the St. Louis Public Schools demonstrated an organizational rigidity and lack of leadership that also handicapped the school system. The school bureaucracy often has been reluctant to change and adapt to new circumstances and demands.

From the Perspective of Civic Progress

Amidst this environment of desegregation battles and institutional rigidities, Civic Progress and business leaders have focused their concerns on discrete events and projects on the educational landscape. The systemic perspective on educational reform that evolved in Boston and Pittsburgh has been absent in St. Louis. Rather, the business community has focused on narrowly defined activities that are more manageable and doable, a pattern repeated in the development arena.

Financial counseling, partnerships, and school board elections are three examples of this targeted involvement. In the mid-1980s, for example, the financial affairs of the school district were in disarray. In response, Civic Progress executives assigned their own financial specialists for a brief period to help redesign the school district's accounting and record-keeping systems. Individual partnerships, through the school district's Partnerships Program offer another means of business involvement. Compared with other cities, however, businesses have not adopted St. Louis schools in the same number and to the same degree of involvement. School administrators seemingly value maintenancing their control over the running of schools and do not encourage adoption. After all, their authority had already been diminished by the federal district court.

School board elections represent a third avenue for business participation. Involvement in this arena, however, has been driven more by a concern over the image of the city than an overall interest in the quality of public education. In 1991, for example, the white citizens' group that had been building support on the school board was poised to win a majority of the seats. Realizing the negative publicity such an outcome would engender, Civic Progress members joined Mayor Vincent C. Schoemehl Jr. and other community leaders in fashioning a slate of four candidates, who became known as "4 Candidates 4 Kids," to oppose the expected antibusing candidates. The slate was race- and gender-balanced and included a former principal and a former community school coordinator (someone who handled after-hours school programs).

Acting as individuals, members of Civic Progress helped to bankroll the slate, making possible extensive advertising, including substantial bulk mailings to potential supporters. The "4 Candidates 4 Kids" crisscrossed the city and attended endless meetings and coffees in search of support. A public relations firm saturated the black areas of the city with mailings, including a piece headlined "The Klan Is Coming" that was designed to increase turnout. The money and effort paid off. The slate was successful, and the electorate also passed a bond issue for the schools—the first in twenty years—on the same day. The tenor of school board meetings began to take a more positive turn, and the quality of education and the future of the schools after desegregation became part of the agenda for the first time.

Corporate leaders appeared comfortable with their involvement in this campaign. A finite effort, it was certainly in keeping with their pursuit of discrete projects in the civic arena. One businessman remarked that "an election campaign was easy, easier than dealing with their (the school system's) bureaucracy." Civic interest in this election was clear-cut. Key also to understanding corporate involvement was the limited commitment required. A community volunteer noted that "businesses would like the schools to be excellent but are not willing to invest much of themselves in efforts to reform." A chief executive officer acknowledged that corporate leaders did not want to play a continuing role in education even though they were aware of the schools' shortcomings. "We're too busy running our own companies," he remarked. "We don't have time."

The Impact of Desegregation

Court-ordered desegregation has had a fundamental effect on the operations of the St. Louis Public Schools. Within the city, desegregation practices have resulted in three types of schools: magnet, "segregated," and "naturally integrated." Magnet schools highlight a particular theme or course of study, while segregated and naturally integrated schools offer more traditional curriculum and, as their informal titles indicate, are either predominantly black or integrated depending upon local residential patterns and student choices of schools.

Magnet schools often are cited as a positive outcome of court-ordered desegregation. Many of these schools have been rated highly, and some have received state and federal awards. The new prekindergarten programs especially have received favorable attention. About 1,200 white children continue to travel from St. Louis County into the city each school day to attend a magnet school. Each school has a special focus, such as international studies or health. Highly touted are new science elementary and middle schools that maintain strong ties to the St. Louis Science Center and the Missouri Botanical Gardens.

There are, however, downsides to the magnet program. White parents in the suburbs are able to place their children in the city's magnet schools with more facility than white parents in the city because they are given priority. Competition for placement at magnet schools, which is done by lottery, is very keen among all city youth. By court design, whites are to constitute a minimum of 45 percent of the student body at each magnet school, yet the city school system is only 22 percent white.

Academic ability is a selection criterion at prestigious Metro High School; teacher recommendations, high grades, and good deportment traditionally have been among admissions requirements. A special lottery is held using the names of those who meet the qualifications. There also is a gifted program at McKinley Classical Academy, a junior high, in which ability is an entrance criterion. Students from McKinley often continue at Metro High. At other magnet schools, including those for the performing arts, there are no special entrance requirements. In general, many city parents have decried the fact that the magnet schools have so many advantages—greater resources, smaller classes, principals able to select the teachers—over other schools in the district.

The reputation of the other two categories of schools—naturally integrated and segregated—is not nearly as laudatory. Many of these schools have operated in dilapidated buildings; they did not experience any rehabilitation until after passage of the 1991 bond issue. Their classrooms have more students than in the magnet schools, and they often lack adequate resources. Books frequently arrive late, and paper and pencils are always in short supply. Some schools, such as the Laclede and the Clay Elementary Schools, exhibit very high performance, but many have a much poorer record. For many years, the physical deterioration at some schools was emblematic of their operation. At Beaumont High School, for example, students in classes on the third floor emerged each day covered with white dust. The ceilings crumbled on top of them as they tried to learn. At Vashon High School, lockers were painted a bright chartreuse—the only paint color available to the school at the time.

A significant goal of the desegregation program is to improve academic performance at the segregated schools. The *St. Louis Post-Dispatch* reports that "between $100 and $200 million of the $1.3 billion in desegregation money has gone toward that goal."[17] Despite such expenditures and cuts in class size, these city schools are not the equals of their suburban counterparts. Drop-out rates are highest at these schools, and academic performance, measured by standardized tests, is lowest. Opponents to ending the desegregation program cite such failings as evidence that the state and city have not effectively implemented the desegregation order.[18]

Without doubt, many parents lack confidence in the city's non–magnet schools; the thirteen thousand children riding buses to suburban school districts are the proof. Some children leave their homes before daylight and do not return until after nightfall. Parents keep selecting this alternative, even though suburban districts themselves vary considerably in quality. As evident in table 6-1, in a number of suburban districts the percentage of city students who graduate is quite low. In addition, the limited presence of black teachers in many suburban districts reduces the availability of role models for city students. In Kirkwood, for example, only 11 percent of teachers are of color, in Mehlville the comparable measure is 1 percent, and there are no teachers of color in Valley Park.[19] Some suburban districts are more amenable to their city charges than others.

Magnet schools and busing open opportunities for African-American students, but many remain in city schools that often fail to provide a satisfactory learning environment. Of the 44,160 African-American schoolchildren in St. Louis public schools in 1996, 41 percent attended segregated, schools and 16 percent were in naturally integrated schools, while only 15 percent attended magnet schools. The remaining 28 percent of African-American schoolchildren attended suburban schools.[20] For those students attending segregated and naturally integrated schools, academic achievement is typically well below their classmates with greater

Table 6-1. Graduation Rates for City Students in Suburban School Districts*

District	Graduation Rate	District	Graduation Rate
Affton	33%	Mehlville	50%
Bayless	46%	Parkway	48%
Brentwood	50%	Pattonville	60%
Clayton	65%	Ritenour	46%
Hancock Place	27%	Rockwood	54%
Kirkwood	53%	Valley Park	23%
Ladue	50%	Webster Groves	57%
Lindbergh	41%		

*For students entering high school in 1992.
Source: *St. Louis Post-Dispatch,* March 3, 1996, 4B.

educational opportunities. Based on national standardized test scores, magnet school students score the highest, followed by Voluntary Transfer Students, and then students at the other city schools.

In general, the impact of desegregation is far from positive for most students. As noted in Chapter 3, educational achievement in St. Louis lags behind Boston and Pittsburgh as well as national norms. In 1994, after a decade of desegregation, 43 percent of St. Louis city students scored in the bottom quartile in reading, and 36 percent scored in the bottom quartile in math. In addition, only about 15 percent of the district's fifth grade students scored a four or better on a district-administered writing test; nearly half scored a one or two, which officials said was "substandard."[21] Attrition from formal education tells a similar story. Using data from the St. Louis Public Schools and the Missouri Coordinating Board of Higher Education, the *Post- Dispatch* reports that for every one hundred students who enter ninth grade in city high schools, only thirty graduate. Of those thirty, thirteen enter college and seven eventually obtain four-year degrees.[22] Gary Orfield and his colleagues attribute part of the poor performance of children in city schools to the fact that higher achieving black students transfer to suburban locations.[23]

Needless to say, the St. Louis school system faces a very difficult mission. Many of its students are from poverty backgrounds, and some are exposed to random violence on a daily basis. The percentage of students qualifying for the free lunch program is higher than in Boston or Pittsburgh. Yet, the question of structuring education to address the special needs of these children is rarely mentioned by district officials or community or corporate leaders. Since Minnie Liddell filed her suit, the issue of desegregation has dominated the agenda.

Institutional Inertia in the School Department

Court battles over desegregation have contributed to the development of a school bureaucracy often characterized as rigid and inflexible. To protect its territorial imperative, the school department is reluctant to change and adapt, preferring existing operating rules rather than venturing into the unknown. A few examples will demonstrate this lack of adaptation.

The failure to accommodate student transfers is one example of bureaucratic rigidity. Like many central city school systems, student mobility is very high in St. Louis. Administrators and teachers estimate that in any given school year about half of all students move to a different residence. Until the fall of 1995, the school district required any student whose family had moved to immediately begin attending (in the middle of a term) a new school based on the new home location. This rule resulted in considerable confusion and disruption of the educational process for students as well as teachers. Yet, a viable option existed: buses transporting children for the purposes of desegregation could also transport students seeking to finish courses at the school where they had begun the semester. Not until 1995 did school administrators implement such a policy. Ironically, this rule change took place in tandem with the first moves to end the desegregation program.

A second example concerns supplies and textbooks, items clearly necessary to the learning process. For many years, a number of schools experienced repeated difficulty in obtaining books and other supplies. Sometimes, texts would not arrive until October or even later in the school year. Finally, in the summer of 1994, district officials created a special task force to monitor vendors and schools' requests for books.[24] Obtaining adequate supplies also is a recurring problem. Teachers continue to reach into their own pockets on a frequent basis to pay for paper and pencils. As with student transfers, problems often have existed for years before ameliorative action is taken.

A third example of organizational rigidity continues today. In its personnel policies, the school system allows teachers who retire in the early weeks of the fall semester to calculate retirement pay at a higher rate than if they had retired at the end of the previous school year. Not surprisingly, teachers often remain on the payroll until they are eligible for the higher rate. The result each fall is that a significant number of classes lose their teachers just as the new year starts. Either substitutes are assigned or classes are combined, in each case producing an environment less amenable to student learning.

Another example that significantly impacts the operations of the school system is actually rooted in state law, which provides that teachers in all school districts receive tenure after three years on the job. For St. Louis only, however, the law also has mandated that principals receive tenure after three years in their position. As a result, the St. Louis school system has had to retain a number of school administrators who fail to perform well. Principals could not be removed; they could only be shuffled from school to school if they failed to adequately perform their responsibilities. In 1995, the St. Louis School Board proposed eliminating this part of the law. Approximately forty principals came to a school board meeting to protest this action, buoyed by an attorney for their union.[25] The school board's proposal was presented as a bill on the state legislature's calendar, but no action was taken then.

Boundary disputes with city government also can derail reform efforts. "Let us run our district" is a frequent comment of school board members and administrators. Exemplifying this bureaucratic sensitivity to outside intervention is the recent failure to coordinate a grant proposal to the National Science Foundation. School officials were asked to apply for a $15 million grant under the foundation's Urban Systemic Initiative to improve science and math classes in central city schools.[26] The National Science Foundation suggested that the city of St. Louis be responsible for disbursing funds if the grant was awarded. School administrators were not in favor of such an arrangement, and the school board voted unanimously not to apply for the grant. Whether this was an attempted power grab on the part of then mayor Freeman Bosley Jr., as some in the school system believed, or whether this suggestion reflected concerns about school district capability, is not clear. Regardless of motivations, the school board and administrators chose not to participate, forgoing a possible opportunity for outside financial support.

Organizational boundary issues also are evident in a recent dispute over establishment of site-based management at St. Louis's fifteen community schools. Community school programs are funded by federal money passed through the city, and they take place in St. Louis Public School buildings. They provide adult classes, recreation, and other activities during after-school hours. In 1992–1993, a task force consisting of aldermen, school board members, and community representatives met and developed a plan to enhance the community schools by integrating their daytime and evening components and increasing neighbor and parental involvement in the schools. The original draft of the task force plan called for extensive site-based management. School administrators, however, interpreted this approach as an infringement upon the district's prerogatives and diluted the site-based management component. A participant supportive of site-based management remarked, "The [school] system took out the way the community would be empowered regarding hiring and staff evaluations. Now it looks like everything else." After protest from task force members, a compromise was reached, but the school district's central office maintained its control over curricular and programming decisions in the regular school component. In the end, community councils at the schools could determine after-school programming but would provide only input on daytime education.

Forming the site-based councils at these community education centers became problematic at times. Central office staff prescribed the composition of the councils—parents, community members, and business people—and drafted model bylaws. Parents were to be a majority on the council, not always an easy feat because of the extensive busing under way in many parts of the city. Frequently, a majority of the daytime student body did not live anywhere near the school. This restriction made parental participation more difficult, particularly participation involving after-school functions. At one new community education center, parental participation became even more difficult after the central office named the school an

English-as-a-second-language facility. Students at this school came from all parts of St. Louis, with only about 20 percent of them living in the neighborhood.

School administrators, by and large, have not wished to dispense with their authority over the community education centers. The McKenzie Group, a national consulting organization, studied the St. Louis school district's efforts at site-based management. Their report noted that principals at community education centers did not become more empowered in staffing or other areas of operation. "Decision-making in the system remains hierarchical and top-down. . . . Principals also indicated that they believe their efforts frequently are undermined by central administrators who reverse decisions made at the local level."[27]

The McKenzie Group also examined another attempt at site-based management in six city schools that are not part of the community centers network. They found this pilot project to be wanting as well. In general, they noted that the St. Louis school system is "a highly centralized and controlled organization" whose administrators "appear to be oriented to regulating and monitoring, rather than providing service."[28] Perhaps fearing a loss of positions in the central office, administrators exhibited reluctance to transfer decision making to the field. Here, as elsewhere, change has not been embraced.

The school department's resistance to change receives little challenge from the local teachers' union. In some school districts, including Pittsburgh and Boston, the teachers' union is an important player in school reform. In St. Louis, however, the union has been neither party to reform nor obstructionist. Rather, it has been a weak player, fraught at times with internal conflict and drawing very little interest from most teachers. The union is an affiliate of the American Federation of Teachers, but Missouri law prohibits collective bargaining by public employees. Employer and union may meet and confer, but they cannot negotiate a contract. The teachers' union often has been divided by internal disputes, including a recent situation in which two members simultaneously claimed to be president. The national office of the American Federation of Teachers sent a person to adjudicate the dispute and act in lieu of an elected president for several months.

The dominant ethos in the St. Louis school department is one of resistance to change, but examples of flexibility do exist. One reform initiative involving the provision of student social services is judged more favorably. Significantly, this program was created and funded by the Missouri Department of Social Services. With a $500,000 annual budget, the Department of Social Services created the Walbridge Caring Community at Walbridge Elementary School in a crime-ridden section of the city known as Walnut Park. The program was soon expanded to include five additional schools in the area.

The purpose of the Walbridge Caring Community is to increase the service network for children and their families and to stabilize the neighborhood. State agency staff are on-site five days a week to handle matters concerning welfare benefits, food stamps, and other social service programs. Staff also provide referrals to health providers. The schools open early and close late in the evening, providing city youth a safe place to relax, engage in recreation, and complete homework. Staff are present to provide help with academics and to monitor recreational activities. Walbridge Caring Community also supports anticrime and antidrug efforts in the community. Monthly marches against drugs crisscross the area, and staff work with police and other public officials to rid the area of drug houses. This program is controlled jointly by the Department of Social Services and the school system, and it focuses on activities not part of regular classroom instruction.

Weaknesses in School Leadership

A lack of leadership within the St. Louis schools has contributed to the system's reluctance to change its established patterns. Weak leadership has been due, in part, to the system's practice of promoting from within the ranks. Although a constructive policy in some school districts, in St. Louis promotion from within has had the effect of fostering both little tolerance for outside initiatives and a narrow vision of school reform. As table 6-2 shows, in 1995 three of the ten highest-ranking officials had been with the St. Louis Public Schools for forty years or more; three others had worked in the system for over thirty years. Seven of the top officials had not held an educational job anywhere else, including David Mahan, superintendent at the time. Furthermore, six administrators completed their graduate study at local institutions. Among the ten top administrators, the average tenure within the system was thirty years. The comparable measure in Pittsburgh was nineteen years, and in Boston it was fifteen years. This entrenched administration has been reluctant to entertain reform initiatives from outside the system and has provided little ground for dynamic leadership.

Weak leadership in the St. Louis Schools has been particularly evident at the top of the system. In 1990, David Mahan was hired as superintendent in large part because he was viewed as "safe."[29] A quiet, mild-mannered product of the system, he served as a healing agent and a distinct contrast to a very vibrant predecessor who received unfavorable coverage in the press. Mahan, however, was not viewed as an innovative leader. According to the *St. Louis Post-Dispatch,* Mahan's critics thought he lacked "the creativity and energy to make the changes needed by a large urban school district that has all the problems of today's big city schools: test scores well below the national average, high drop-out rates and neighborhood violence that too often finds its way into the schools."[30] As only one of two whites in top administrative positions, Mahan was able to interact well in a majority black system. He also was well received by some prominent business and community leaders. However, his mild-mannered, conciliatory style failed to win a desired three-year contract extension, prompting his departure in 1996.

The search for Mahan's successor was not without its own pitfalls. The school board wished to hire someone with experience in an urban district, and the unspoken criterion for many members was to hire someone black. A consulting firm handled the nationwide search and drew forty-six applicants. The board selected

Table 6-2. Profile of Top Ten St. Louis Public Schools Administrators in 1995

Position	Race/Sex	Years in Education	Years in Current System	Highest Degree Earned	Institution Attended
Superintendent	White male	36	36	Ed.D.	Washington U.
Chief of Staff	Black male	34	33	M.A.	Lincoln U.
Associate Superintendent	Black male	33	33	Ph.D .	U. of Wisconsin
Associate Superintendent, Curriculum	Black male	42	42	M.A.	St. Louis U.
Associate Superintendent, Personnel	Black female	24	11	Ph.D.	St. Louis U.
Executive Assistant	Black male	42	42	M.A.	St. Louis U.
Executive Director, Curriculum Services	Black male	40	40	M.A.	St. Louis U.
Executive Director, State/Federal Programs	Black male	25	25	Ph.D.	Iowa State U.
Executive Director, Community Relations	Black male	29	29	M.A.	U. of Missouri– St. Louis
Treasurer	White male	24	11	M.B.A.	Iona College

three finalists, all black males. Each, however, had left a prior position unwillingly. Public criticism of the process mounted. Alderman Phyllis Young, representing a diverse ward near downtown St. Louis, requested that the school board reexamine other applicants or reopen the search. Commenting on her stance, the *St. Louis Post-Dispatch* editorialized: "If the current finalists included a prospective superintendent who clearly could lead the St. Louis schools through what promises to be turbulent times, her request would make no sense. As things stand, board members would be wise to pay attention."[31]

The school board proceeded, nonetheless, and hired Cleveland Hammonds Jr. from among the three finalists. Hammonds is an African-American originally from nearby Alton, Illinois, who more recently served as superintendent of the Birmingham, Alabama, schools. He was denied a contract renewal in Birmingham, but many board members attributed this fact to circumstances beyond his control. The new superintendent had a strong background in community education, an important concern of many school board members.

Hammonds arrived at his new job in the fall of 1996, a time of preoccupation with the possible end to desegregation. In the spring of 1997 he announced an administrative reorganization in which all top administrators would compete for newly defined positions. The results were announced to school personnel on June 5, 1997. Hammonds changed a number of top personnel, including several administrators with strong political connections. Many observers believed that such action would have been impossible only a couple of years before. Hammonds is thought to be focused on reform, but he moves slowly.

Despite these recent changes, the St. Louis school district is still described negatively by the press, most residents, elected officials, and many others. Although the district receives positive publicity for such programs as the Walbridge Caring Community and certain prizewinning schools, many parents still leave the city when children reach school age, or they try to utilize alternatives to the city's public schools. As the St. Louis system nears a likely end to its desegregation program, many in the community, including business leaders, do not expend a great deal of effort on public education and its shortcomings.

BUILDING A NETWORK FOR EDUCATIONAL REFORM

An institutional network designed to foster innovation in public education requires commitment from a number of sectors, both inside and outside the school system. Certainly, if a school system is a willing player, the task is easier. If the past is a guide, however, the St. Louis Public Schools are reluctant participants. The school department lacks flexibility and is most desirous of maintaining its autonomy. It is very difficult for an entrenched bureaucracy to change its ways quickly, if at all. Leadership within the school system also has met with limited success in network building. The school board, the superintendent, and the teachers' union have lacked a vision and will to engage the community in extensive reform.

Limitations within the school system, however, can be overcome by aggressive action from outside agents. The turn to mayoral control of school systems in Boston, Chicago, and other cities as well as state takeovers of school districts in New Jersey and other states point to such possibilities. In St. Louis there are a number of actors—the mayor, city council, business community, and others—who might assume a proactive reform role. A brief look at each, however, shows that St. Louis faces considerable obstacles in this area as well.

City Government

A city's mayor can play a key role in creating a cross-sector network. As the chief elected official of the city, the mayor occupies a pivotal position to focus community attention on municipal problems. Two ingredients, however, are particularly critical to the exercise of mayoral influence: institutional authority and personal interest. In the case of St. Louis, these ingredients have not combined in support of strong mayoral leadership for public education.

Institutionally, the St. Louis charter gives the mayor weak formal powers. The mayor shares budgetary and contractual authority with the comptroller and the president of the board of aldermen, and must work with twenty-eight city legislators and the various county officeholders. In addition, the mayor often turns to state and federal officials, who make important funding and organizational decisions that affect the city. In general, the mayor relies extensively upon informal powers, such as persuasion and coalition building, to achieve success. Furthermore, the mayor's formal power with regard to the school system is limited to two areas: selection each year of an auditor for the system, and appointment of individuals to fill a vacancy on the school board if an incumbent leaves office before his or her term expires. These powers are contained in state statute. Otherwise, the public schools and city government are legally and fiscally separate.

The second key ingredient—personal interest—refers to the level of interest and involvement sought by an individual mayor. Mayoral interest in public education has varied among recent mayors. In general, however, it has been limited and episodic. Mayor Vincent C. Schoemehl Jr. (1981–1993), for example, expressed concern for the school system, but his involvement was primarily reactive through such actions as interim appointments to the school board and support for the "4 Candidates 4 Kids" slate in 1991. Although a dynamic mayor in a number of areas, Schoemehl made no real impression on the school system. Like many in public office, he had attended parochial schools as had his children.

Freeman Bosley Jr., clerk of the Circuit Court, was elected to succeed Schoemehl and became the city's first black mayor (1993–1997). Education was a pivotal part of his campaign platform. At campaign stops he stressed the relationship of education to other key issues, such as jobs and crime. He also was the first graduate of the St. Louis Public Schools to hold the city's highest office in many years. His wife and mother both are teachers in the school district. In his four years in office, Bosley visited many of the city's schools. He spoke of them as neighborhood anchors that could serve the general community as well as their students; he was a strong supporter of the community education centers mentioned earlier.

Bosley, however, was a critic of busing. He linked extensive busing under desegregation to increased neighborhood instability. In his reelection campaign, he ran a commercial in which he decried lengthy bus trips for city children, asserting that money for busing would be better spent in the classroom. His desire to end busing helped shape community debate on this critical issue as well as the general future of the schools after the court is no longer steward. He certainly tempered divisions over desegregation that had followed along racial lines.

Bosley's relationship with the school board varied according to the issues involved. He took a keen interest in the 1996 search for a new superintendent, meeting with each of the three finalists. Some board members, however, worried about his intentions. People close to the school district noted that his office often expressed the desire to learn of possible photo opportunities at the schools. Exchanges between the mayor and school board were often curt, if not divisive. In March 1996, for example, the school board passed a resolution asking the mayor to consider the impact of tax abatements on education and "to establish a task force of business, civic and education leaders to study education and economic development."[32] The mayor responded in a sharply worded letter critical of the school system: "The problems that the schools face don't necessarily require more money—they require better management."[33]

Bosley's 1997 reelection campaign faltered in the Democratic primary. His opponent was Clarence Harmon, the city's first African-American police chief. Both candidates touted educational reform as critical to the future of the city. Bosley, however, was hurt by several scandals and charges of cronyism. As a result, Harmon defeated Bosley handily in the Democratic primary, winning 96 percent of the white vote and 17 percent of the black vote. Harmon went on to win the general election in April. Mayor Harmon pledged closer coordination with the school system, including creation of an education liaison position with cabinet-level status. Yet, the 1997–1998 school year opened with no one appointed to that position. Harmon finally selected a former school board member, a white woman, for the post; she would serve as a volunteer.

On the legislative side, St. Louis's twenty-eight aldermen have occasional involvement with the school district, but as with the mayor, their involvement is typically limited to narrowly defined issues or single events that emerge on the agenda. Two aldermen, for example, served on the community schools task force, and the city council appropriates about $800,000 per year from federal community development block grant funds to support after-school programs at the community education centers. That appropriation is generally routine, though occasionally its continuation has been questioned by several aldermen. Also, aldermen frequently are criticized by school board members and administrators for granting tax abatements for commercial or residential development. School board members perceive this practice as money lost to the school system, while city officials see abatements as important development tools.

Although sometimes critical of the system, African-American aldermen generally take a greater interest in the public schools than their white counterparts. Their constituents' children are more likely to attend public schools. In general, however, the public schools have not absorbed a great deal of aldermanic energy in the past few years. Although there are exceptions, white aldermen and some of their black counterparts generally avoid an area in which they have little control and receive few tangible benefits.

State Government

State officials play an important role in city education, covering such key issues as financial support and academic requirements. The St. Louis delegation to the Missouri Legislature currently numbers sixteen, three state senators and thirteen state representatives. In recent years, only one state senator from St. Louis, William L. Clay Jr., has served consistently on the education committee. Clay has shepherded bills to improve pensions for city teachers, and he has unsuccessfully filed suit in federal court to challenge at-large elections to the school board.

Otherwise, many in the state legislative delegation have eschewed dealings with the school system, largely because of the lack of support from the system's administration. The relative lack of representation on key legislative committees gives

St. Louis little voice on questions of state aid and mandated requirements. There also is no urban caucus through which legislators from Kansas City and St. Louis could work together on school issues and other matters of common concern.

As the future of desegregation began to be debated, the governor's office became more critical to the future of St. Louis's schools. Elected in 1992, Mel Carnahan was the first Democratic governor in many years. His Republican predecessors ably represented the low-tax, low-spending style of Missouri politics. Soon after taking office, Carnahan faced a judicial request to enhance and equalize state funding for local school districts. Rather than have a judge determine the formula, he pushed a plan through the legislature that included tax increases. The additional funding did not accrue to St. Louis, however, because of its receipt of substantial desegregation monies. Unlike a number of other recent candidates for statewide office, Carnahan did not campaign against desegregation and its costs. However, he has not been a strong leader for reform.

Missouri's attorney-general and U.S. Senate candidate in 1998, Jeremiah (Jay) Nixon, is another important state government actor. Nixon has made an end to state funding of desegregation central to his agenda. He has argued his case in court and advocated a diminished role for the state in the St. Louis schools. For example, he has not favored the redirection of most of the desegregation monies from the state (at least a third of which goes to busing) to other needs of the St. Louis system.

Business Community

The city's corporate leaders are a potentially significant source of leadership on educational issues. However, thus far, this resource is largely untapped. Civic Progress, as noted earlier, has formed a low-cohesion regime with local elected officials. It has no office or staff of its own, and its interaction with municipal government is centered around finite downtown development projects of limited duration. This type of limited business-government relationship, similar to the one in New York City, could be linked to the factional machine-style politics practiced in both cities.[34]

Members of Civic Progress are not completely aloof from educational issues. The association's education chairman has had monthly meetings with the superintendent and visits city schools regularly. Individual business-school partnerships also are quite common. One business, the Maritz Corporation, has become particularly involved with the school system. As a purveyor of organizational development training, Maritz developed a program called "Be There" to improve student attendance. "Be There" met with mixed results, having better success in the elementary grades. For the 1997–1998 school year, Maritz announced that all students attending school on the first day of the year would be included in a drawing for a large-screen television set. Despite the incentive, 25 percent of students failed to report.

The full energy of Civic Progress, however, has never been extended on be-half of public education in the city. For many businesses, the changing economy creates pressures that divert attention away from civic activities. One corporate executive notes the many strains on corporate leaders today: "It takes more time to compete now; it is a much fiercer struggle." Other executives and a longtime student of St. Louis politics echo this view. In an op-ed column in the *Post-Dispatch,* Robert Salisbury, professor emeritus of political science at Washing-ton University, remarked: "A generation ago it was useful to both their institutional interests . . . for the leaders of the major organizations to take on heavy civic re-sponsibilities. If St. Louis prospered, their enterprises would also. They depended on local customers, they hired local people and their corporate image was closely linked with the community's."[35] Today, as Salisbury and others note, the busi-ness world is much different. Top executives often do not come from St. Louis; corporate mergers and takeovers shift headquarters outside the city; markets and operations often are global in nature. The identification of corporate leaders with St. Louis civic affairs has diminished considerably.

Thus, there is no compact between corporations and the public schools as exists in Boston. Interactions between businesses and the school district are lim-ited in scope and intensity. In fact, some businesses assume a larger educational role as part of their own personnel function. One top executive commented that Southwestern Bell considers seventeen applicants for each person it hires; many applicants fail to pass basic skills tests. He added that "maybe they'll just have to train them themselves." The executive did not proffer reform of the public schools as a solution; in general, school reform does not appear to be particularly salient to corporate leaders.

Currently, many Civic Progress members are championing "2004," a celebra-tion of the centennial of St. Louis's World's Fair. Among the task forces planning this celebration is one entitled Learning, which covers education at all levels. Members of this task force include representatives from school systems in Illinois and Missouri, including St. Louis County and city schools, along with rep-resentatives from area colleges and universities. Whether they will address the problems of the central city's schools in any depth remains to be seen, although a suitable end to the desegregation program has appeared as part of the agenda of the 2004 chairman, former senator John Danforth.

Higher Education and Other Community Organizations

Several universities participate in efforts to enhance certain schools, frequently magnet schools. For example, the Wilkinson School is an award-winning magnet school with students from prekindergarten programs through second grade. Since its inception as a magnet school, Wilkinson has had a strong relationship with Maryville University. Maryville provides in-service training for the Wilkinson staff, participates in program evaluations and school staff meetings, and utilizes members of Wilkinson's staff to help train future teachers at its campus. In a similar vein, Dewey Elementary School, a magnet facility with an international studies and foreign languages theme, works closely with faculty from Washington University. Dewey also receives training on using the concept of multiple intelligences in instruction in conjunction with New City School, a progressive private K-6 facility located in the city.

Other area universities and colleges also support public school programs. St. Louis University's School of Education works with a number of schools, and the University of Missouri–St. Louis, aided by a grant from the National Science Foundation, supports improved instruction in science and math at Beaumont High School, a segregated school. A student from Beaumont won a top prize at the annual Missouri Science Fair in 1994, a first for a city student. Students from city schools also participate in summer institutes at this university.

Participation by universities and other institutions of higher education is generally within limited parameters. These outside agents do not work with systemic initiatives but with a limited number of schools and specific programs. Some of the activity is actively encouraged by the federal district court as part of its continuing oversight of the desegregation program. In general, these relationships do not affect the general curriculum, which continues to be tightly protected by district administrators.

Other community organizations also work with the school system, although again in a limited and targeted fashion. The Mathews-Dickey Club, a provider of athletics and related activities for central city children, sponsors a program for school dropouts. The archdiocese offers another example in its summer program for preteenage girls. And finally, the Conference on Education, a nonprofit organization, studied parental involvement at two city schools and issued a report critical of school system administrators in this area.

In general, establishing a supportive network for the St. Louis Public Schools is indeed difficult. The fate of CHANGE is an example. Launched in 1992, CHANGE was an informal network of individuals from different sectors focused on improving the community schools. In its early days, school board members and others concerned with the public schools attended its meetings, and it played an important role in the redesign of the community schools. By the spring of 1997, however, its early energy had dissipated; it was no longer holding regular meetings and seemed unable to move beyond its original focus on the community schools.

THE END OF DESEGREGATION AND FUTURE PROSPECTS

In 1996, efforts to end the court-ordered desegregation settlement began in earnest when Attorney General Jay Nixon filed suit in federal district court. In seeking to end the settlement, Nixon focused particularly on high state costs to support the busing of students between St. Louis and its suburbs. Some critics of Nixon's action charged that the original integration goals set down in the court order had yet to be achieved. Others noted that an end to the transfer program would shift thirteen thousand city youth back to city schools where the school district admitted there was no space for them. Furthermore, a decline in state support also would jeopardize the school district's magnet programs.

Even some suburban districts lobbied for continuation of the desegregation program. For many of these districts, desegregation funds were a significant part of their budget. The largest of the suburban districts affected, Parkway, served about thirty-three hundred city children. In 1995–1996, Parkway received $19 million in state desegregation funds.[36] In addition to the loss of funding, an end to the desegregation program would reduce racial diversity in suburban classrooms. In Parkway, just over 18 percent of students are currently African-American; before cross-district busing, that figure was 3 percent.[37]

Attorney General Nixon's action sparked a number of proposals. On one front, the federal district court appointed recently retired Washington University Chancellor William Danforth to outline a possible resolution. Danforth's proposal, however, which included alternative state funding to replace the loss of desegregation funds, failed to pass the state legislature. The legislature itself added to the debate by creating a special joint committee to examine desegregation in both St. Louis and Kansas City. In 1997, the committee proposed to replace the desegregation program with several key financial and governance changes. Chief among these changes was an additional appropriation of $1,000 per student to each city for educating at-risk children. In addition, the committee proposed that the mayor of St. Louis appoint a chief executive officer for the schools and that the school board be reduced to an advisory role. According to this proposal, after five years, control of the schools would revert to a new school board with members elected from seven districts.

Perspectives on the proposed changes varied widely, particularly for those changes regarding governance. Mayor Harmon appeared willing to assume control of the schools, but he was quick to point out many other demands on his time. The *St. Louis Post-Dispatch* supported mayoral control but not the transition to a new district-based school board.[38] Not surprisingly, school board members were opposed to a mayoral takeover, calling it an injection of politics into education. Interestingly, no major corporate leader joined the public debate.

In 1998, legislators went back to the drawing board and crafted another proposal, which was accepted and approved by the governor in the summer of that year. The new settlement, which followed by two years the desegregation settlement in Kansas City, preserves certain elements of the Voluntary Transfer Program while removing the constant monitoring of a federal judge. Key features of the settlement include:

The continuation of the Voluntary Transfer Program with more narrowly defined attendance zones. In a decade, voters in suburban school districts will vote on whether they wish to continue participating in this program.

A request to St. Louis voters to approve either an eighty-five-cent property tax increase or a one-half percent sales tax (or a combination of these) as a condition for additional state aid.

The creation of a special three-member board, with members appointed by the mayor, president of the board of aldermen, and school board, to assume the role of the school board if the St. Louis schools lose their accreditation in 1999.

The reconstitution of the school board into a seven-member body elected by districts rather than at-large.

An end to tenure for principals and the allowance of charter schools in the city.[39]

This settlement, adopted by the Missouri legislature in May 1998, set the parameters for local negotiations to end St. Louis's desegregation program. To actually terminate the program, all parties to the original suit had to come to an agreement that the federal judge would then accept or reject. In January 1999, these parties—including the suburban school districts—reached a settlement, which took place just before St. Louis city voters adopted a one-half percent sales tax, part of the fiscal component of the settlement. Many civic, business, and political leaders urged passage of the settlement. The most vocal opposition came from the teachers' union representing teachers employed by the St. Louis Public Schools. The union argued that St. Louis city schools would receive fewer dollars after the settlement took effect. In March 1999, Judge Stephen Limbaugh signed the settlement despite last-minute objections from the union and from St. Louis's mayor.

Implementing this settlement poses a major challenge to city and state officials. Residents of St. Louis face school governance changes as well as additional financial burdens. Furthermore, stronger leadership within the schools is critical to the success of this settlement, but leaders must work within the city's institutional framework, which remains fragmented. In addition, the city's traditional political culture has been rewarded by the return to district elections for school board members, tying the schools more closely to the ward system (four wards will constitute each school board district).

Other recent developments in St. Louis point toward a greater recognition of the problems of governmental fragmentation and weak business associations. Some civic leaders are studying the issue of charter reform and the need for a strong-mayor system of government. Whether this effort will succeed is unknown, but the problem is recognized. Further, Civic Progress is embarking on its own internal changes. Richard Liddy, its current president, has spoken of the need for a new and larger organization and the formation of teams to address area problems, such as regionalism and education. Members are discussing the possibility of hiring regular staff and moving their meetings from an exclusive country club.[40] Civic Progress's plans immediately faced a challenge, however. In late August 1998, all but one African-American leader ended participation in the organization's Dialogue Committee, stopping a thirty-year practice of meetings between Civic Progress and leaders of the African-American community. These leaders were convinced that race did not occupy a prominent place in Civic Progress's new agenda.[41]

Culture and tradition do not bode well for either a stronger, more centralized city government or a business elite. Yet, development of such institutions might provide the only hope for developing a genuine civic capacity to deal with St. Louis's public schools. To date, the low cohesion of the city's leadership and their lack of a deeply shared interest in the school system leaves slim ground for optimism. Fragmentation and structural constraints are profound impediments; institutions remain weak and incapable of generating or supporting strong leadership. The school system's bureaucracy, the city's unreformed politics, and the business community's intermittent involvement in civic affairs do not bode well for cohesive action. The divide of race remains a continuing impediment for a school district that is almost 80 percent black. Although local political contests have long carried racial overtones, race is not addressed forthrightly. Perhaps the desegregation settlement will mark a watershed, but the outlook for the development of civic capacity to address the problems of the St. Louis Public Schools is guarded at best.

7

Civic Capacity and Urban Education: Lessons from Three Cities

As rustbelt cities, Pittsburgh, Boston, and St. Louis share a number of common political and economic experiences. Machine-style politics is part of the political heritage of each city, and the economic transformation from manufacturing to services has occurred in each, albeit to different degrees. As a new century approaches, each also shares a similar challenge faced as well by most central cities in the United States: how to improve achievement in its public schools. This challenge is complicated by a changing student population. The student body in each city has been growing preponderantly poor, leaving many students with limited support outside the school building. Furthermore, many students, if not most, are members of minority groups, marking a racial transformation of the school system with implications for the development of broad community support.

A key step in meeting this challenge is the extension of civic capacity to include public education. As outlined in earlier chapters, this approach requires a civic vision and supportive leadership at the governance level as well as capacity and resources at the programmatic level. Our three cities have faced this challenge with quite different results. Pittsburgh's relative success stands in sharp contrast to the failures in St. Louis, while recent positive steps in Boston have followed a number of stalled efforts.

In all three cities, the task of building and activating civic capacity on behalf of public education has proved to be a major test for community institutions and leaders. Each case study offered a different experience in which institutions and leadership combined, or failed to combine, in the development of civic capacity. In this chapter we bring these experiences together to explore more fully how civic capacity can incorporate public education. Our analysis begins with a review of the ranking of the cities, followed by a closer look at the development of institutions in each—formal organizations, associations, and networks—and how these institutions became involved, or failed to become involved, in supporting public education. We also consider the prevailing political culture in each city and how it establishes a context for institution building and leadership. Finally, we examine leadership, which plays a critical role in alliance building and the development of capacity. Our three-city comparison yields a number of important lessons for understanding the development of civic capacity in supporting urban education.

RANKING THE CITIES

At the conclusion of Chapter 3 we ranked our three cities according to their support for school reform. Pittsburgh ranked highest, followed by Boston and then St. Louis. We relied upon three indicators to make this assessment: each city's level of financial support for public education, the presence and extent of innovation within each school system, and the perceptions of local elites as to community support for education.

Our case studies provided an explanation for this ranking. In particular, the historical development of institutions and the role of leaders in supporting public education varied quite dramatically in Pittsburgh, Boston, and St. Louis. In Pittsburgh, our top-ranked city, the Allegheny Conference on Community Development provided critical support for school reform while fostering a climate of collaboration and cross-sector support for education and other community initiatives. The conference was joined by leadership from within the school district, particularly from the superintendent's office. This combination of institutional support and strong leadership was central to the development and activation of civic capacity in Pittsburgh.

The Boston and St. Louis case studies offered quite different experiences. In Boston, the development of cross-sector institutions, like the Boston Compact, provided a potential base for civic support of public education. Yet, educational and community leadership were often lacking, and a skeptical, and sometimes cynical, attitude toward public education served to minimize this potential. In more recent years, however, strong leadership has combined with key institutions to increase community support for public education. In St. Louis, the public education experience has followed the same pattern as that of overall civic capacity: episodic efforts amidst few cross-sector institutions and limited leadership. Court-ordered busing and race have dominated the educational agenda, leaving little room for the development of more broad-based support for the city's schools.

Desegregation: An Example of Civic Response

These differences in the development of civic capacity are evident in how each community responded to demands for the desegregation of their schools. In the 1970s, Pittsburgh, Boston, and St. Louis, like many other American cities, had school systems with a high degree of racial segregation. Pressures to desegregate came from residents, state government, and federal courts. Although each of the three cities faced pressures, community responses varied, depending in large part upon the different levels of civic capacity in each city.

In Pittsburgh, the pressure to desegregate the schools reached its peak in 1980 when the Pennsylvania Human Relations Commission, frustrated by the school district's inability to address this issue, demanded a desegregation plan within ninety days. The community was sharply divided over desegregation strategies, and the school board was unable to resolve differences. Faced with a continued stalemate and growing divisions, a Citizens Advisory Committee was created under the direction of Robert Pease, executive director of the Allegheny Conference on Community Development. The conference granted Pease a paid leave to devote his full attention to this critical task.

The Allegheny Conference on Community Development turned its considerable resources to addressing the desegregation issue. In addition to "loaning" its executive director, the conference sponsored a number of other efforts to resolve this issue. The assistant director of the conference, for example, chaired a committee that developed and helped implement a magnet school program. To borrow a sports metaphor, the conference stepped up to the plate to help the city address this very critical issue. For forty years the conference had provided a forum for addressing the problems of the region, particularly in the economic development arena; it then applied that experience and capacity to public education. The conference offered an institutional forum as well as leadership to help resolve a divisive racial issue that was dividing the community. The civic capacity of Pittsburgh was meeting a new challenge.

In Boston, the desegregation experience was quite different. The Boston School Committee opposed desegregation demands from minority residents as well as state government. As in Pittsburgh, this volatile issue was dividing the community. However, unlike Pittsburgh, the dominant business association, the Vault, did not enter the fray. In fact, members of the Vault avoided the issue, viewing it as outside their domain. Instead, desegregation became a federal court issue, and in 1974 Judge Garrity issued the first of many orders designed to achieve racial desegregation. For all practical purposes, the federal court controlled the school system for the next ten years. These were very difficult years characterized by divisions and turmoil in the school community.

The civic leaders and institutions of Boston were unable to address this challenge. Most business leaders avoided the desegregation issue altogether, arguing that it was a concern of city residents, not the business community. Resources that revived Boston's economy in the 1960s would not be turned, at least initially, to address the problems of public education. The broad civic orientation of the Allegheny Conference on Community Development was absent in Boston during the early phases of desegregation. Slowly, however, civic support for education did develop. In 1982 the Boston Compact was created, combining leadership with cross-sector resources from business, government, and the schools. These first steps in building civic support for public education were incremental and tentative. Compared with Pittsburgh, Boston was just beginning a process of turning its civic resources to educational concerns.

The St. Louis experience with desegregation points to an almost complete lack of civic institutions and leadership to address this issue. In fact, St. Louis and the state of Missouri brought a legacy of de jure segregation into the debate on school desegregation. Not surprisingly, a dual educational system was generally accepted by many in the city. A federal court case that began in 1972 finally ended in a consent decree in 1982, resulting in an expanded school magnet program and extensive busing between St. Louis and its surrounding suburbs. The magnet schools and Voluntary Transfer Program have dominated the educational agenda since 1982.

The desegregation plan in St. Louis has been a court-ordered and state-supported (by court order) remedy for past segregation in the schools. St. Louis's key business association, Civic Progress, has not been a player in school desegregation except to work behind the scenes to prevent any violence when the buses rolled. In contrast to Pittsburgh and, to a lesser extent Boston, civic institutions and resources have played little role. Rather, the federal district court has been the key actor. Civic capacity has been largely absent in St. Louis's desegregation experience.

Race and Civic Capacity

The desegregation experiences in our three cities highlight the importance of race in urban America and also point to a possible alternative explanation for successes and failures in the extension of civic capacity to public education. Pittsburgh, Boston, and St. Louis, like most American cities, have become the homes of a growing minority population. Race relations are a major social, economic, and political concern of urban policy makers and school officials. As noted earlier, many urban schools systems, including the three in this study, have minority populations larger than the comparable proportion for the overall city population. Business and political leaders, however, have remained predominantly white.

In this setting, it might be argued that the development of civic capacity and its extension to the schools reflect the tenor of race relations more than the status of institutions and leadership. For example, the poor development of civic capacity in one city might reflect the lack of interest by white political and business leaders in a minority-dominated school system. Following this line of argument, the more minority students in a school system, the less likely is the development of civic capacity.

On the surface, this argument appears to fit our ranking of the three cities. Pittsburgh has the lowest concentration of minority students and the highest development of civic capacity; Boston is in the middle on both measures; St. Louis has the highest proportion of minority students and the least civic capacity and fewest reform efforts. We recognize that race is an important issue, yet the development of civic capacity is not simply race-driven as this correlation might indicate. Indeed, there are important examples in our three cities in which the development of civic capacity did not follow this line of argument. Rather, as we have argued throughout this book, institutions and leaders played a critical role at these junctures.

A second look at the desegregation experiences of Pittsburgh and Boston provides one example. In Pittsburgh, the turning point in the desegregation case was in 1980 when the Allegheny Conference on Community Development stepped forward to take a key role in helping the community craft a plan acceptable to state authorities. In Boston, the turning point was in 1974 when Judge Garrity issued his first ruling and effectively assumed control of the school system. At both dates, the proportion of minority students in the two school systems was comparable—50 percent in Pittsburgh and 48 percent in Boston. Yet, the responses by political, business, and community leaders, as outlined previously, were very different. Race was not the key explanatory factor. Rather, Pittsburgh's institutional development set the stage for that community's response, while the lack of a comparable infrastructure in Boston contributed to a response driven by courts rather than local institutions and leaders.

Mayor Menino's leadership in Boston in the 1990s offers another example. Throughout his tenure as mayor, Menino has been a strong and consistent advocate for public education. He has worked with business and community leaders to extend the civic capacity of the community to include public education. Menino launched this effort, however, at a time when 80 percent of the students were members of minority groups. Again, race was not the deciding factor. Rather, a major institutional change—granting the mayor appointive power over the school committee—was critical. This new institutional setting, combined with the mayor's authority under a strong-mayor form of government, created leadership opportunities that Menino has used to expand the city's civic capacity.

This is not to argue that race is irrelevant. Indeed, the question of race compounds the attainment of civic capacity as it does most questions of contemporary urban life. Race does matter. All three cities have histories of racial divisions and discord that impact the development of civic capacity. Our argument, however, is that the role of race in explaining the development of civic capacity is best understood through the prism of institutions and leadership. Racial divisions often are manifest through institutions, and leaders must consider racial groups in their formulation of a vision to lead the community. Divisions among racial groups clearly complicate the task of building and extending civic bonds that are central to civic capacity. To understand how this challenge is met, we use institutions and leadership as our explanatory tools. To that end, we first offer a comparison of institutions among our three cities.

INSTITUTIONAL TERRAIN

Institutions provide the context for civic alliances at a governance level as well as the development of resources and capacity at a programmatic level. As outlined in Chapter 2, the institutional terrain is composed of three major types of institutions: formal organizations, associations, and networks. The cross-sector nature of networks is particularly important, but each institutional type plays a part in a community's civic capacity. A comparison of the institutional terrain in our three cities highlights its critical role as well as relative presence in each city. Table 7-1 summarizes the key institutional actors in each city and their relative efficacy during the most successful years in the development of civic capacity, as well as the role of leadership, which is the subject of the next section in this chapter.

Formal Organizations

Formal organizations, such as city governments and school departments, are a key part of the foundation for civic capacity. Different organizations and the individuals who work in them are connected and interrelated to create associations and networks that in turn establish the critical cross-sector nature of a city's civic capacity. Weak formal organizations undermine a city's civic structure. In our three cities, such weaknesses, as well as important strengths, are quite evident. Our discussion focuses on three major organizations—city governments, school departments, and school boards—that played an important role in each city.

City government. Structures of city government vary among the three cities and have important implications for the task of building civic capacity. In Pittsburgh and Boston, a strong-mayor form of government creates a quite different set of incentives and opportunities for action than does the weak-mayor system in St. Louis. The mayors in Pittsburgh and Boston have higher political visibility and greater available resources than does their counterpart in St. Louis.

Pittsburgh and Boston share a common form of city government, but the involvement of city officials in public education has evolved down quite different paths. In Pittsburgh, the mayor and other city officials have been reluctant to enter school debates. The school department is seen as outside the domain of city hall; it is governed by a separately elected board and is fiscally independent. City officials may voice their opinions on specific school issues, particularly when they involve a potential tax increase, but they shy away from more direct involvement in the schools. From Pittsburgh's perspective, this approach is an advantage for the school system. Educational debates are less likely to become entwined in broader political divisions and controversies in city government. A division of responsibilities between city hall and the school department appears to have served Pittsburgh well.

Boston has charted a different course. Since 1992 the mayor of Boston has appointed the members of the school board and has effectively controlled the

Table 7-1. Institutions and Leaders: Their Efficacy in Extending Civic Capacity to Public Education

	Pittsburgh 1980s		Boston 1993–1998		St. Louis No period of high efficacy	
Period of Highest Efficacy	Name	Efficacy	Name	Efficacy	Name	Efficacy
Institutions						
Formal Organizations	Strong-mayor city gov't.	Low	Strong-mayor city gov't.	High	Weak-mayor city gov't.	Low
	Pittsburgh School Dept.	High	Boston School Dept.	Moderate	St. Louis School Dept.	Low
	Pittsburgh Fed. of Teachers	High	Boston Teachers' Union	Moderate	St. Louis Teachers' Union	Low
	Pittsburgh School Board	Moderate	Boston School Committee	Moderate	St. Louis School Board	Low
	University of Pittsburgh	High	Higher Education Consort.	Moderate		
			Private Industry Council	Moderate		
Associations	Allegheny Conference on Community Development	High	Vault	Low–Moderate	Civic Progress	Low
Networks	Allegheny Conference Education Fund	High	Boston Compact	High	CHANGE	Low
	Council on Public Education	Moderate	Boston Plan for Excellence in the Public Schools	Moderate–High		
	New Futures (1990s)	Low	Citywide Educational Coalition	Moderate		
	Policy Council (1990s)	Low	Critical Friends	Moderate		
Political Culture characterized as	• Civic responsibility and cooperation	High	• Mix of individualism and civic responsibility	Moderate	• Parochial and individualistic	Low
	• Moderate racial divisions		• Moderate to high racial divisions		• High racial divisions	
Leaders	Superintendent Wallace	High	Mayor Flynn	Moderate	Mayor Bosley	Moderate
	Board President Milliones	High	Mayor Menino	High	Mayor Harmon	Low
	ACCD Director Pease	High	Superintendent Payzant	High	Superintendent Mahan	Low
	PTU President Fondy	High				

choice of superintendent. City hall has become a major player in school politics. The key distinction between Boston and Pittsburgh is the institutional relationship between city government and the school department. In Boston, the school department is fiscally dependent upon city government. The Boston School Committee controls the allocation of funds within the school budget, but the total amount of funds allocated to the schools must be approved by the mayor and city council.

This budgetary link between the schools and city government has been the source of tensions and disagreements for many years. When the Boston School Committee was an elected body (prior to 1992), members of the committee would frequently complain that city hall was not providing adequate funds for the schools. City officials, on the other hand, complained that school funds were not used in an efficient and effective manner by the school committee. Replacement of the elected committee by an appointed committee was the resolution to this issue. By granting the mayor this authority over another organization, Boston has followed a very different path for developing civic capacity.

In St. Louis, a weak-mayor system clearly has contributed to the city's limited ability to develop broad, cross-sector institutions. The mayors of St. Louis have a limited platform for policy development and civic leadership. They must share the political platform with a number of other officials elected citywide, including the president of the board of aldermen and the city comptroller. In addition, the twenty-eight aldermen elected from wards further fragment political discourse and often focus debates around ward-specific concerns. This unreformed system has a long legacy of patronage that continues to influence the policy process. In general, this environment is not conducive to discussions about broad civic concerns, such as education. The mayors of St. Louis have played a limited role in the educational debates of the city. Recent discussions about a mayoral takeover of the school system raised a number of questions as to the ability of the mayor to assume such a major responsibility. Furthermore, the recent settlement to end the desegregation program involved old-style politics as much as a concern for student achievement.

School departments. School departments constitute a second formal organization that play a critical role in the civic capacity matrix. The schools themselves, after all, are the sites where reform efforts must be implemented. Without support from teachers, administrators, and other departmental personnel, educational reform has little chance of succeeding. The key questions, then, are whether school departments are receptive to reform initiatives, and whether departments possess the capabilities, among teachers and administrators, to effectively implement those initiatives.

In response to these questions, the Pittsburgh school department receives quite high marks. The department has maintained a strong professional orientation, and it is generally receptive to educational innovations. As noted in Chapter 3, the Pittsburgh school system has adopted the most innovative practices among our three school districts. This openness to school reform reflects a high level of professionalization that was nurtured by Superintendent Wallace. During Wallace's tenure a number of professional development programs were put in place, although several were curtailed in later years. A professional orientation, however, has survived even during major shifts in organizational structure, from Wallace's centralized administration to Superintendent Brennen's focus on school-based management.

The Pittsburgh schools also benefited from a supportive teachers' union. Teacher strikes in the 1960s and 1970s were replaced in the 1980s and 1990s with a more cooperative relationship between the union and school administration. The president of the teachers' union developed a strong working relationship with Superintendents Wallace and Brennan and supported the school system's push for professionalization. Union support for teacher training and school-level management programs was met with salary increases for teachers. This cooperative relationship helped support the overall professional orientation of the school department, which in turn made the department an important component in the city's civic support for public education.

The Boston school department is moving in the direction of Pittsburgh, but an emerging emphasis on professionalization competes with a deep-seated skepticism that the system can actually change. Since the early 1980s the school department has been directed by four different superintendents, each of whom brought his or her own organizational approach to the system. Thus, the Boston school department has experienced a range of centralized and decentralized organizational structures. Unlike Pittsburgh, however, these changes often have been met with skepticism and occasional resistance. Many administrators and teachers in the system view these organizational changes as temporary and lacking in overall purpose and direction. In the last three years, a more concerted effort has been undertaken to strengthen the school department and enhance professional development. Superintendent Payzant reorganized the department in 1996, and school-based management is now in all schools, although implementation is variable. In addition, a new Center for Leadership Development was created to develop and sponsor professional development programs for administrators, teachers, and staff. Enhanced professional development has met with general support, although some observers, like Critical Friends, call for more extensive change to improve performance in the school department.

Like Pittsburgh, the Boston schools have a strong teachers' union that has played an increasingly significant role in professional development and overall school reform. Collective bargaining sessions remain intense and disagreements are common, but the teachers' union has become a player in strengthening the school system. The 1994 and 1997 teachers' contracts included participation by the union in a number of key school reforms, including school-based management, pilot schools, learning standards, and the Center for Leadership Development.

The school department in St. Louis has a reputation and track record quite different from its counterparts in Pittsburgh and Boston. In general, the St. Louis school system is limited in its receptivity to school reforms. Professional development is not a priority in the system, and new initiatives often fail to receive support. Recent attempts to implement school-based management, for example, received negative evaluations. The system is highly centralized and reluctant to transfer significant authority to individual schools.

In general, the St. Louis school department has not embraced reforms or initiatives coming from outside parties. The department has a history of promoting from within and drawing its administrators from a relatively narrow pool of local graduates. While rewarding internal candidates has certain merit, it can stultify the system's openness to new ideas and initiatives. To a significant degree, the St. Louis Public Schools have become an employment outlet for those with connections. Furthermore, the local teachers' union is not a key actor in supporting professional development or reform. Denied by state government the ability to negotiate a collective bargaining contract, the teachers' union is in a weak position to influence the school department and has been further hampered by internal disagreements. In comparison to Pittsburgh and Boston, the St. Louis school department has not been a positive contributor to the city's civic capacity.

School boards. A third important actor at the organizational level is the school board. Although part of a school system, school boards merit separate attention because of their potential role in developing community support for education. They provide a key political connection between the school system and the community, and they are the chief policy-making body for the school system. Furthermore, school boards are a frequent target of parental complaints regarding school practices. The role of school boards in forging civic capacity is sometimes limited,[1] yet they remain local organizations that can play a key role in the development of school-community support structures.

In each of our three cities, the school board was a factor—sometimes supportive, sometimes less so—in developing and extending civic capacity to include public education. In Pittsburgh, the elected school board was an important actor in responding to reform initiatives from the superintendent's office. The school board consisted of a diverse group that represented a wide range of interests in the city. During the first eight to ten years of Superintendent Wallace's tenure, the school board was generally supportive. Growing criticisms of Wallace's centralization, however, contributed to his departure, and the board was split along racial lines over the hiring of Louise Brennan. Yet, despite such divisions, the school board played a generally positive role in supporting educational reform. In large part, this support was a testament to the guiding influence of the school board president, who was usually successful in developing a working relationship with the incumbent superintendent. More recently, the board has lacked strong leadership, and internal conflict has inhibited decisive action.

The Boston experience exemplifies the importance of institutional congruence between key organizations. More specifically, the disharmony between the elected school board and the city's mayor was a major stumbling block to the development of community support for education. The elected board was viewed by many as dysfunctional. As described previously, the problem was not so much that the board was elected and included members with political ambitions, but rather that the board was fiscally dependent upon city hall. This fiscal dependence undermined the political authority of the board, which was elected to set policy for the schools. Resolving this issue was critical to the development of civic support for the schools.

This school governance model is quite different from Pittsburgh's. Whereas Pittsburgh relied upon a clear separation between city hall and the school system, in Boston the two became more closely connected. Indeed, Boston's Mayor Menino has asked the voters to judge him by the success or failure of the city's public schools. In Pittsburgh, such a statement would be an unacceptable incursion across institutional boundaries. In Boston, however, the mayor's comment is consistent with the connections that now bind city hall and the school system.

In St. Louis, a weak and often divided school board has contributed to that city's inability to develop civic support for the public schools. Board elections from 1983 to 1991, for example, were dominated by candidacies of those opposed to desegregation. Polarization between advocates and foes of busing diluted the ability of the board to shape school policy. In addition, board members are often overwhelmed with personnel issues at the expense of policy development. In general, the St. Louis school board has failed to exercise strong policy leadership or establish deep-rooted connections with other community institutions.

Other formal organizations. There are a number of other formal organizations that helped provide the basic infrastructure for the associations and networks that developed in each city. In Pittsburgh, local foundations and the University of Pittsburgh provided critical support for school reform. As noted in Chapter 4, Pittsburgh ranks fortieth in population but first in grants from independent foundations and among the top ten in grants from corporate and community foundations. Many local foundations have adopted a systemic, community-wide approach to awarding grants that is particularly conducive to broad-based civic projects that include education as a key component. The University of Pittsburgh also has played an important supportive role. The Learning Research and Development Center at the university, for example, played a key role during the early Wallace years by conducting a district-wide needs assessment. Wallace used this assessment to develop policy initiatives, and the center continued to play a role in implementation of these initiatives.

In Boston, the Private Industry Council has played an important role in the incorporation of education into that city's civic capacity. Created in 1979, the Private Industry Council soon became an institutional buffer between the business community and the school department. Business leaders placed trust and confidence in the council as a conduit for business support for education. In doing so, businesses minimized direct financial contributions to the schools, a less attractive option because of concerns over the fiscal capabilities of the school department. The council continues to support a variety of education-related programs, including school-business partnerships and staff support for the Boston Compact.

Importantly, not all organizations necessarily have a positive effect on the development of civic capacity. Federal courts, for example, played a complicated role in our communities, particularly in Boston and St. Louis. While court intervention was critical in the march toward equality of opportunity in education, its effect was often less positive for the development of civic capacity. In Boston and St. Louis, the federal court became an outside party perceived by many as imposing conditions and requirements on the community. Court orders were mandates, not locally generated strategies and goals. Federal courts could force communities to address long-standing practices of segregation, but they were less adept at laying the groundwork for community collaboration. As one study of six big-city school districts found, building the community infrastructure for major school improvement efforts typically begins only after desegregation battles have been resolved in the courts.[2] In the case of St. Louis, resolution also required action by state government, which did not come until 1998. In general, judicial intervention can plant the seeds for change, but individuals and organizations within the community must build and sustain a structure of support for the schools.

Associations

Associations constitute a second group of key actors in the institutional terrain. Defined as a collection of organizations within one sector and united by a common purpose, associations in our three cities, particularly business associations, played a critical role in the development of civic capacity. Pittsburgh's Allegheny Conference on Community Development, a business association, set the highest standard. From its founding in 1943, the conference has required chief executive officers—not substitutes from within a corporation—to serve on its executive committee. This "no-substitutes" policy ensured that top decision makers were at the table for discussions and decisions. In addition, the conference benefits from a full-time staff who provide support ranging from secretarial and legal advice to policy analysis. An executive director oversees operations and provides important input to the conference's deliberations and initiatives.

The conference also benefits from a sophisticated and fairly comprehensive view of community development. In its early years the conference focused on physical development in the region, but it has responded to changing times and demands. In the late 1950s, for example, it entered the housing arena, and in the 1960s and 1970s it became involved in unemployment and minority support initiatives. Economic development has always been central to the agenda of the conference, but it has responded to changing concerns in the community.

In general, the Allegheny Conference on Community Development has established a very successful action model of expanding its agenda and supporting the creation of new institutions to carry on its initiatives. For example, it supported the creation of a nonprofit agency, ACTION-Housing, Inc., to address issues of affordability in the housing market. Other organizations that the conference helped launch include the Regional Industrial Development Corporation, Pittsburgh Partnership for Neighborhood Development, Mon Valley Initiative, and Health Policy Institute. In general, the conference serves as a catalyst for change, bringing together the "right combination of ideas, people and funding to improve Pittsburgh and its surrounding region."[3]

Neither Boston nor St. Louis has reached this standard. In both cities the key business associations have made contributions, but they have not created the same collaborative environment achieved in Pittsburgh. Boston's major business association, the Vault, has limited staff support. Lacking its own personnel, businesses in the Vault loan their staff for various activities on an as-needed basis. This situation limits the ability of the Vault to identify key areas for action, formulate alternatives, and implement initiatives. When the Vault did become involved with the schools through the Boston Compact, staff at the Private Industry Council became the de facto support structure. This support was critical to the success of the compact as well as its ability to continue to the present day. Without the organizational support of the Private Industry Council it is doubtful that this collaborative effort—a network—would have survived.

In comparison to the Allegheny Conference on Community Development, the Vault also has not demonstrated a comprehensive vision of community development. The Vault's early focus was on economic development, but its inclination and capacity to expand into other policy arenas has been limited. As noted earlier, the Vault stood on the sidelines during the desegregation battles of the 1970s. When businesses did become involved with the schools, it was as much at the prodding of the federal district court as it was a planned initiative from the business community. Furthermore, as the economy has changed in the past decade, the Vault has become less relevant. Today, in fact, the Vault has been declared dead by a number of participants and observers.

To a significant degree, the Vault did not institutionalize itself. It was born in a reactive mode to economic problems in the late 1950s and never successfully assumed the more proactive stance that characterized the Allegheny Conference on Community Development in Pittsburgh. Whereas the conference publishes an annual report outlining its activities, the Vault has rarely published any document under its own name. The Vault has declined to create an identity for itself; indeed, its very secretive and closed nature has diminished its ability to pursue a more activist course. The Private Industry Council has provided an important surrogate role, principally in the educational and workforce training areas, but at a lower profile and level of community awareness.

In St. Louis, Civic Progress has played an even less active role in the city's development. Although in existence since the early 1950s, Civic Progress assumed a limited role in the community after the mid-1960s. Like the Vault, Civic Progress has no independent staff; it relies upon staff from a local public relations firm. Furthermore, connections with the political community are intermittent. Some mayors have had good working relationships with Civic Progress, while others have had more distant ties.

Civic Progress has operated primarily in a project-specific fashion. It has not developed a broad, systemic view of urban development. Rather, the orientation is to focus on key projects principally in the economic realm, such as a sports stadium, that capture the attention of the members. The association has not completely eschewed education and social policy, but its involvement has followed this project focus. For example, individual school partnerships are supported by a number of companies, but these partnerships do not address more general systemic problems of public education. Civic Progress also became involved with several school board elections, but it was a reactive strategy to prevent the board from falling under the control of a divisive group opposed to desegregation. Compared with the Allegheny Conference on Community Development and, to a degree, the Vault, Civic Progress has not played a key role in shaping the debate on educational reform in St. Louis.

Networks

Networks are at the heart of a city's civic capacity. They provide a critical forum for collaboration and joint action by actors from different sectors in the community. Both Pittsburgh and Boston have developed important networks that link education with other sectors. In fact, in both cities several networks have formed in a similar fashion. The key business associations described above—the Allegheny Conference on Community Development and the Vault—have spawned, or helped to spawn, one or more networks. In Pittsburgh, the conference established the Education Fund in 1978 to support a variety of school programs, including grants to teachers for curriculum innovations, support for business-school partnerships, and a leadership development program for principals. In Boston, a similar cross-sector approach emerged. In 1984 the business community, with general support from the Vault, launched the Boston Plan for Excellence in the Public Schools. The plan supported a number of programs, such as grants for curriculum development, that were closely akin to those supported by the conference's Education Fund.

Networks, however, are very fragile institutions. As the Casey Foundation found in its New Futures initiative, cross-sector coalitions that attempt comprehensive reform face "the path of most resistance."[4] Vested interests, fiscal constraints, and political differences are commonplace. In particular, the broader the membership in a network, the more difficult it is to sustain initiatives and programs. Pittsburgh's Education Fund and the Boston Plan included two primary actors, the business community and the schools, while other organizations played a limited role. When a network brings together more parties from different sectors of the city, the task becomes increasingly difficult. Different actors bring different priorities to the table as each defines educational problems and solutions through their own interests and perspective. It is a major challenge to translate this diversity into a common agenda and vision. As we have found, and will discuss later, leadership plays a key role in meeting that challenge.

Both Boston and Pittsburgh have struggled to develop a broad-based network, although Boston has been more successful. The Boston Compact, begun in 1982, includes not only the school system and business community, but also city government, labor, and higher education. In the mid- to late 1980s, the compact struggled to stay together. The business community, in particular, was dissatisfied with the slow pace of school reform and limited improvement on measures of school achievement. The compact, however, survived that period and is now in its third period of renewal. It maintains a relatively low profile but continues to be a significant part of the community's civic capacity, principally in the forum it provides to develop a common school agenda among different sectors in the community.

In Pittsburgh, a New Futures initiative was launched in 1987 to bring to the table not only the school department and the Allegheny Conference on Community Development but also local foundations and city and county officials, particularly in the workforce development area. New Futures, however, failed to make significant strides in improving public education. The major stakeholders were not committed to the collaboration. Each had programmatic initiatives they championed, but interest was lacking at the governance level for the development of a common agenda that would support serious programmatic coordination. After several years, New Futures was dissolved.

In 1992, the Allegheny Policy Council for Youth and Workforce Development became the new showcase for cross-sector collaboration. With representatives from the Allegheny Conference on Community Development, school department, city, county, foundations, and University of Pittsburgh, the Policy Council took a broader, regional approach to education and workforce development. The conference's Education Fund as well as a number of other initiatives were placed under the Policy Council. In its first few years, however, the Policy Council also has failed to establish itself as a forceful new actor in the education and workforce arena. Again, broad, cross-sector collaboration that includes the business community and other key actors is difficult to build and sustain.

Both cities also have been the site of collaborations based on community advocacy. In Pittsburgh, the Council on Public Education began in 1963 and has served as a strong outside voice on the direction and effectiveness of school policies and programs. As a coalition of parents, educators, and civic leaders, the council has sponsored, among other activities, informational newsletters to the public on school matters, school board election forums, and task forces on key issues before the school system. It currently plays a very significant role in the training of the school councils established under Pittsburgh's site-based management plan.

In Boston, the Citywide Educational Coalition performs a similar function. Supported by parents, educators, businesses, and other community organizations, the coalition began in 1973 during the early days of desegregation and has served as a major information clearinghouse on the schools as well as an advocate for positive change. More recently, the new organization called Critical Friends has brought together representatives from key organizations in the city, principally outside the business community, to provide critical analyses of the school system and advocate for key reforms.

These community-based networks have strong staying power, and they often have the ear of school and government leaders. As outside advocates, however, their ability to bring about change in the school system is generally limited. Their major resource is public attention and pressure; reports and newsletters are their primary tools. The two actors with the most resources—government and business—are not key parties to such networks. Lacking consistent support from these two actors, such community-based networks must rely upon their public advocacy role to support school reform.

Despite the limitations of community-based networks and the generally fragile nature of broad, cross-sector coalitions, the networks in Pittsburgh and Boston have played a significant role in supporting school reform. Each network has offered an opportunity for key members of the community to join forces around a common educational agenda. In so doing, each network also brings together the different resources of its members. Financial support and management expertise from business, for example, can be joined with tutoring and scholarship support from universities and colleges. Although successes are mixed with setbacks, these networks nevertheless provide an important support structure for school reform.

St. Louis has been much less successful in developing an infrastructure of networks. Business interest in public education has been primarily episodic, a pattern similar to what has taken place in the development arena, with little attention to developing long-lasting coalitions. Networks that do develop often falter or are quite limited in scope. The fate of CHANGE represents the typical scenario in St. Louis. This broad network included individuals and organizations from government, business, the school department, the school board, and neighborhoods. A flurry of activity at the outset faded as the network lost its funding. It did not create an enduring platform for discussion and action and never expanded its agenda beyond changes to the community education centers. Walbridge Caring Community is a more positive outcome, but it is more narrowly defined and, equally important, is funded by state government. In St. Louis generally, the institutional infrastructure for the development of education-based networks is absent.

Political Culture

A city's political culture helps shape the development of institutions as well as opportunities for leadership. The local orientation toward politics—the beliefs, values, and traditions of the community—sets the stage for political discourse and action. As noted earlier, cities vary in this orientation. In some communities there is a predisposition toward the development of networks through collective decision making and collaborative activities, while in other communities people are inclined toward a parochial or individualistic orientation to politics.[5] Both orientations, as we note below, are present in our three cities.

Among the many factors that shape a city's political culture, two of the most important are existing institutional arrangements and race. The current institutional environment, particularly existing governmental structures, establishes basic patterns of power and communication among political actors. A strong-mayor system, for example, nurtures a political orientation in which active leadership and centralized power are likely. Existing networks, as in Pittsburgh and Boston, foster further collaborative approaches to addressing political problems. In addition to the existing institutional environment, a community's race relations have an important impact on the development of political culture. Race is particularly important because it can establish group identities that, in turn, become the focus of political action. Sharp racial divisions, as in St. Louis, can become a major and often insurmountable hurdle to the development of collaborative strategies to address citywide concerns.

Among our three cities, political cultures varied significantly and helped to shape the world of institutions and leaders. In Pittsburgh, the existing institutional environment, shaped largely by the Allegheny Conference on Community Development, fostered a political culture of "civic responsibility, cooperation, and a strong dose of deference."[6] As noted earlier, one interviewee referred to the conference as a "state of mind," a striking reference to this institution's impact on the culture and orientation of the community. Indeed, the premise of the conference was twofold: discussion across organizational boundaries and a high level of expertise. Both of these characteristics became ingrained in the general civic orientation of the broader community. When key issues, such as school desegregation, faced community leaders, the dominant orientation was to foster broad, cross-sector discussions and identify a targeted response to address the concern. This orientation did not guarantee success, but it did establish a pattern of collaborative discourse and action that was central to Pittsburgh's civic capacity.

Pittsburgh, however, has had its divisions. The civic-mindedness of the community has given way, on occasion, to disagreements and disputes. Race, for example, has been a source of division. When Louise Brennan replaced Richard Wallace as superintendent of the schools, there was a strong negative reaction from many in the African-American community who wanted an African-American superintendent. Within a year, however, Brennan won over most of her early critics with an educational agenda that featured decentralized decision making in the school system. The collaborative, civic-oriented nature of the community remained dominant as parents, educators, and civic leaders adjusted to new leadership in the school department. Later, the neighborhood school issue brought race back into the education debate, but once again compromises have been reached.

In Boston, the political culture historically has been less supportive of cross-sector collaboration. Described by one observer as "private-regarding," Boston's political orientation highlights a tension between strong individualism and a community focus.[7] Collaboration across sectors often is difficult to sustain. As two community leaders noted after a trip to Atlanta, Boston "does not experience the same collaborative drive or promotion of our many successes" as takes place in Atlanta.[8]

Both governmental structures and racial divisions have contributed to this political orientation. As noted earlier, the school department's fiscal dependence on budgetary approval from city hall confused accountability for school performance. Neither city hall nor the school system would assume full responsibility, and this lack of clear accountability nurtured a negative political orientation toward the school system. In addition, Boston has a history of difficult race relations that overshadows many efforts at community building. As noted in the case study, race is a division line in the city that plays out in politics, education, and other areas. The legacy of court-ordered desegregation and busing has become a part of the local political culture. This cultural orientation manifested itself in a distancing from the school system and a high degree of skepticism, indeed cynicism, that the schools could improve.

As we have seen, however, these hurdles are not insurmountable. A city's political culture can shift, albeit slowly. Boston has achieved a significant level of cross-sector collaboration, and support for the schools is growing. Racial divisions remain significant, but institutional changes between city hall and the school system—mayoral appointment of the school committee—have provided clearer accountability and fostered a more positive orientation toward the schools. Critical to this cultural shift are political and educational leadership, a point we will discuss shortly.

In our third city, St. Louis, political culture has been shaped by the city's governmental structure as well as its legacy of de jure racial segregation. Unlike Boston and Pittsburgh, St. Louis has retained its weak-mayor form of government. This unreformed city government reflects a long-standing political orientation favoring patronage and neighborhood politics. Individual wards remain central to the city's political dynamic. A citywide vision and perspective is less apparent. Broad citywide coalitions and cross-sector collaborations tend to be incongruent with St. Louis's political fragmentation.

Historically a very Catholic city, St. Louis has a high proportion of white students who have never attended the public schools. As the school population became increasingly black, more white families distanced themselves from the schools. In addition, many African-Americans left the city's schools, preferring private education or a bus ride to the suburbs. Indeed, almost half of school-age children in St. Louis do not attend the city's public schools. Building citywide coalitions has been difficult in this environment.

LEADERSHIP

Leadership plays a key role in the development of civic capacity. In building a civic coalition, leaders help to develop a common vision and problem definition among diverse actors. Leaders identify similar interests and work toward a collective vision of the city's future. In building requisite capacity, leaders help identify existing institutions to implement the city's collective vision, or they create new institutions to address this task. In either case, leaders combine critical resources in support of a civic agenda.

The relationship between leaders and institutions is interactive. On the one hand, institutions provide the setting for the exercise of leadership. Institutions define the context for leaders and often constrain their actions. Superintendent Payzant in Boston, for example, confronted an institutional environment that included the school department, school board, teachers' union, local government, and other organizations, associations, and networks. To a significant degree, these institutions defined the range of possible actions open to the superintendent. Institutions, however, can be altered. Leaders possess the potential to redesign and recreate institutions, thereby changing the environment within which they operate. Superintendent Payzant reorganized the school department in a decentralized fashion that altered the lines of authority and responsibility. Although often difficult, institutional redesign is a hallmark of strong leadership.

Leadership is the catalyst for building and activating civic capacity. For this activity to occur, however, our case studies point to three key ingredients. First, an alignment of leaders from different sectors in the city is critical. A single leader in one sector, be it the superintendent, mayor, or business leader, is insufficient. One individual may be the spark to begin a coalition-building process, but he or she needs help to create and implement a common vision and agenda that span diverse interests in the community. The double helix metaphor reminds us of the importance of leadership and support from both inside and outside the school system. To repeat a phrase often heard in Boston, educational reform requires that "all the planets line up." Similarly, building civic capacity requires participation from leaders in key sectors of the community.

Second, successful leadership in developing civic capacity calls for the crafting of a common problem definition that can guide the strategies and actions of both leaders and institutions. Educational problems, indeed any problems, are the product of human perceptions and interpretations. A successful leader shapes those perceptions and interpretations to bring different actors together around a common understanding of the task at hand. Given the diversity of perspectives on the goals and methods of public education, this task can be formidable. In our comparative study, those problem definitions that best served this role were ones that maintained high visibility, received ongoing political sponsorship, and included viable solutions.

And third, successful leadership requires a connection to institutional resources and the ability to ensure that those resources are effectively managed. In building coalitions and support, leaders typically operate at a governance level discussing various policy options. A successful leader, however, also reaches to the programmatic level to connect with tools and resources needed to implement policies and address identified problems. Successful implementation rests upon this connection. Leaders must be able to manage these tools and resources or hire an individual to perform the managerial role.

Our case studies provide several examples where leadership supported the development and activation of civic capacity. In Pittsburgh, the 1980s were years of strong leadership in which civic capacity was extended into the public education arena. Superintendent Richard Wallace was at the center of this effort, but leadership in other sectors also contributed. In Boston, a different model of leadership emerged in which the political and educational worlds have become more interconnected. Mayor Thomas Menino plays a key role here, as does the superintendent of the school system. These examples are elaborated below.

Richard Wallace and Leadership in Pittsburgh

In Pittsburgh in the 1980s, leadership played a central role in expanding civic capacity to include public education. During this decade a number of factors combined to facilitate this critical role for leadership. One major factor was the alignment and long tenure of key leaders in the community, all of whom were supportive of collaborative reform efforts. The alignment and longevity of leaders were indeed striking: Superintendent Wallace served from 1980–1992, Teachers' Union president Al Fondy from 1968–present; School Board president Jake Milliones from 1983–1989; and Allegheny Conference on Community Development executive director Robert Pease from 1968–1990. This continuity allowed an unprecedented sharing of ideas and strategies among this group. Their support for public education was strong and consistent throughout the 1980s. Sustained leadership was critical; as Superintendent Wallace noted, it "takes a decade to institutionalize changes that can produce and sustain positive results for students."[9]

These leaders also were connected to key resources in the institutional environment. Among them, they controlled or had access to school department resources, teachers, and various business resources. The Allegheny Conference on Community Development, in particular, played a key role. Beginning with grant programs through the Education Fund and support for a desegregation plan, the conference provided a "stamp of approval" that facilitated various community connections through foundations and other sources to support the schools.

In addition, the conference applied its model of civic support that included deference to the school department as the lead institution responsible for education in the city. The conference incorporated education into its agenda but relied upon the school department to deliver the product. This model of turning to existing or newly created institutions to implement a civic agenda had been used in housing and other policy arenas. It facilitated a critical connection between leadership at a governance level and implementation through the school department at a programmatic level. For public education, this approach would prove particularly conducive, since it matched the independent nature of Superintendent Wallace's leadership.

Wallace was the linchpin of the reform effort. His leadership skills touched all aspects of a superintendent's role: political, educational, and managerial. Politically, he maintained strong working relationships with actors in the educational field as well as in the outside strand of the double helix. He was well respected by business leaders, who supported the search that led to his appointment as superintendent. He also worked well with other educational leaders, including the presidents of the school board and teachers' union. He recognized the political pressures experienced by other leaders and respected the limits to their actions.

Wallace also was an energetic educational leader and effective manager. Throughout his tenure, he brought a vision to the superintendency that focused on teaching and learning. As he concluded, "There is no substitute for constant reinforcement of a vision and an excellence agenda; it is critical to successful leadership."[10] He carried this vision forward through a number of educational improvements within the school system, including personnel development, basic skills performance, enrollment policies, and discipline. Managing these reform initiatives was another challenge that Wallace met. He closely monitored the implementation of school policies and brought other managers into the school department to assist in this process.

Through these leadership roles, Wallace developed a problem definition that united the community. Crafting a definition began at the outset of his tenure when he hired the University of Pittsburgh to develop a comprehensive assessment of the school system. This assessment became the core of the problem definition. It provided an outline of key strategies to address the educational challenges of the school system, and it raised the overall issue of academic excellence to a position of high visibility on the community's agenda. Wallace and the school board became the sponsors for this definition as they initiated a number of programmatic initiatives to improve teaching and learning in the schools. Based upon the needs assessment, there was a decade of "virtual unanimity among the board on educational matters."[11] This "data-oriented leadership" became a central feature of Pittsburgh's success story.[12]

Political Leadership in Boston

In Boston, the best example of leadership followed a political path featuring Mayor Thomas Menino. Before this leadership could emerge, however, several major hurdles had to be overcome. In the late 1980s and early 1990s, a key stumbling block was turnover among leaders in top institutional positions. Superintendents did not last more than three or four years; the president of the school committee changed frequently; leadership of the Vault also changed every few years; and Mayor Flynn left office in 1993. This environment was very different from what existed in Pittsburgh. Frequent turnover made it difficult for key leaders to establish strong working relationships and to create a common vision of how education fit into the fabric of the community.

In addition, the connection between leaders and institutional resources was fragmented. The fiscal dependence of the school committee on city hall blurred accountability. As noted earlier, elected school committee members criticized city officials for not providing adequate funds, and in turn, the mayor and city council criticized the school committee for not effectively using the resources they did receive. This "blame game" was an annual ritual at budget time. Mayors assumed a low profile in the educational arena, and superintendents and school committee members complained of limited support from the city.

This failure in governance was part of a problem definition that set the stage for proactive leadership. Increasingly, leaders in the community pointed to a fundamentally flawed governance structure as central to the weak performance of the schools. Mayor Raymond Flynn became the key sponsor of this problem definition and raised its visibility. Importantly, this problem definition provided a viable solution: replace the elected school committee with a body appointed by the mayor. Thus, in 1992, after considerable debate, Boston replaced its elected school committee with one appointed by the mayor. The mayor's new appointive authority was congruent with the fiscal authority he already possessed. The mayor, then, assumed a central role in extending civic capacity to public education, which was a very different path than Pittsburgh took. Whereas Pittsburgh extended its civic capacity by maintaining a *separation* between the educational and governmental arenas, Boston achieved the same goal by formalizing an *interdependence* between the two spheres.

This new institutional environment fostered leadership opportunities. Mayor Menino stepped into this setting and took a high-profile position in support of public education. His 1996 state of the city message offered a new problem definition in which the city's renewal depended upon improvement in the schools. Public education, as the mayor said, was the "hub" of the "urban wheel." The mayor appointed a school committee and was instrumental in hiring Thomas Payzant as superintendent. Payzant quickly became an educational leader in the community. He developed a strong working relationship with the mayor, school committee, business leaders, and other community leaders. He established and continually reiterated a positive vision of educational reform that focused on teaching and learning. Payzant also assumed a strong managerial role by reorganizing the school department and pushing forward with various initiatives for improvement.

By 1996 an alignment of leaders was emerging in Boston. The mayor and superintendent were working together, and members of the school committee, who were appointed by the mayor, were also supportive. This alignment was viewed quite favorably by the business community, which had long demanded more accountability in public education. In this new environment, the Boston Compact was renewed, and business leaders gave their support to the Boston Plan for Excellence in the Public Schools and its focus on whole-school change and the Annenberg Foundation grant. The gradual demise of the Vault did not detract from this support. The Boston Plan for Excellence in the Public Schools assumed an important institutional role, and the Private Industry Council continued to support partnerships, academies, summer jobs, and other school-to-career initiatives.

Episodes of Truncated Leadership in Pittsburgh and Boston

Both Pittsburgh and Boston have experienced other episodes in which leadership played an important role, albeit for a more limited period of time and with less sweeping results. In Pittsburgh, the superintendency of Louise Brennen (1992–1997) displayed significant flashes of leadership, although her supportive environment faded midway through her tenure in office. Brennen's leadership style was much different from the directive approach of Wallace. She was more process oriented and a consensus builder who advocated decentralization and greater reliance on school-based management.

Brennen's leadership faltered, however, in the face of rising demands and a changing institutional environment. The restructuring plan sponsored by Brennan, for example, was met with dissension by many parents and educators. In addition, the civic support structure for education was in flux under the newly formed Allegheny Policy Council. The Allegheny Conference Education Fund lost its identity, and the attention provided to education by key leaders in the city decreased compared with previous years. The connection to resources was weakened, and to further complicate the superintendent's task, the school system faced recurring budget deficits throughout her tenure, prompting periodic layoffs and program reductions. By 1995, only three years into her superintendency, Brennen received a two-year terminal contract.

Boston in the early 1980s offers an example in which strong leadership made an important impact on the school system but was not sustained for more than a few years. The formation of the Boston Compact in 1982 can be attributed primarily to the leadership of two individuals, William Edgerly, chairman of the Vault, and Robert Spillane, superintendent of the schools. Edgerly, a business leader in the city, presented public education as a critical link in the economic future of the city. He persuaded other members of the Vault to follow his vision and support the school system through the quid pro quo provisions of the compact. Spillane, hired as superintendent in 1981, was willing to work with the business community and hold the school system accountable for student achievement. He spoke the language of the business community and was a believer in the critical role of broad-based community support for school improvement.

Furthermore, the Private Industry Council was in place to serve as the institutional home for the compact.

This episode of strong leadership, however, did not last long. Spillane left Boston in 1985, only three years after the compact had started. The Boston Compact and the Private Industry Council were at fragile, formative stages and thus relatively weak institutional platforms for leadership. Furthermore, Spillane was replaced by a superintendent more interested in strategic planning processes than in nurturing support from the business community. Edgerly continued to play a key role in the Vault, but he became disenchanted with the school department for failing to meet the goals of the compact. By 1985, court orders and desegregation debates returned to center stage, displacing much of the dialogue that had fostered the compact. This experience left an important legacy—the Boston Compact—but it would be a number of years before key ingredients would come together again in support of civic-minded leadership.

The Lack of Leadership in St. Louis

St. Louis, in contrast to Pittsburgh and Boston, has a pattern of limited and narrowly focused leadership. The city has never had a significant episode in which leaders attempted to expand civic capacity to include public education. A sustained alignment of like-minded leaders has never developed; the connection to institutional resources remains weak in this city's fragmented political structure; and a problem definition calling for broad community support for public education has never received strong sponsorship. The project-specific nature of the urban regime in St. Louis has not been conducive to cross-sector institution building and, in like fashion, has been unsupportive of civic-oriented leadership. A narrow focus on specific development projects has left a legacy of parochialism. The fragmented political system supports this orientation, leaving St. Louis with what one observer described as a "structured anarchy of political influence."[13] This environment is not conducive for leadership.

The St. Louis experience highlights the dependent and embedded nature of leadership. Leaders, to a significant degree, are captives of the institutional environment within which they operate. Existing patterns of politics and policy making typically are rooted in established institutions and the prevailing political culture. In St. Louis, this situation has narrowed the potential for leadership. The typical tendency is to preserve the status quo. The choice of David Mahan as superintendent in 1990, for example, was described by the local newspaper as "safe."[14] Superintendent Hammonds, hired in 1996, has launched several reform initiatives, but progress has been limited because of institutional inertia and past practices.

The recent debate over possible state or mayoral control of the school system is equally instructive. Mayor Harmon's first response to a possible takeover by his office was not very favorable; he said he had "a lot on his plate," but he would do it. The mayor's reluctance is not surprising, given the lack of institutional support for public education in the broader civic arena. This environment is quite different than the situation in Boston, where Mayor Menino can count on significant support from civic partners in his quest to improve the public schools.

Leadership and Civic Capacity

Leadership played a key role in extending civic capacity to include public education. In Pittsburgh and Boston, leaders inside and outside the school system shaped and supported a problem definition in which educational improvement became a goal for the community. At a governance level, leaders from different sectors in the community adopted a common vision to strengthen the schools. At a programmatic level, leaders extended institutional resources and assistance to the school system. Using existing or newly created institutions, capacity was developed to address educational challenges.

Leadership, however, operates within a dynamic world. Leaders are constantly coping with change. Their counterparts in other institutions come and go, for example, and the fiscal environment is subject to fluctuations. Furthermore, the local economy is battered by national and international trends, and demands from residents in the community often change in content and intensity. Leaders cannot control these and many other changes in their surrounding environment, but they must be able to respond. An effective leader accommodates change while striving to achieve established goals. Maintaining a steady course is critical; building civic capacity is a long-term process requiring a number of years. The challenge is to maintain focus on long-term goals while also adjusting to the demands of a dynamic environment.

Meeting this challenge is difficult. Leadership is highly situational and contextual. In all three cities, leaders were limited and constrained by their institutional environments as well as historical precedents. Even the actions of Superintendent Wallace and Mayor Menino were fundamentally shaped by their environments, historical opportunities, and the actions of previous leaders. Wallace's superintendency took advantage of the opening provided by the desegregation settlement and the consensus opinion for a strong superintendent; Menino's leadership built upon the work of Mayor Flynn in establishing an appointed school committee as well as the powers inherent in a strong-mayor form of government. Individual vision and skills are important for success, but it is the larger institutional and historical setting that establishes the context for leadership.

CONCLUSION: CIVIC CAPACITY AND URBAN EDUCATION

We began our inquiry with urban regimes and their focus on economic development. The cross-sector coalitions of a regime support governmental authority in the development and implementation of a civic agenda, which most often highlights the economic development of the city. The creation of coalitions and the implementation of a civic agenda test the civic capacity of a city.

Our attention turned to a single question: Can civic capacity be extended to incorporate public education as a focal concern of an urban regime? Our short answer is yes, although qualifications are needed. In two of our cities—Pittsburgh and Boston—public education achieved this status, but it was not achieved easily, nor was it sustained indefinitely. In St. Louis, weak institutions and limited leadership worked against the development of civic capacity for public education.

Creating civic capacity in support of public education is a true test of leadership and institution building. This test is apparent on both sides of the civic capacity equation. On the civic side, leadership plays a central role in defining a cross-sector, community-wide vision—a civic vision—that includes public education. This task is critical at the governance level in a community. In Boston, Mayor Menino's support for education was critical, and his reference to education as the hub of the urban wheel captured this vision. In Pittsburgh, the Allegheny Conference on Community Development played a civic leadership role when it entered the desegregation battle and defined education as central to the future of the city.

The civic challenge is to replace the individual interests of business leaders, politicians, educators, community activists, and others with collective interests that include support for school reform. A problem definition must be crafted that encourages broad participation to address the key challenges and obstacles to improving public education. As evident in all three cities, this is an ongoing task. Businesses, for example, experience periods of economic change that can pull corporate executives away from community concerns. Furthermore, business leaders are often uncomfortable with a collaborative environment in which decision making is slow and subject to frequent public scrutiny. The leadership task is to develop a "social-purpose politics" in which the advancement of public education is the defining goal of the regime.[15]

On the capacity side of the equation, the key task is to develop resources that can help realize an educational reform agenda. This challenge exists primarily at the programmatic level. Institution building is central. Networks, associations, and formal organizations play a critical role, whether through the strengthening of existing institutions or the creation of new ones. In Boston, the institutional alignment among the school committee, superintendent, and mayor was critical, as was the development of institutions such as the Boston Compact and Private Industry Council. In Pittsburgh, the school department significantly strengthened its capacity, and the Allegheny Conference on Community Development incorporated education into its capacity-building approach to community development. Leadership also played a role in building capacity for school reform. On the inside strand of the double helix, for example, Superintendent Wallace in Pittsburgh provided vision and actions to enhance the professional quality of that city's school department.

Political culture shapes the context for building civic capacity. A city's dominant political orientation creates a predisposition toward different types of discourse, such as community-wide collaboration or individualistic concerns, which in turn impact the development of a civic vision. This orientation also influences the receptivity to capacity building. Pittsburgh offers the most favorable example. The corporatist model that evolved after World War II included a cultural orientation that favored elite collaboration and collective responsibility for addressing community concerns. When education was presented for possible incorporation into the civic agenda, it was viewed through this lens of civic responsibility.

An important lesson from our three-city comparison is the availability of different paths for the incorporation of education into a city's civic capacity. Pittsburgh followed a corporatist path based upon institutional expertise and autonomy, strong and continuous leadership, and civic cooperation. The Allegheny Conference on Community Development set the stage with its broad orientation and support for community development, and Superintendent Wallace provided leadership throughout the 1980s for a school department that established institutional expertise in the educational arena. Importantly, this path was built around a separation of governmental and educational actors. The mayor and city council maintained a distance from school policies and politics, while Wallace and other educators were the recognized experts for school reform. The business community through the conference played a facilitative and supportive role.

Boston followed a political path that offers a quite different model of incorporating education into a city's civic capacity. The business community played a supportive role, but it lacked the strong presence and dominant influence of the Allegheny Conference on Community Development in Pittsburgh. The political traditions and institutional connections in Boston were quite different. A critical issue was to resolve the dysfunctional relationship between city hall and the school system. Granting the mayor authority to appoint members of the school committee became the turning point that integrated the schools into city politics in a fashion consistent with Boston's political orientation. The mayor assumed fiscal and political accountability for the schools and became the key actor to link institutions—city hall, the school department, and the business community—in support of the public schools. Boston's path integrated, rather than separated, political and educational arenas.

Each path is viable, although each faces key challenges. For the corporatist path, a major challenge is to build flexibility and responsiveness into the system. In a corporatist arrangement, institutions and leaders often become fixed around established policies and programs. This fixed or durable character has the positive effect of encouraging the development of expertise and strong institutions, but it can also discourage the consideration of alternative proposals and practices. In Pittsburgh, for example, by 1990 pressures for school-based decision making had mounted, but the school department under Superintendent Wallace was reluctant to embrace this alternative decision-making design. Wallace's leadership style and the school department were more centralized, an orientation quite consistent with the corporatist nature of Pittsburgh's civic regime. Responsiveness did come, but it required new leadership in the superintendent's office and came amidst a disruption in the close institutional links among the schools and business community.

The corporatist path also can insulate reform efforts from the larger political arena. The emphasis on expertise and organizational development can come at the expense of incorporating new leaders and institutions into broad policy discussions. In Pittsburgh, for example, the New Futures initiative stalled largely because key leaders in the community could not agree on a common agenda. Regional problems competed with city problems, and the members of New Futures focused more on their own programmatic initiatives than on broad policy issues. The strengths of Pittsburgh's reform efforts, programmatic expertise and school leadership, neglected the changing dynamic at a governance level. In this instance, the separation of educational reform from the political arena came at a cost.

Leadership plays a central role in addressing the rigidities and insulation of a corporatist system. Strong and bold leadership is needed to make school departments, public-private partnerships, and other organizations more responsive to outside pressures. This task is difficult, and leaders must balance organizational responsibilities with the need to respond to a changing environment. A key test of leadership becomes redesigning an institution to appropriately respond to external demands.

In the political path, as in Boston, the challenge is quite different. Rather than a concern for responsiveness and flexibility, the goal is to build continuity into the system. In particular, continuity in political leadership—principally in the mayor's office—is critical. Mayoral turnover can undermine the support structure for the schools. Boston will face this test when Mayor Menino leaves office. A new mayor might relegate the schools to a lower rank on the priority list, thereby weakening a key link between the schools, city hall, and the larger community. Alternatively, a new mayor might move to replace school reforms with a new set of strategies. New mayors, similar to other leaders, often favor an agenda that bears their own mark. In either case, the school system becomes subject to the political character of city hall.[16]

Strong institutions can play an important role in meeting this challenge. The central task is to construct supportive institutions that will bring continuity to a system despite changes in leadership. And yet, these institutions also must not stifle individual leaders. One strategy is to strengthen network connections between city hall, the school department, and the business community. The Boston Compact and Boston Plan for Excellence in the Public Schools provide some of these connections. The goal is to sustain support for major reform efforts despite changes in key leadership positions.

The lesson for cities that engage in school reform is to look closely at their own constellation of leaders, institutions, and culture. The political path with mayoral control has proved popular in recent years—in Chicago and Cleveland, for example—but each city must pay close attention to its own civic traditions and political character. The task is to build a civic support structure for the schools that is consistent with and draws the best from that city's own style of leadership, institutional matrix, and political culture.

The challenges, however, to incorporating education into the civic capacity of a city are formidable. Successful leadership, in particular, is problematic. Leadership plays a central role in building and activating civic capacity, but it is highly dependent on the institutional environment as well as earlier acts of leadership. Leaders rarely operate from a clean slate. Equally problematic is the task of building and sustaining institutional networks. Network collaboration across sectors raises a diversity of opinions and perspectives on the nature of educational problems and solutions. Creating common ground is an ongoing task. And finally, the overall economic and social problems of central cities remain. Entrenched poverty amidst a continuing decline in blue-collar jobs makes mobility for many urban youth unlikely. Extensive social problems cannot be combated by the schools alone. To build civic capacity within this economic, institutional, and leadership environment is indeed a formidable challenge, but it is one that merits the attention and resources of urban leaders.

Appendix 1
Research Design and
Interview Schedule

The primary research for this book was conducted by the authors as part of an eleven-city study of civic capacity and educational reform. In addition to Pittsburgh, Boston, and St. Louis, the eleven cities included Baltimore, Washington, D.C., Detroit, Atlanta, Denver, Houston, Los Angeles, and San Francisco. Grant support was received from the National Science Foundation, and the project was directed by Clarence Stone from the University of Maryland with the assistance of Jeff Henig from Washington University and Bryan Jones from the University of Washington.

In each city, the research design followed a common strategy: collection of data involving government, economic, community, and education-related matters as well as interviews with individuals involved in government, business, and community affairs. In-person interviews were conducted with forty to fifty individuals in each city. Interviewees were identified from three groupings: general influentials (leaders in business, government, academics, and the general community), community activists (leaders and other individuals involved in community-based organizations) and program specialists (professional educators and staff in educational and social service organizations).

The same set of questions was asked of individuals in each group in each city. In addition, there was some overlap of questions among the three groups. For example, one of the questions reported in Chapter 3—What would enable your city to make a greater effort in education?—was asked of interviewees in all three groups, while the other question—What do you see as the major problems facing your city?—was asked only of general influentials and community advocates. Most questions were open-ended and required the coding of responses before answers could be tabulated and compared across cities.

Appendix 2

Programmatic Effort in Support of Educational Innovation

The following questionnaire was used to rate the levels of educational innovation in each city as of January 1995. Each author "scored" his or her own city using the number at the beginning of each statement. In general, the higher the number (three or four, depending upon the question), the more systemic and comprehensive was the reform effort. Table 3-16 in Chapter 3 summarizes the scores for each city.

A. PRESCHOOL AND EARLY CHILDHOOD DEVELOPMENT

1. Essentially confined to federally funded Head Start, with perhaps a scattering of other unconnected efforts to prepare students for K–12.
2. Essentially confined to federally funded Head Start and state-funded programs such as all-day or four-year-old kindergarten, with perhaps a scattering of other unconnected efforts.
3. In addition to federally and state-funded programs, a significant number of pilot and demonstration projects to reach poverty-level students, and special efforts to meet the health and social needs of preschoolers.
4. Something approximating a comprehensive approach to reach most economically disadvantaged preschool children at a very early age through programs of learning readiness and health and social services, including possibly a follow-through effort in K–4 via Title I funds.

_____ (ranking for city and its school system)

B. POSTSCHOOL TRANSITION; SCHOOL-TO-WORK AND SCHOOL-TO-COLLEGE

1. Little more than standard vocational education and Private Industry Council training, with perhaps a few scattered college-scholarship programs for needy students.
2. Beyond the standard programs, a significant number of school-business and school-based partnerships, with mentor and other efforts to prepare and motivate students for the work world; plus a significant number of scholarship opportunities.
3. Some system-level efforts to include business and other partners in citywide school-to-work and school-to-college transition programs; includes an attempt to assess workforce needs and college readiness.
4. Institutionalized system-level plan, perhaps through a citywide compact involving business and/or other partners, with a comprehensive approach to encouraging and supporting needy students to go on to college or to channeling them into the job market by providing apprenticeships and actual jobs.
    _____ (ranking for city and its school system)

C. PARENTAL INVOLVEMENT IN THE EDUCATION OF THEIR OWN CHILDREN

Explanation—Aside from participation in organizations such as the PTA or participation in planning and site-level decision making (covered separately below), parents can be encouraged to be involved in their children's school in various ways: by being in communication with teachers, counselors, and others at the school; by monitoring their children's school performance and homework; by encouraging their children to read and limiting TV watching; and by helping with schoolwork much as a tutor would. Options include:

1. Little more than scattered efforts initiated by a few principals and teachers to encourage closer parent contact.
2. A small but significant number of pilot and demonstration projects that call for systematic efforts to invite parents into schools at the beginning of the year with follow-ups; by sending out newsletters to parents; by establishing a hot line for parents to call with questions about homework or other school activities and issues; or by establishing special classes for parents to refresh or improve their own personal and academic skills for working with their children.
3. A large number of the kinds of demonstration and pilot projects described above.
4. A substantial move toward establishing a system-wide program of parent involvement along the lines described above.
    _____ (ranking for city and its school system)

D. ADMINISTRATIVE DECENTRALIZATION AND SBM (SITE-BASED MANAGEMENT)

Explanation—Taking the position that local context is important, reformers have embraced the view that micromanaging from the top and central rule-making are inappropriate on many matters. In its strongest form (SBM), decentralization has the aim of shifting to the building level most of the decisions about such matters as budget priorities, control of uses of the building, class scheduling and curriculum, staff organization, and even professional staff development. In the reformer's ideal, the main task of the central administration would be that of sponsoring and evaluating innovations, enhancing school level capacity, and developing/refining and applying good measures of outcome. There is a range of possibilities:

1. Decentralization is mostly talk; the central administration continues to set procedures, promulgate rules, and control spending in some detail.
2. The school system has made some modest moves; for example, by providing a number of schools with autonomy through becoming pilots or negotiating a relaxation of rules and regulations.
3. Some administrative decentralization is available for all schools, although budget and personnel authority are limited. The extent to which schools take advantage of decentralization is uneven.
4. The district is embarked on a systematic and system-wide move toward genuine decentralization, which includes some far-reaching steps such as relaxation of union contract provisions and training and development for teachers and principals to take on a significant decision-making role in budgeting, curriculum, and personnel.
   _____ (ranking for city and its school system)

E. PARENTAL PARTICIPATION IN SCHOOL GOVERNANCE

Explanation—SBM also includes the participation of parents and perhaps other community representatives in the decision process at the school level. It is not parental control but parental inclusion in planning and priority setting. Reform calls for official channels of participation. The terminology varies: school-improvement teams, local school councils, school-site councils, and so forth. Practice also varies:

1. Parental participation in school governance is scant. Even if there is an official channel, it is mostly pro forma or concerned with trivial issues such as decorating the front entrance.

2. Parental participation is uneven. In some schools, there is genuine participation in significant decisions, either due to energetic parents or selective encouragement, but there is no system-wide effort.
3. The school system has developed pilot programs to strengthen parental participation and has made some selective moves, but has not yet developed a system-wide program.
4. The system is embarked on a district-wide program to make parental participation real that includes training or development for parents. There is a special effort to see that low-income parents are included, and that principals encourage extensive parental participation and are held accountable for their actions.
   _____ (ranking for city and its school system)

F. SCHOOL-LINKED SERVICES; SCHOOL AS A COMMUNITY CENTER FOR MULTIPLE SERVICES

Explanation—Part of the reform initiative, seeking to lessen the isolation of the school from the community, is a set of proposals to couple a variety of social, health, and community services to schools: health programs, day care and after-school care, counseling and family services, and adult education, among others. These may be on the school site or off-site but still linked to the schools. The range includes:

1. Very little beyond the traditional school nurse.
2. A variety of pilot or specially funded projects, targeted at some of the city's neediest population.
3. A broad collaboration between the school system and various public and nonprofit agencies to move toward institutionalized, comprehensive, integrated, and school-linked services, with special attention to the poorest areas of the city.
   _____ (ranking for city and its school system)

G. EVALUATION RESEARCH AND ITS USE

1. Mandated state and/or federal data collection, plus occasional reports on topics of special interest; reports may be done under contract with external agents.
2. A variety of reports and evaluations, especially of pilot projects, and an attempt to collect more rigorous data. Some reports may be done under contract with external agents.
3. A systematic effort to study programs and practices in order to develop baseline data, address needs, identify problems, provide findings, and make evaluations available for use by a variety of actors.
   _____ (ranking for city and its school system)

H. CHOICE PROGRAMS

1. There are a few magnet schools, but most students are assigned to schools based on residence and racial balance.
2. There are a variety of magnet programs and "theme" schools that parents can select, and there are some transfer opportunities. But dissemination of information about the programs is inconsistent, and the level of transfers is low.
3. The system may have a "controlled choice" plan to avoid racial concentration. Federal court orders may include suburban schools as part of the choice available to students.
4. The system has embraced or is moving toward a district-wide program of choice, which includes system efforts to see that parents are provided information about the schools and the special features they have. Vouchers and abolishment of assigned schools may or may not be part of a choice plan.
   _____ (ranking for city and its school system)

I. PRIVATIZATION

Explanation—Can occur in a variety of forms, from transportation and cafeteria service to school management. Privatization can be quite narrow, as in specific services such as tutoring students with reading handicaps; or can cover only selected schools; or could cover a broad service.

1. Only a few narrowly targeted services, such as special education programs, are offered by private companies.
2. There is significant privatization of one or two broad services, such as transportation and cafeteria workers, or there is a significant set of schools within the system that have a variety of privatized services, including the management of some schools.
3. Privatization is widespread throughout the system and includes some management as well as various services.
   _____ (ranking for city and its school system)

J. PEDAGOGY AND ASSESSMENT PRACTICES

Explanation—Many reformers talk about the need to promote active learning and shift away from exclusive reliance on "teacher talk." They argue that today's world calls for problem-solving skills and higher level thinking. Accountability can be served by multiple forms of testing and assessment so long as they focus on desired outcomes. Though the term is a red flag to the religious right, *outcome-based testing* is the phrase often used. One form of this approach, especially encouraged by Sizer's Coalition of Essential Schools, is to make use of *portfolios and exhibitions*—collections of projects and documented activities that show student proficiency in a variety of skills. Three alternative patterns follow:

1. With the exception of scattered classrooms, the system relies on standard forms of testing and assessment; it is making no move toward varied forms of assessment.
2. There are pilot schools (e.g., Coalition of Essential Schools) making use of performance-based testing, including some reliance on portfolios.
3. Performance-based testing, including some reliance on portfolios, currently exists or is in the process of becoming system-wide practice, though some conventional testing may be retained for some purposes.
   _____ (ranking for city and its school system)

Notes

CHAPTER 1. CITIES, SCHOOLS, AND CIVIC CAPACITY

1. Kenneth Jackson, *Crabgrass Frontier: The Suburbanization of the United States* (New York: Oxford University Press, 1985), 4.

2. Ibid., 87–96.

3. U.S. Department of Housing and Urban Development, *The State of the Cities* (Washington, D.C.: U.S. Department of Housing and Urban Development, 1997), 13.

4. Dennis R. Judd and Todd Swanstrom, *City Politics: Private Power and Public Policy* (New York: HarperCollins, 1994), 158.

5. Barry Bluestone and Bennett Harrison, *The Deindustrialization of America* (New York: Basic Books, 1982), 6.

6. Ibid., 35.

7. John Kasarda, "Urban Change and Minority Opportunities," in *The New Urban Reality,* ed. P. Peterson (Washington, D.C.: Brookings Institution, 1985), 44.

8. A thoroughgoing account of this process can be found in Bluestone and Harrison, *The Deindustrialization of America.*

9. Judd and Swanstrom, *City Politics,* 341.

10. Paul E. Peterson, "The Urban Underclass and the Poverty Paradox," in *The Urban Underclass,* ed. C. Jencks and P. Peterson (Washington, D.C.: Brookings Institution, 1991), 21. For some social scientists and politicians, the term "underclass" has taken on political overtones to demarcate a group of individuals and families totally removed from mainstream culture. The authors of this book are not adopting that position here; our focus is on the conditions and consequences of chronic unemployment in central cities.

11. Christopher Jencks, "Is the Underclass Growing?" in *The Urban Underclass,* 30.

12. William Julius Wilson, *The Truly Disadvantaged* (Chicago: University of Chicago Press, 1987), 7.

13. Wilson, *Truly Disadvantaged,* 20.

14. Jencks, "Is the Underclass Growing?" in *The Urban Underclass,* 53.

15. William Julius Wilson, *When Work Disappears: The World of the New Urban Poor* (New York: Alfred A. Knopf, 1996), xvi.

16. Ibid., 19.

17. Ibid., 21.

18. Ibid., 24.

19. U.S. Department of Education, National Center for Education Statistics, *The Condition of Education, 1993* (Washington, D.C.: U.S. Department of Education, 1993), 116; U.S. Department of Commerce, Bureau of the Census, *1990 Census of Population, Social and Economic Characteristics: Urbanized Areas, Section 1* (Washington, D.C.: Government Printing Office, 1990), pub. no. 1990-CP-2-1C, 70.

20. Annie E. Casey Foundation, *City Kids Count: Data on the Well-being of Children in Large Cities* (Baltimore: Annie E. Casey Foundation, 1997), 5.

21. Distressed neighborhoods are defined as census tracts with all of the following characteristics: high poverty rate (above 24.7%); high percentage of female-headed families (above 36.8%); high percentage of males unattached to the labor force (above 45.4%); high percentage of families receiving public assistance (above 17.6%). See Annie E. Casey Foundation, *City Kids Count,* 115.

22. Ibid., 5

23. Ibid.

24. Council of the Great City Schools, *National Urban Education Goals: 1992–93 Indicators Report* (Washington, D.C.: Council of the Great City Schools, 1994).

25. Virginia Edwards, ed., *Quality Counts '98: The Urban Challenge and Public Education in the 50 States* (Washington D.C.: *Education Week* and Pew Charitable Trusts, 1998), 14.

26. Harvey Kantor and Barbara Brengel, "Urban Education and the 'Truly Disadvantaged': The Historical Roots of the Contemporary Crisis," in *The "Underclass" Debate,* ed. M. Katz (Princeton, N.J.: Princeton University Press, 1993), 367.

27. Council of the Great City Schools, "Signs of Progress: Preliminary Evidence of Urban School Comeback," *Urban Indicator* 4, no. 2 (Washington, D.C.: Council of the Great City Schools, 1998).

28. Charles Kerchner, "Education as a City's Basic Industry," *Education and Urban Society* 29, no. 4 (August 1997): 429.

29. Clarence N. Stone, "Paradigms, Power, and Urban Leadership," in *Leadership and Politics,* ed. B. Jones (Lawrence: University Press of Kansas, 1989), 148.

30. Floyd Hunter, *Community Power Structure* (Chapel Hill, N.C.: University of North Carolina Press, 1953).

31. Robert A. Dahl, *Who Governs?* (New Haven, Conn.: Yale University Press, 1961).

32. Harvey L. Molotch, "The City as a Growth Machine: Toward a Political Economy of Place," *American Journal of Sociology* 82, no. 2 (1976): 310.

33. John R. Logan and Harvey L. Molotch, *Urban Fortunes: The Political Economy of Place* (Berkeley: University of California Press, 1987).

34. Paul E. Peterson, *City Limits* (Chicago: University of Chicago Press, 1981).

35. See Susan Fainstein, R. C. Hill, D. Judd, and M. Smith, eds., *Restructuring the City: The Political Economy of Urban Development* (New York: Longman, 1986), or Todd Swanstrom, *The Crisis of Growth Politics: Cleveland, Kucinich, and the Challenge of Urban Populism* (Philadelphia: Temple University Press, 1985).

36. John H. Mollenkopf, *The Contested City* (Princeton, N.J.: Princeton University Press, 1983).

37. Stephen L. Elkin, *City and Regime in the American Republic* (Chicago: University of Chicago Press, 1987), 7–8.

38. Ibid., 8.

39. Clarence N. Stone, *Regime Politics: Governing Atlanta, 1946–1988* (Lawrence: University Press of Kansas, 1989), 3.

40. Ibid., 5.

41. Ibid., 229.

42. Clarence N. Stone, "Summing Up: Urban Regimes, Development Policy, and Political Arrangements," in *The Politics of Urban Development*, ed. C. Stone and H. Sanders (Lawrence: University Press of Kansas, 1987), 269–90.

43. Stone, *Regime Politics,* 17, 21.

44. Robyne S. Turner, "Growth Politics and Downtown Development: The Economic Imperative in Sunbelt Cities," *Urban Affairs Quarterly* 28 (September 1992): 3–21.

45. Barbara Ferman, *Challenging the Growth Machine: Neighborhood Politics in Chicago and Pittsburgh* (Lawrence: University Press of Kansas, 1996), 4.

46. Stone, *Regime Politics,* 9.

47. Bryan D. Jones and Lynn W. Bachelor, *The Sustaining Hand: Community Leadership and Corporate Power,* 2d ed., rev. (Lawrence: University Press of Kansas, 1993), 11–13.

48. Ibid., 13.

49. Kenneth A. Sirotnik, "Improving Urban Schools in the Age of 'Restructuring,'" *Education and Urban Society* (May 1991): 264.

50. Paul T. Hill, Arthur E. Wise, and Leslie Shapiro, *Educational Progress: Cities Mobilize to Improve Their Schools* (Santa Monica, Calif.: Rand, 1989), 11.

51. David Tyack and Larry Cuban, *Tinkering Toward Utopia: A Century of Public School Reform* (Cambridge, Mass.: Harvard University Press, 1995).

52. Maurice R. Berube, *American School Reform: Progressive, Equity, and Excellence Movements, 1883–1993* (Westport, Conn.: Praeger, 1994).

53. Ernest Boyer, *High School* (New York: Harper and Row, 1983); James P. Comer, *School Power* (New York: Free Press, 1980); John Goodlad, *A Place Called School* (New York: McGraw-Hill, 1984); Arthur Powell, Eleanor Farrar, and David Cohen, *The Shopping Mall High School* (Boston: Houghton Mifflin, 1985); and Theodore R. Sizer, *Horace's Compromise* (Boston: Houghton Mifflin, 1984).

54. Diane Ravitch, *The Troubled Crusade: American Education 1945–1980* (New York: Basic Books, 1983), and Chester E. Finn Jr., *We Must Take Charge: Our Schools and Our Future* (New York: Free Press, 1991).

55. Finn, *We Must Take Charge,* xv, 19.

56. National Commission on Excellence in Education, *A Nation at Risk: The Imperative of Educational Reform* (Washington, D.C.: Government Printing Office, 1983).

57. Larry Cuban, "Reforming Again, Again, and Again," *Education Researcher* (January 1990): 9.

58. Michael G. Fullan with Suzanne Stiegelbauer, *The New Meaning of Educational Change,* 2d ed. (New York: Teachers College Press, 1991), 265–70.

59. William A. Firestone et al., *Education Reform from 1983–1990: State Action*

and District Response (New Brunswick, N.J.: Consortium for Policy Research in Education, 1991), 38.

60. Joseph Murphy and Philip Hallinger, *Restructuring Schooling: Learning from Ongoing Efforts* (Newbury Park, Calif.: Corwin Press, 1993), 3.

61. Murphy and Hallinger, *Restructuring Schooling,* 8.

62. John E. Chubb and Terry M. Moe, *Politics, Markets, and American Schools* (Washington, D.C.: Brookings Institution, 1990).

63. Jeffrey R. Henig, *Rethinking School Choice: Limits on the Market Metaphor* (Princeton, N.J.: Princeton University Press, 1994), 200–201.

64. Jeffrey R. Henig, "Civic Capacity and the Problem of Ephemeral Education Reform" (paper presented at the annual meeting of the Urban Affairs Association, Portland, Oregon, May 3–6 1995), 1.

65. Andrew Porter et al., "Reforming the Curriculum: Will Empowerment Policies Replace Control?" in *The Politics of Curriculum and Testing,* ed. S. Fuhrman and B. Malen (New York: Falmer Press, 1991), 11–36.

66. Douglas Archbald and F. M. Newmann, *Beyond Standardized Testing: Assessing Authentic Achievement in the Secondary School* (Reston, Va.: National Association of Secondary School Principals, n.d.).

67. William Cooley and William Bickel, *Decision-Oriented Educational Research* (Boston: Kluwer-Nijhoff, 1986).

68. Jane Hannaway and Martin Carnoy, Preface, in *Decentralization and School Improvement: Can We Fulfill the Promise?* ed. J. Hannaway and M. Carnoy (San Francisco: Jossey-Bass, 1993).

69. Council of the Great City Schools, *National Urban Education Goals,* 93.

70. Betty Malen et al., "What Do We Know About School-Based Management? A Case Study of the Literature—A Call for Research," in *Choice and Control in American Education 2: The Practice of Choice, Decentralization, and School Restructuring,* ed. W. Clune and J. Witte (New York: Falmer Press, 1990), 289–342.

71. Hans Weiler, "Control Versus Legitimation: The Politics of Ambivalence," in *Decentralization and School Improvement,* 69.

72. Lisabeth Schorr, *Within Our Reach: Breaking the Cycle of Disadvantage* (New York: Doubleday, 1988), xxii.

73. Robert L. Crowson and William Lowe Boyd, "Structures and Strategies: Toward an Understanding of Alternative Models for Coordinated Children's Services," in *Coordination Among Schools, Families, and Communities: Prospects for Educational Reform,* ed. J. Cibulka and W. Kritek (Albany: State University of New York Press, 1996), 137–69.

74. "Survey Shows School-Based Health Centers Increasing," *Urban Educator* 6, no. 3 (April 1997): 8.

75. Crowson and Boyd, "Structures and Strategies," in *Coordination Among Schools, Families, and Communities,* 142.

76. John C. Weidman, "Facilitating the Transition from School to Work," in *Investing in U.S. Schools: Directions for Educational Policy,* ed. B. Jones and K. Borman (Norwood, N.J.: Ablex, 1994), 37–49.

77. Edwards, *Quality Counts '98,* 6.

78. Terrel H. Bell, cited by Lisbeth B. Schorr, *Within Our Reach: Breaking the Cycle of Disadvantage* (New York: Doubleday, 1988), 220.

79. Kantor and Brengel, "Urban Education and the 'Truly Disadvantaged,'" in *The "Underclass" Debate*, 367.

80. Frederick Hess, "Initiation Without Implementation: Policy Churn and the Plight of Urban School Reform" (paper presented at the Conference on Rethinking School Governance at the Kennedy School of Government, Harvard University, 1997), 3.

81. Henig, "Civic Capacity," 14–15.

82. Clarence N. Stone, "The Politics of Urban School Reform: Civic Capacity, Social Capital, and the Intergroup Context" (paper presented at the annual meeting of the American Political Science Association, San Francisco, August 29–September 1, 1996), 8.

83. Wilbur Rich, *Black Mayors and School Politics* (New York: Garland Publishing, 1996), 5.

84. Ibid.

85. Clarence N. Stone, "Introduction: Urban Education in a Political Context," in *Changing Urban Education*, ed. C. Stone (Lawrence: University Press of Kansas, 1998).

86. Tyack and Cuban, *Tinkering Toward Utopia*, 109.

87. Council of the Great City Schools, "A Marshall Plan for Urban Schools: A Framework for Improving America's Urban Public Schools" (Washington, D.C.: Council of the Great City Schools, 1997).

88. Michael Casserly, "From the Director . . . ," *Urban Educator* 6:6 (August 1997): 3.

89. Council of the Great City Schools, *National Urban Education Goals*, xvii.

90. James Comer, *Waiting for a Miracle* (New York: Penguin Putnam, 1997).

91. David C. Berliner and Bruce Biddle, *The Manufactured Crisis: Myths, Fraud, and the Attack on America's Public Schools* (Reading, Mass.: Addison-Wesley, 1995).

92. Philip Meranto, *School Politics in the Metropolis* (Columbus, Ohio: Charles E. Merrill, 1970), 5.

93. James G. Cibulka, "The Reform and Survival of American Public Schools," in *The Politics of Education and the New Institutionalism: Reinventing the American School*, ed. R. Crowson, W. Boyd, and H. Mawhinney (Washington, D.C.: Falmer Press, 1996), 12.

94. Richard C. Hunter, "The Mayor Versus the School Superintendent: Political Incursions into Metropolitan School Politics," *Education and Urban Society* 29, no. 2 (February 1997): 217–32.

95. David B. Tyack, *The One Best System: A History of American Urban Education* (Cambridge, Mass.: Harvard University Press, 1974), 176.

96. Edwards, *Quality Counts '98*, 23.

97. Erik Hanushek, *Making Schools Work: Improving Performance and Controlling Costs* (Washington, D.C.: Brookings Institution, 1994).

98. Karl Weick, "Administering Education in Loosely Coupled Schools," *Phi Delta Kappan* 63, no. 10 (June 1982): 673–76. Also see Richard McAdams, "A Systems Approach to School Reform," *Phi Delta Kappan* 79, no. 2 (October 1997): 138–42.

99. Richard Elmore, *Steady Work: Policy, Practice, and the Reform of American Education* (Santa Monica, Calif.: Rand, 1988).

100. Weick, "Administring Education in Loosely Coupled Schools," 675.

101. Clarence N. Stone, "Field Research Guide for the Civic Capacity and Urban Education Project," September 1993, 5.

102. Annenberg Institute for School Reform, *Reasons for Hope, Voices for Change: A Report of the Annenberg Institute on Public Engagement for Public Education* (Providence, R.I.: Annenberg Institute for School Reform, 1998), 16.

CHAPTER 2. BUILDING CIVIC CAPACITY: INSTITUTIONS AND LEADERSHIP

1. Quoted in Derrick Jackson, "Energized about education," *Boston Globe,* November 1, 1996, A27; emphasis added.
2. W. Richard Scott, *Institutions and Organizations* (Thousand Oaks, Calif.: Sage, 1995), 33.
3. James March and Johan Olsen, *Rediscovering Institutions: The Organizational Base of Politics* (New York: Free Press, 1989), 22.
4. March and Olsen, *Rediscovering Institutions,* 38.
5. Robert Putnam, *Making Democracy Work: Civic Traditions in Modern Italy* (Princeton, N.J. : Princeton University Press, 1993), 8.
6. Scott, *Institutions and Organizations,* 24–32.
7. Sven Steinmo, Kathleen Thelen, and Frank Longstreth, *Structuring Politics: Historical Institutionalism in Comparative Analysis* (New York: Cambridge University Press, 1992). Also see Scott, *Institutions and Organizations.*
8. Grahame Thompson, Jennifer Frances, Rosalind Levacic, and Jeremy Mitchell, Introduction, in *Markets, Hierarchies, and Networks: The Coordination of Social Life,* ed. Thompson, Frances, Levacic, and Mitchell (London: Sage, 1991), 14.
9. David Knoke and James Kuklinski, *Network Analysis* (Newbury Park, Calif.: Sage, 1982), 13. See David Knoke, *Political Networks: The Structural Perspective* (New York: Cambridge University Press, 1990).
10. Leon Lindberg, John Campbell, and J. Rogers Hollingsworth, "Economic Governance and the Analysis of Structural Change in the American Economy," in *Governance of the American Economy,* ed. Campbell, Hollingsworth, and Lindberg (New York: Cambridge University Press, 1991), 25.
11. Linda Jacobson, "New alliance endeavors to put schools first," *Education Week,* October 1, 1997, 21.
12. Ibid.
13. In the theoretical literature, the term "hierarchy" often is used instead of formal organizations. We prefer, however, to use the term "formal organization" and reserve the use of hierarchy to describe a particular way of organizing authority among a group of individuals. Formal organizations are often structured in a hierarchical fashion, but that is not always the case. In education, for example, most schools are structured hierarchically, with principals at the top of the organization chart, but some schools have experimented with authority structures in which teachers collectively operate the school. Both are formal organizations, but only the first is structured in a hierarchical fashion.
14. March and Olsen, *Rediscovering Institutions,* 18.
15. Charles Lindblom, "The Market as a Prison," *Journal of Politics* 44 (1982): 324–36.
16. Barbara Ferman, *Challenging the Growth Machine: Neighborhood Politics in Chicago and Pittsburgh* (Lawrence: University Press of Kansas, 1996), 8.
17. James Q. Wilson, *Bureaucracy* (New York: Basic Books, 1989), 302.
18. For a general discussion of this topic, see Daniel Elazar, *The American Mosaic: The Impact of Space, Time, and Culture on American Politics* (Boulder, Colo.: Westview Press, 1994). See also Daniel Elazar, *American Federalism: A View from the States,* 2d ed. (New York: Thomas Crowell, 1972).

19. Margaret Weir, "Ideas and the Politics of Bounded Innovation," in *Structuring Politics,* 191.

20. Harold Wolman, "Local Government Institutions and Democratic Governance," in *Theories of Urban Politics,* ed. D. Judge, G. Stoker, and H. Wolman (Thousand Oaks, Calif.: Sage, 1995).

21. Daniel Elazar, *Building Cities in America* (Lanham, Md.: Hamilton Press, 1987), 66.

22. Putnam, *Making Democracy Work,* 182.

23. Joseph Rost, *Leadership for the Twenty-First Century* (New York: Praeger, 1991).

24. James MacGregor Burns, *Leadership* (New York: Harper and Row, 1978), 19. For a similar definition, see Rost, *Leadership for the Twenty-First Century,* 102.

25. David Rochefort and Roger Cobb, eds., *The Politics of Problem Definition* (Lawrence: University Press of Kansas, 1994), 15.

26. Jean Blondel, *Political Leadership: Towards a General Analysis* (Beverly Hills, Calif.: Sage, 1987), 25.

27. Thomas Cronin, "Reflections on Leadership," in *Contemporary Issues in Leadership,* 3d ed., ed. W. Rosenbach and R. Taylor (San Francisco: Westview Press, 1993), 12.

28. Jameson Doig and Erwin Hargrove, "Leadership and Political Analysis," in *Leadership and Innovation: A Biographical Perspective on Entrepreneurs in Government,* ed. Doig and Hargrove (Baltimore: Johns Hopkins University Press, 1987).

29. Blondel, *Political Leadership,* 30.

30. Burns, *Leadership,* 126.

31. See Chapter 1 and Karl Wieck, "Educational Organizations as Loosely Coupled Systems," *Administrative Science Quarterly* 21, no.1 (1976): 1–18.

32. Benjamin Levin and J. Anthony Riffel, *Schools and the Changing World: Struggling Toward the Future* (Washington, D.C.: Falmer Press, 1997).

33. Carol Livingston, *Teachers as Leaders: Evolving Roles* (Washington, D.C.: National Education Association, 1992).

34. Samuel Krug, "Leadership Craft and the Crafting of School Leaders," in *Phi Delta Kappan* (November 1993): 240–44.

35. Twentieth Century Fund, *Report of the Twentieth Century Fund Task Force on School Governance* (New York: Twentieth Century Fund Press, 1992).

36. Kenneth Wong, Robert Breeben, Laurence Lynn, and Gail Sunderman, *Integrated Governance as a Reform Strategy in the Chicago Public Schools: A Report on System-wide School Governance Reform* (Chicago: University of Chicago Department of Education, 1997), 22.

37. M. William Konnert and John J. Augenstein, *The Superintendency in the Nineties: What Superintendents and Board Members Need to Know* (Lancaster, Pa.: Technomic, 1990), 134.

38. Susan Moore Johnson, *Leading to Change: The Challenge of the New Superintendency* (San Francisco: Jossey-Bass, 1996). Larry Cuban similarly outlined three components to the leadership role of the superintendent: instructional, management, and political. See Cuban, *The Managerial Imperative and the Practice of Leadership in Schools* (Albany: State University of New York Press, 1988).

39. Larry Cuban, "The District Superintendent and the Restructuring of Schools: A Realistic Appraisal," in *Schooling for Tomorrow: Directing Reforms to Issues That Count,* ed. T. Sergiovanni and J. Moore (Boston: Allyn and Bacon, 1989), 258.

40. Ibid., 264.

41. Sharon Rallis, "Professional Teachers and Restructured Schools: Leadership Challenges," in *Educational Leadership and Changing Contexts of Families, Communities, and Schools,* ed. B. Mitchell and L. Cunningham (Chicago: University of Chicago Press, 1990), 186.

42. Steve Farkas, *Divided Within, Besieged Without: The Politics of Education in Four American School Districts* (New York: Public Agenda Foundation, 1993), v, 1.

43. Johnson, *Leading to Change,* 166.

44. Charles Mathesian, "Handing the Schools to City Hall," *Governing* (October 1996): 36–40; Richard Hunter, "The Mayor Versus the School Superintendent: Political Incursions into Metropolitan School Politics," *Education and Urban Society* 29, no. 2 (February 1997): 217–32.

45. Johnson, *Leading to Change,* 168.

46. Michael Fullan, *The New Meaning of Educational Change,* 2d ed. (New York: Teachers College Press, 1991), 210.

47. Annenberg Institute for School Reform, *Reasons for Hope, Voices for Change: A Report of the Annenberg Institute on Public Engagement for Public Education* (Providence, R.I.: Annenberg Institute for School Reform, 1998), 55.

48. Barbara Jackson, *Balancing Act: The Political Role of the Urban School Superintendent* (Washington, D.C.: Joint Center for Political and Economic Studies, 1995), 2.

49. Clarence N. Stone, "Paradigms, Power, and Urban Leadership," in *Leadership and Politics,* ed. B. Jones (Lawrence: University Press of Kansas, 1989), 154.

50. Bryan D. Jones and Lynn W. Bachelor, *The Sustaining Hand: Community Leadership and Corporate Power,* 2d ed. (Lawrence: University Press of Kansas, 1993), 19.

51. Barbara Ferman, *Governing the Ungovernable City: Political Skill, Leadership, and the Modern Mayor* (Philadelphia: Temple University Press, 1985).

52. Ibid., 202.

53. Clarence N. Stone, "Political Leadership in Urban Politics," in *Theories of Urban Politics,* ed. D. Judge, G. Stoker, and H. Wolman (Thousand Oaks, Calif.: Sage, 1995), 110.

54. John Mollenkopf, *The Contested City* (Princeton, N.J: Princeton University Press, 1983), 6.

55. Howard Gardner, *Leading Minds: An Anatomy of Leadership* (New York: Basic Books, 1995), 36.

56. Burns, *Leadership,* 405.

57. Ibid., 454.

CHAPTER 3. THE SETTING: PITTSBURGH, BOSTON, AND ST. LOUIS

1. In the *1963 Census of Services,* which was the source for these data in the *County and City Data Book,* only a selected group of services was included. Omitted from this census were establishments and employment in medical care and other health services, legal services, education, museums, and nonprofits. In the *1982* and *1992 Census of Services,* however, these areas were included. Caution should be used, then, in comparing the 1963 data with subsequent years. In the case of Boston, particularly, it is likely that the 1963 data understate the presence of services in that city.

2. Theodore Hershberg, "The case for new standards in education," *Education Week,* December 10, 1997, 52.

3. Jack Beatty, *The Rascal King: The Life and Times of James Michael Curley* (Reading, Mass.: Addison-Wesley, 1992).

4. Roy Lubove, *Twentieth-Century Pittsburgh: Government, Business, and Environmental Change* (New York: John Wiley and Sons, 1969).

5. Lana Stein, *Holding Bureaucrats Accountable: Politicians and Professionals in St. Louis* (Tuscaloosa: University of Alabama Press, 1991).

6. Our analysis of problem perceptions in each city is based on interviews conducted by the authors. In each city approximately forty-five individuals involved in city politics, education, business, and the broader community were interviewed using a survey instrument that included a number of common questions. These questions probed interviewees' perceptions of and experiences with educational and political change in each city. See appendix 1 for an overview of the project design.

CHAPTER 4. PITTSBURGH'S PUBLIC SCHOOLS: A FRAGILE BALANCE OF LEADERSHIP AND INSTITUTION BUILDING

1. Bill Zlatos, "Wallace wins national education award," *Pittsburgh Press,* December 5, 1990.

2. Paul T. Hill, Arthur E. Wise, and Leslie Shapiro, *Educational Progress: Cities Mobilize to Improve Their Schools* (Santa Monica, Calif.: Rand, 1989), 11.

3. Donald Stevens Jr., "The Role of Nonprofit Corporations in Urban Development: A Case Study of ACTION-Housing, Inc. of Pittsburgh" (Ph.D. diss., Carnegie-Mellon University, 1987), 24.

4. Roy Lubove, *Twentieth-Century Pittsburgh: Government, Business, and Environmental Change,* vol. 1 (Pittsburgh: University of Pittsburgh Press, 1995); John F. Bauman and Margaret Spratt, "Civic Leaders and Environmental Reform: The Pittsburgh Survey and Urban Planning," in *Pittsburgh Surveyed: Social Science and Social Reform in the Early Twentieth Century,* ed. M. Greenwald and M. Anderson (Pittsburgh: University of Pittsburgh Press, 1996).

5. Michael Weber, "Rebuilding a City: The Pittsburgh Model," *in Snowbelt Cities: Metropolitan Politics in the Northeast and Midwest Since World War II,* ed. R. Bernard (Bloomington: Indiana University Press, 1990), 231.

6. Lubove, *Twentieth-Century Pittsburgh,* vol. 1, chap. 6.

7. Weber, "Rebuilding a City," in *Snowbelt Cities,* 231.

8. Edward K. Muller, "Historical Aspects of Regional Structural Change in the Pittsburgh Region," in *Regional Structural Change and Industrial Policy in International Perspective,* ed. J. Hesse (Baden-Baden, Germany: Auflage, 1988), 38.

9. Barbara Ferman, *Challenging the Growth Machine: Neighborhood Politics in Chicago and Pittsburgh* (Lawrence: University Press of Kansas, 1996), 49.

10. Roy Lubove, *Twentieth-Century Pittsburgh: The Post Steel Era,* vol. 2 (Pittsburgh: University of Pittsburgh Press, 1996), 73.

11. "Community Ties, Income Affect Level of Giving in 50 Big Cities,"*Chronicle of Philanthropy* (February 22, 1994), 51–68.

12. Alberta M. Sbragia, "Pittsburgh's 'Third Way': The Nonprofit Sector as a Key

to Urban Regeneration," in *Leadership and Urban Regeneration*, ed. D. Judd and M. Parkinson (Newbury Park, Calif.: Sage, 1990).

13. *Allegheny Conference on Community Development: 1983 Report* (Pittsburgh: Allegheny Conference on Community Development, 1984), 2.

14. Ferman, *Challenging the Growth Machine,* 54.

15. Charles Taylor Kerchner, "Pittsburgh: Reform in a Well-Managed Public Bureaucracy," in *A Union of Professionals: Labor Relations and Educational Reform,* ed. C. Kerchner and J. Koppich (New York: Teachers College Press), 45.

16. Richard D. Gutkind, "Desegregation of Pittsburgh Public Schools, 1968–1980" (Ph.D. diss., University of Pittsburgh, 1983).

17. Ibid., 63–64.

18. Both Pease and Bergholz had personal ties to education. Pease's father and later his son were public school teachers, and David Bergholz's wife was a professional educator.

19. Valerie S. Lies and David Bergholz, "The Public Education Fund," in *American Business and the Public School: Case Studies of Corporate Involvement in Public Education,* ed. M. Levine and R. Trachtman (New York: Teachers College Press, 1988), 78.

20. *Ten-Year Report: Allegheny Conference Education Fund* (Pittsburgh: Allegheny Conference on Community Development, 1988). Pease credits Bergholz's wife, Eleanor, with the minigrant idea, again exemplifying the highly personalized nature of the policy initiation process. The ACEF was viewed as so successful that in 1983 the Ford Foundation gave the ACCD a grant to spread the model to other cities across the country. The Public Education Fund (PEF) was housed at ACCD until 1988, at which time it changed to a technical assistance provider and moved to Washington, D.C.

21. The position remains an important one in the school system today, and the same individual occupies it.

22. Richard C. Wallace Jr., *From Vision to Practice: The Art of Educational Leadership* (Thousand Oaks, Calif.: Corwin Press, 1996), 21.

23. Dr. Wallace had spent a portion of his career in educational research and development at Syracuse University and the University of Texas and knew not only the benefit of such analysis but also the personnel at LRDC. The methodology used was a "democratic view" survey that resulted in over 1,000 respondents, ranging from board members to school nurses, business leaders to households with non–public school children. See William Cooley and William Bickel, *Decision-Oriented Educational Research* (Boston: Kluwer-Nihjoff, 1986), 183–96.

24. Indicating the close working relationship Dr. Wallace established with the University of Pittsburgh, he hired Paul LeMahieu, whose dissertation documents the development of the MAP program, to head his testing and research division. Paul B. LeMahieu, "A Study of the Effects of a Program of Student Achievement Monitoring Through Testing" (Ph.D. diss., University of Pittsburgh, 1983), 7–12.

25. Tina Calabro, "Closing the Racial Achievement Gap: Is the School District Doing Enough to Improve the Achievement of African-American Students?" *Public Voices Public Schools: An Independent Look at the Pittsburgh Public Schools* (January/February 1994).

26. Cooley and Bickel, *Decision-Oriented Educational Research,* 18.

27. LeMahieu, "A Study of the Effects of a Program of Student Achievement Monitoring Through Testing," 11.

28. Kerchner, "Pittsburgh: Reform in a Well-Managed Public Bureaucracy," in *A Union of Professionals,* 47.

29. The bulk of the funding for the teacher centers, however, came from the school system's own budget—$10 million in 5 years.

30. He remains with the system as director of development and strategic planning. Over the next decade, the Pittsburgh Public Schools raised nearly $30 million in private funds. They have set an annual goal of $3–$5 million.

31. Charles Taylor Kerchner and Krista Caufman, "Building the Airplane While It's Rolling Down the Runway," in *A Union of Professionals*, 16.

32. Wallace, *From Vision to Practice*.

33. Zlatos, "Wallace wins national education award."

34. Wallace, *From Vision to Practice*, 99.

35. Quoted in Kerchner and Caufman, "Building the Airplane," in *A Union of Professionals*, 19.

36. Rexford G. Brown, *Schools of Thought: How the Politics of Literacy Shape Thinking in the Classroom* (San Francisco: Jossey-Bass, 1993), 196.

37. Joy Dryfoos, "School-Based Social and Health Services for At-Risk Students," *Urban Education* (April 1991): 132–33. As of 1994, thirteen were in operation with six more planned. The goal is for all schools to have a health partnership by the year 2000.

38. Pittsburgh was most likely selected because its civic leadership had already turned to educational issues. It was reported that the AEC sought to test this commitment by asking that the ACCD "get its leadership together" for an initial meeting with just three weeks' notice. The fact that they could accomplish this task was an indication that Pittsburgh had the required civic capacity.

39. Annie E. Casey Foundation, "A Strategic Planning Guide for a New Futures Initiative," 1987.

40. Brown, *Schools of Thought*.

41. Wallace, *From Vision to Practice*, 35.

42. Bill Zlatos, "School board's bickering could scare off candidates," *Pittsburgh Press*, April 12, 1992.

43. "McDonald requires probe of board improprieties," *Pittsburgh Press*, May 20, 1990.

44. Bill Zlatos, "Board weighs cost of joining group it helped start," *Pittsburgh Press*, December 18, 1990.

45. "Valerie McDonald tells Wallace: 'Sue Me,'" *Pittsburgh Press*, March 16, 1991.

46. The jobs component of New Futures, Pittsburgh Promise, was modeled on the Boston Compact. One evaluation of this initiative contended that institutional commitments were very weak. Unlike the Boston example, the Pittsburgh signers were expressing their personal support rather than the commitment of their institutions. Particularly detrimental, in terms of getting employer commitment, was the absence of support from the Allegheny Conference on Community Development. See Alan Melchior, *An Evaluation of the Pittsburgh Promise* (Waltham, Mass.: Brandeis University, Center for Human Resources, 1991).

47. This problem was faced by all New Futures sites and one that the Casey Foundation has sought to prevent in subsequent projects. See Annie E. Casey Foundation, *The Path of Most Resistance: Reflections on Lessons Learned from New Futures* (Baltimore: Annie E. Casey Foundation, 1995).

48. For a comprehensive assessment of the Pittsburgh New Futures experience, see the various evaluations completed by the Center for the Study of Social Policy in

Washington, D.C.: "New Futures in Pittsburgh: A Mid-Point Assessment," 1991; "Pittsburgh New Futures Initiative: Year Three Evaluation Report," 1991; "Pittsburgh New Futures: Year Four Evaluation," 1992; and Melchior, *An Evaluation of the Pittsburgh Promise*.

49. Tina Calabro, "Louise Brennen: Daughter of the System," *Pittsburgh,* December 30, 1992–January 6, 1993.

50. Ernest R. House, *The Politics of Educational Innovation* (Berkeley, Calif.: McCutchan, 1974).

51. Pittsburgh Public Schools, *News,* July 29, 1993.

52. Calabro, "Louise Brennen: Daughter of the System."

53. In 1993, two high schools were selected to develop restructuring models, and in 1994, one middle school was chosen. In 1995, ten Pittsburgh schools were selected to become part of a nationwide project called The New American Schools/National Alliance Initiative. The three-year project, funded by the New American Schools Development Corporation and local foundations, would add ten additional schools each subsequent year.

54. In 1993, Pennsylvania became one of the first states in the nation to adopt outcomes-based education (OBE). Over the next three years, each of the 501 school districts had to submit a strategic plan that showed how it would implement OBE. Pittsburgh volunteered to be in the first round of systems submitting a strategic plan.

55. Pittsburgh Public Schools, "Strategic Implementation Plan for Restructuring," November 1994, 4.

56. Council members also receive training from two neighborhood-based community development corporations as well as a citywide education advocacy group, the Pittsburgh Council on Public Education (PCPE). PCPE, with foundation and school district funding, has created a citywide network called the PCPE Alliance.

57. Carmen J. Lee, "Transferred city principals express dissatisfaction," *Pittsburgh Post-Gazette,* August 8, 1995.

58. John M. R. Bull, "Principals' transfers touch off a protest," *Pittsburgh Post-Gazette,* July 31, 1995.

59. Allegheny Policy Council, "Allegheny Policy Council Takes on Full Agenda for 1994," news release, February 18, 1994.

60. Carmen J. Lee, "Brennen contract extended 2 years," *Pittsburgh Post-Gazette,* February 27, 1995.

61. Wirt and Kirst refer to school boards as "arroyos," or dry riverbeds. Most of the time they remain empty, but during a storm they provide a path for excess water. See Frederick M. Wirt and Michael W. Kirst, *Schools in Conflict* (Berkeley, Calif.: McCutchan, 1982), chap. 5.

62. Carmen J. Lee, "Survey to study student decline," *Pittsburgh Post-Gazette,* April 10, 1995.

63. Of a total annual transportation budget of approximately $25 million, one-third is for busing for integration. The remainder is to transport students to magnet schools and to transport private school students.

64. Frank Reeves, "Murphy urges end to school busing," *Pittsburgh Post-Gazette,* June 2, 1995; "Three councilmen support end to school busing," *Pittsburgh Post-Gazette,* June 1, 1995.

65. Pittsburgh Public Schools, "Draft Report on the Attract and Hold Recommendations," December 1995.

66. "Dis-integration?" editorial, *Pittsburgh Post-Gazette,* December 22, 1995.

67. Carmen J. Lee, "Busing report drawing criticism," *Pittsburgh Post-Gazette,* December 15, 1995.

68. Pittsburgh Public Schools, *News,* April 4, 1996.

69. Mackenzie Carpenter, "School vote fails to yield busing defeat," *Pittsburgh Post-Gazette,* May 22, 1997.

70. Carmen J. Lee, "Busing foes look to next election," *Pittsburgh Post-Gazette,* January 23, 1997.

71. Carmen J. Lee, "Annual dropout rate reaches 10-year low," *Pittsburgh Post-Gazette,* January 8, 1998.

72. Carmen J. Lee, "Running out of options for schools," *Pittsburgh Post-Gazette,* October 22, 1996.

73. One of the attractive elements of the initial redistricting plan was saving $10 million per year by eliminating busing for desegregation. This savings projection, however, was later reduced to $4 million.

74. In a ceremony at the White House, Allderdice was designated as a 1996 Blue Ribbon School of Excellence.

75. Tom Barnes, "City audit of school management ignites sparks," *Pittsburgh Post-Gazette,* October 25, 1995.

76. Mark Belko, "Murphy will allow school board audit," *Pittsburgh Post-Gazette,* November 4, 1995.

77. "Substitute teachers: Council and Flaherty shouldn't meddle in school affairs," editorial, *Pittsburgh Post-Gazette,* October 24, 1995.

78. Belko, "Murphy will allow school board audit."

79. Tom Barnes and Carmen J. Lee, "Council votes to audit books of city schools," *Pittsburgh Post-Gazette,* October 19, 1995.

80. Carmen J. Lee, "Appointed board for schools sought," *Pittsburgh Post-Gazette,* January 28, 1997.

81. Darlene Harris, "A slap in the face," letter to the editor, *Pittsburgh Post-Gazette,* February 2, 1997.

82. Jean Fink, "Our system is viable," letter to the editor, *Pittsburgh Post-Gazette,* February 2, 1997.

83. Carmen J. Lee, "School closing and construction proposal unveiled, criticized," *Pittsburgh Post-Gazette,* August 22, 1997.

84. Carmen J. Lee, "City schools' budget keeps tax rate same," *Pittsburgh Post-Gazette,* November 27, 1996.

85. "Hard lessons ahead: Pittsburgh schools are struggling to balance the books," editorial, *Pittsburgh Post-Gazette,* November 5, 1996.

86. See Ferman's discussion of the limits of "unidimensional progressivism" in *Challenging the Growth Machine,* 135–52.

87. Lubove, *Twentieth-Century Pittsburgh,* 2:76.

88. *A Strategy for Growth: An Economic Development Program for the Pittsburgh Region* (Pittsburgh: Allegheny Conference on Community Development, 1984).

89. Lubove, *Twentieth-Century Pittsburgh,* vol. 2, chaps. 2–4.

90. *Toward a Shared Economic Vision for Pittsburgh and Southwestern Pennsylvania: A Report by the White Paper Committee for the Allegheny Conference on Community Development* (Pittsburgh: Allegheny Conference on Community Development, 1993).

91. *The Greater Pittsburgh Region: Working Together to Compete Globally* (Pittsburgh: Allegheny Conference on Community Development, 1994).

92. Tom Barnes and John M. R. Bull, "City task force targeting safety service, pension fund to end $39 million deficit," *Pittsburgh Post-Gazette,* October 3, 1996.

93. "Painting by numbers," editorial, *Pittsburgh Post-Gazette,* February 24, 1998.

94. Mackenzie Carpenter, "New superintendent will face a contentious board," *Pittsburgh Post-Gazette,* May 13, 1997.

95. Pittsburgh Public Schools, *News,* December 17, 1996.

96. Carmen J. Lee, "Community to aid schools' chief search," *Pittsburgh Post-Gazette,* December 18, 1996.

97. John G. Craig Jr., "To the point," *Pittsburgh Post-Gazette,* December 22, 1996.

98. The board was quick to note that in 1980 Wallace had been ranked last of the twelve candidates recommended to the board. See Eleanor Chute, "School pick 'dynamic,'" *Pittsburgh Post-Gazette,* June 5, 1997.

99. Carmen J. Lee and Mackenzie Carpenter, "School search: A good look," *Pittsburgh Post-Gazette,* June 15, 1997.

100. Bill Heltzel, "Healer of deep wounds," *Pittsburgh Post-Gazette,* June 8, 1998.

101. Rebecca Baker, "Most likely to succeed," *Pittsburgh City Paper,* August 27–September 3, 1997.

102. Carmen J. Lee, "New city school superintendent is off to a promising start," *Pittsburgh Post-Gazette,* October 6, 1997.

103. Mackenzie Carpenter, "Rough start for school chief," *Pittsburgh Post-Gazette,* August 30, 1998.

104. Financial and Educational Program Assessment Panel, "Grading the Graders: Evaluating the Pittsburgh Public School System," October 1998, 7.

CHAPTER 5. BOSTON'S PUBLIC SCHOOLS: EMERGING INSTITUTIONS AND LEADERSHIP

1. Barbara Ferman, *Governing the Ungovernable City: Political Skill, Leadership, and the Modern Mayor* (Philadelphia: Temple University Press, 1985); Thomas O'Connor, *Building a New Boston: Politics and Urban Renewal, 1950–1970* (Boston: Northeastern University Press, 1993); Cynthia Horan, "Coalition, Market, and State: Postwar Development Politics in Boston," in *Reconstructing Urban Regime Theory: Regulating Urban Politics in a Global Economy,* ed. M. Lauria (Thousand Oaks, Calif.: Sage, 1997).

2. O'Connor, *Building a New Boston;* John Mollenkopf, *The Contested City* (Princeton, N.J.: Princeton University Press, 1983).

3. Mollenkopf, *Contested City.*

4. Ibid., 165–66.

5. Boston Urban Study Group, *Who Rules Boston?* (Boston: Institute for Democratic Socialism, 1984).

6. Peter Schrag, *Village School Downtown: Boston Schools, Boston Politics* (Boston: Beacon Press, 1967); Jonathan Kozol, *Death at an Early Age: The Destruction of the Hearts and Minds of Negro Children in the Boston Public Schools* (New York: New American Library, 1985 [1967]); Martin Meyerson and Edward Banfield, *Boston: The Job Ahead* (Cambridge, Mass.: Harvard University Press, 1966).

7. Schrag, *Village School Downtown,* 72.

8. Robert Wood, "Professionals at Bay: Managing Boston's Public Schools," *Journal of Policy Analysis and Management* 1, no.4 (1982): 455.

9. Alan Lupo, *Liberty's Chosen Home: The Politics of Violence in Boston* (Boston: Beacon Press, 1988), 95.

10. Ronald Formisano, *Boston Against Busing: Race, Class, and Ethnicity in the 1960s and 1970s* (Chapel Hill, N.C.: University of North Carolina Press, 1991).

11. U.S. District Court, *Morgan v. Kerrigan,* June 5, 1975.

12. Marilyn Gittell, *Limits to Citizen Participation* (Newbury Park, Calif.: Sage, 1980), 202.

13. 379 F. Supp. 410 (1974) *Morgan v. Hennigan,* 410.

14. Formisano, *Boston Against Busing.*

15. Robert Dentler and Marvin Scott, *Schools on Trial: An Inside Account of the Boston Desegregation Case* (Cambridge, Mass.: Abt Books, 1981).

16. *Morgan v. Kerrigan.*

17. Charles Willie, *The Sociology of Urban Education* (Lexington, Mass.: D. C. Heath, 1978); U.S. Commission on Civil Rights, *Hearings,* June 16–20, 1975, held in Boston, 177–98.

18. Dentler and Scott, *Schools on Trial.*

19. Formisano, *Boston Against Busing.*

20. Ibid.

21. U.S. Commission on Civil Rights, *Hearings,* 184.

22. Ibid.

23. Sandra Waddock, "Public-Private Partnerships as Social Product and Process," in *Research in Corporate Social Performance and Policy,* vol. 8, ed. J. Post (Greenwich, Conn.: JAI Press, 1986).

24. Eleanor Farrar and Anthony Cipollone, "After the Signing: The Boston Compact 1982 to 1985," in *American Business and the Public School,* ed. M. Levine and R. Trachtman (New York: Teachers College Press, 1988), 95.

25. Alan Melchior, "The Boston Compact," unpublished, prepared for the Massachusetts Governor's Task Force on Private Sector Initiatives, February 1983, 27.

26. Eleanor Farrar and Anthony Cipollone, "The Business Community and School Reform: The Boston Compact at Five Years" (Madison, Wis.: National Center on Effective Secondary Schools, 1988).

27. Farrar and Cipollone, "After the Signing," in *American Business and the Public School,* 98.

28. Melchior, "The Boston Compact."

29. Edward Dooley, *The Culture of Possibility. The Story of the Boston Plan for Excellence in the Public Schools: The First Ten Years* (Boston: Boston Plan for Excellence in the Public Schools).

30. *1995 Annual Report* (Boston: Boston Plan for Excellence in the Public Schools, 1995).

31. Farrar and Cipollone, "The Business Community and School Reform."

32. Farrar and Cipollone, "After the Signing," in *American Business and the Public School,* 97.

33. Wood, "Professionals at Bay," 464.

34. Dentler and Scott, *Schools on Trial,* 98.

35. Clarence N. Stone, *Regime Politics: Governing Atlanta, 1946–1988* (Lawrence: University Press of Kansas, 1989), 229.

36. The appointed school committee, which took effect in 1992 and was mentioned in Chapter 3, will be discussed later in this chapter.

37. Muriel Cohen, Brian Mooney, and Diego Ribadeneira, "Boston schools on the brink: Infighting diverts focus from education," *Boston Globe,* May 22, 1991, 23.

38. Mayor's Advisory Committee, *The Rebirth of America's Oldest Public School System: Redefining Responsibility* (Boston: City of Boston Mayor's Office, 1989), 30.

39. *Facts and Figures, 1992* (Boston: Boston Municipal Research Bureau, 1992), 56.

40. "Shortchanging the school children," editorial, *Boston Globe,* August 30, 1990, 26.

41. Cohen, Mooney, and Ribadeneira, "Boston schools on the brink," five-part series, *Boston Globe,* May 19–23, 1991.

42. Mayor's Advisory Committee, *The Rebirth of America's Oldest Public School System,* 1.

43. Ibid., 27.

44. Samuel Tyler, "Statement of the Boston Municipal Research Bureau Before the City Council Committee on Public Education," April 8, 1991, 2.

45. *Facts and Figures, 1992,* 66.

46. Diego Ribadeneira, "City schools face fund cutoff for lag in assigning plan," *Boston Globe,* January 24, 1990, 17.

47. Diego Ribadeneira, "Boston schools' candidate: quits race, citing politics," *Boston Globe,* November 30, 1990, 1.

48. U.S. Commission on Civil Rights, *Hearings,* 510.

49. Formisano, *Boston Against Busing;* U.S. Commission on Civil Rights, *Hearings,* 506–30; Martha Weinberg, "Boston's Kevin White: A Mayor Who Survives," in *Boston 1700–1980: The Evolution of Urban Politics,* ed. R. Formisano and C. Burns (Westport, Conn.: Greenwood Press, 1991).

50. Ray Flynn, "A Vision for Public Education Reform," presentation to the Boston business community, January 29, 1993, 19.

51. John Portz, "Problem Definitions and Policy Agendas: Shaping the Education Agenda in Boston," *Policy Studies Journal* 24, no. 3 (Autumn 1996): 371–86.

52. Ibid.

53. "Time to abolish the school committee," editorial, *Boston Globe,* January 16, 1991, 10; "For an appointed school committee," editorial, *Boston Globe,* April 10, 1991, 18.

54. Portz, "Problem Definitions and Policy Agendas"; and John Portz, "Civic Capacity and Public Education in Boston," in *Innovation in Urban Education: The Impact of Research on Practice in Schools* (Boston: Northeastern University Center for Innovation in Urban Education, 1994).

55. Brian Mooney, "70% in Boston poll back 'radical' school reforms," *Boston Globe,* April 12, 1989, 29.

56. Philip Clay, "Boston: The Incomplete Transformation," in *Big City Politics in Transition,* ed. H. Savitch and J. Thomas (Newbury Park, Calif: Sage, 1991).

57. Flynn, "A Vision for Public Education Reform," 19.

58. James Jennings, "Urban Machinism and the Black Vote: The Kevin White Years," in *From Access to Power: Black Politics in Boston,* ed. J. Jennings and M. King (Cambridge, Mass.: Schenkman Books, 1986), 97.

59. Irene Sege, "Census tells tale of two Bostons," *Boston Globe,* May 4, 1991, 26.

60. Sarah Snyder, "Business to schools: We want results," *Boston Globe,* October 25, 1988, 33; Boston Private Industry Council, "Organizational Fact Sheet: History and Program Development."

61. Charles Stein, "A compact unfulfilled," *Boston Globe,* October 19, 1993, 43.

62. *Facts and Figures, 1995* (Boston: Boston Municipal Research Bureau, 1995), 57.

63. Jerry Ackerman, "Company mergers may take civic toll," *Boston Globe,* July 3, 1995, 1.

64. Rosabeth Moss Kanter, *Greater Boston's Challenges in the Global Economy: Strengthening the Infrastructure for Collaboration* (Boston: Harvard University Graduate School of Business Administration, 1994).

65. Jordana Hart, "Harrison-Jones sees a lack of respect for role," *Boston Globe,* January 19, 1995, 1.

66. "A failing grade for Harrison-Jones," editorial, *Boston Globe,* December 21, 1994, 22.

67. "At last, schools that mean business," editorial, *Boston Globe,* November 1, 1996, A26.

68. "Massachusetts Business Roundtable: Six views from the top," *Boston Globe,* December 1, 1996, F1.

69. Boston Compact Steering Committee, *Strategic Plan for the Boston Compact* (Boston: Boston Private Industry Council, 1994).

70. Mayor Menino was acting mayor at the time. Under a state education law passed in June 1993, as mayor he was authorized to sit as a member of the school committee and vote on the approval or disapproval of collective bargaining contracts.

71. "A contract full of promise," editorial, *Boston Herald,* June 23, 1994, 30.

72. Mayor Thomas Menino, "State of the City Address," City of Boston Mayor's Office, January 17, 1996.

73. *Reorganization Plan for the Boston Public Schools* (Boston: Boston School Department, 1996).

74. Thomas Payzant, *The Connection,* radio talk show on WBUR, February 19, 1996.

75. Thomas Payzant, "Memorandum: Changes in Senior-Level Management Positions," July 15, 1998.

76. *Focus on Children: A Comprehensive Reform Plan for the Boston Public Schools* (Boston: Boston School Department, 1996), 3.

77. Ibid., 17.

78. Thomas Payzant, "Memorandum: Material for Discussion of Whole-School Change," October 31, 1997.

79. *21st Century School Grants: A Framework* (Boston: Boston Plan for Excellence in the Public Schools, 1996).

80. Karen Avenoso, "Schools to get $10m for reform," *Boston Globe,* October 29, 1996, A1.

81. Thomas Payzant, "Memorandum: Boston Annenberg Challenge Status Report," October 2, 1998.

82. Boston Public Schools, "Promotion Policy," *Superintendent's Circular,* School Year 1998–1999, no.1, September 1, 1998.

83. Beth Daley, "School panel passes new promotion plan," *Boston Globe,* June 25, 1998, B2.

84. Thomas Payzant, "Boston is taking strong steps toward better schools," *Boston Globe,* September 8, 1998, A19.

85. Richard Chacón, "Menino: School panel to be 'more accessible,'" *Boston Globe,* November 7, 1996, B13.

86. Critical Friends, "The Culture of the Boston Public School System," unpublished analysis, November 18, 1996.

87. Boston Municipal Research Bureau, "Raising the Bar for Education in Boston," *Special Report,* no. 98–3, April 8, 1998, 4.

88. Critical Friends, "Status Report on Boston's Public Schools After Two Years of Reform," October 1997.

89. Beth Daley, "Hub school reform lags, panel says," *Boston Globe,* December 4, 1997, A1.

90. Karen Avenoso, "Boston students lag in tests," *Boston Globe,* June 25, 1996, A1.

91. "Payzant's candid friends," editorial, *Boston Globe,* December 12, 1997, A26.

92. Beth Daley, "Hub test scores show elementary gain," *Boston Globe,* October 8, 1998, B3.

93. Beth Daley, "Gap widens in Boston test scores," *Boston Globe,* September 25, 1998, A1.

94. Jordana Hart, "School chief aims to end racial gap," *Boston Globe,* October 29, 1998, A1; Derrick Jackson, "Payzant's brave rescue attempt," *Boston Globe,* October 30, 1998, A27.

95. Paul Watanabe, *A Dream Deferred: Changing Demographics, Challenges, and New Opportunities for Boston* (Boston: University of Massachusetts, 1996), 32.

96. Beth Daley, "Boston schools face test to aim higher," *Boston Globe,* December 22, 1997, B6.

97. Critical Friends, "The Culture of the Boston Public School System."

98. Jon Keller, "On Harrison-Jones: Another look at who said what," *Boston Globe,* January 22, 1995, City Weekly, 3.

99. Adrian Walker, "Menino calls race relations the overriding issue for the city," *Boston Globe,* September 19, 1994, 1.

100. See Hubie Jones, "What is 'reform' with so little effect?" *Boston Globe,* July 26, 1998, D4. For a more positive assessment, see Chad Gifford and Ray Hammond, "In Boston's public schools, a new focus on what needs to be done," *Boston Globe,* September 25, 1998, A31.

101. Sarah Snyder, "Where have all the powers gone?" *Boston Globe,* December 27, 1988, 37.

102. Sean Flynn, "Mr. Boston," *Boston Magazine* 89, no. 5 (May 1997): 55.

103. Hubie Jones and Paul Guzzi, "A lesson in leadership," *Boston Globe,* December 29, 1997, A17.

104. Kanter, *Greater Boston's Challenges in the Global Economy,* 128.

105. Alan Lupo, "Menino bids to retain an appointed school board," *Boston Globe,* February 11, 1996, City Weekly, 1.

106. Beth Daley, "Backers of 8-year contract say schools need stability," *Boston Globe,* August 21, 1998, B6.

107. Thomas Menino, "City of Boston: Inaugural Address," City of Boston Mayor's Office, January 5, 1998.

CHAPTER 6. ST. LOUIS'S PUBLIC SCHOOLS: WEAK SECTORS AND LOW COHESION

1. The three universities are Washington University, St. Louis University, and the University of Missouri–St. Louis.

2. "A desegregation timetable," *St. Louis Post-Dispatch,* June 9, 1997, 7A.

3. James Neal Primm, *Lion of the Valley: St. Louis, Missouri,* 2d ed. (Boulder, Colo.: Pruett, 1990): 435–39.

4. "A desegregation timetable."

5. Ibid.

6. Larry Tye, "St. Louis provides a lesson in suburb-to-city schooling," *Boston Globe,* December 5, 1995, 1.

7. Nicholas A. Masters, Robert H. Salisbury, and Thomas H. Eliot, *State Politics and the Public Schools* (New York: Alfred A. Knopf, 1964), 12.

8. See Lana Stein, *Holding Bureaucrats Accountable: Politicians and Professionals in St. Louis* (Tuscaloosa: University of Alabama Press, 1991).

9. Masters, Salisbury, and Eliot, *State Politics and the Public Schools,* 34–35.

10. David Tyack and Larry Cuban, *Tinkering Toward Utopia: A Century of Public School Reform* (Cambridge, Mass.: Harvard University Press, 1995), 8.

11. Theodore J. Lowi, "Machine Politics—Old and New," *Public Interest* (Fall 1967): 83–92.

12. Philip Meranto, *School Politics in the Metropolis* (Columbus, Ohio: Charles E. Merrill, 1970).

13. Tyack and Cuban, *Tinkering Toward Utopia,* 9.

14. Daniel J. Monti, *A Semblance of Justice: St. Louis Desegregation and Order in America* (Columbia: University of Missouri Press, 1985), 157.

15. Ibid.

16. E. Terrance Jones, "Community Leadership," in *St. Louis Currents: The Community and Its Resources* (St. Louis: Leadership St. Louis, 1986), 4.

17. William H. Freivogel, "School desegregation dilemma," *St. Louis Post-Dispatch,* March 3, 1996, 4B.

18. Ibid.

19. Ibid.

20. Ibid.

21. Joan Little, "City students post better test scores but still trail national, state averages," *St. Louis Post-Dispatch,* October 12, 1994, 13A.

22. "What happens to St. Louis city public high school students," *St. Louis Post-Dispatch,* March 3, 1996, 4B.

23. Gary Orfield, Susan Eaton, and the Harvard Project on School Desegregation, *Dismantling Desegregation: The Quiet Reversal of Brown v. Board of Education* (New York: New Press, 1996), 89.

24. Joan Little, "Schools rewrite the book on texts," *St. Louis Post-Dispatch,* August 19, 1994, 12A.

25. Joan Little, "Principals oppose tenure law change," *St. Louis Post-Dispatch,* March 15, 1995.

26. William Allen, "Infighting hindered St. Louis's effort for schools grant," *St. Louis Post-Dispatch,* December 25, 1994, 1A.

27. "An Organizational Review of the St. Louis Schools," prepared by the McKenzie Group, Washington, D.C., September 11, 1995, 11.

28. Ibid., 9.

29. Joan Little, "The quiet man: David Mahan gives city schools stability; His critics say they want to see energy," *St. Louis Post-Dispatch,* February 12, 1995, 4B.

30. Ibid.

31. *St. Louis Post-Dispatch,* February 10, 1996, 6C.

32. Jerry Berger and Marianne Riley, "Mayor's letter attacks school management," *St. Louis Post-Dispatch,* March 25, 1996, 1A.

33. Ibid.

34. See John Hull Mollenkopf, *A Phoenix in the Ashes: The Rise and Fall of the Koch Coalition in New York City Politics* (Princeton, N.J.: Princeton University Press, 1992), 18–19.

35. Robert H. Salisbury, "Our fading civic leadership," *St. Louis Post-Dispatch,* November 26, 1995.

36. Carolyn Bower, "Desegregation end implies layoffs, cuts," *St. Louis Post-Dispatch,* January 15, 1996, 1W.

37. D. J. Wilson, "Dismantling deseg," *Riverfront Times,* February 28–March 5, 1996, 17–23.

38. "Broken schools fail children," *St. Louis Post-Dispatch,* December 21, 1997, B2.

39. Virginia Young, "House advances charter amendment," *St. Louis Post-Dispatch,* May 8, 1998; Susan C. Thomson, "Three who may oversee city schools are selected," *St. Louis Post-Dispatch,* August 29, 1998.

40. Margie Manning and Rick Desloge, "New Civic Progress," *St. Louis Business Journal,* August 10–16, 1998, 1; Margie Manning, "Liddy, CP ponder new group," *St. Louis Business Journal,* September 14–20, 1998, 3.

41. "A racial watershed," *St. Louis Post-Dispatch,* September 3, 1998, B6.

CHAPTER 7. CIVIC CAPACITY AND URBAN EDUCATION:
LESSONS FROM THREE CITIES

1. Clarence N. Stone, "Civic Capacity and Urban School Reform," in *Changing Urban Education,* ed. C. Stone (Lawrence: University Press of Kansas, 1998), 255.

2. Paul T. Hill, Arthur E. Wise, and Leslie Shapiro, *Educational Progress: Cities Mobilize to Improve Their Schools* (Santa Monica, Calif.: Rand, 1989).

3. *1983 Report* (Pittsburgh: Allegheny Conference on Community Development, 1984), 5.

4. Annie E. Casey Foundation, *The Path of Most Resistance: Reflections on Lessons Learned from New Futures* (Baltimore: Annie E. Casey Foundation, 1995), 1.

5. See Daniel Elazar, *Building Cities in America* (Lanham, Md.: Hamilton Press, 1987).

6. Barbara Ferman, *Challenging the Growth Machine: Neighborhood Politics in Chicago and Pittsburgh* (Lawrence: University Press of Kansas, 1996), 20.

7. Barbara Ferman, *Governing the Ungovernable City: Political Skill, Leadership, and the Modern Mayor* (Philadelphia: Temple University Press, 1985). The reference to

"private-regarding" is from Edward Banfield and James Q. Wilson, *City Politics* (Cambridge, Mass.: Harvard University Press, 1966).

8. Hubie Jones and Paul Guzzi, "A lesson in leadership," *Boston Globe,* December 29, 1997, A17.

9. Richard C. Wallace Jr., *From Vision to Practice: The Art of Educational Leadership* (Thousand Oaks, Calif.: Corwin Press, 1996), 93.

10. Ibid., 21.

11. Ibid., 131.

12. Ibid., 120.

13. Andrew Glassberg, "St. Louis: Racial Transition and Economic Development," in *Big City Politics in Transition,* ed. H. Savitch and J. Thomas (Newbury Park, Calif.: Sage, 1991).

14. Joan Little, "The quiet man: David Mahan gives city schools stability; His critics say they want to see energy." *St. Louis Post-Dispatch,* February 12, 1995, 4B.

15. Clarence N. Stone, "Introduction: Urban Education in a Political Context," in *Changing Urban Education,* ed. C. Stone (Lawrence: University Press of Kansas, 1998), 12.

16. Richard C. Hunter, "The Mayor Versus the School Superintendent: Political Incursions into Metropolitan School Politics," *Education and Urban Society* 29, no. 2 (February 1997): 217–32.

Index